BEN JONSON

BEN JONSON
By Gerard Honthorst
(*Original at Knole Park*)

[front

BEN JONSON

By

JOHN PALMER

AUTHOR OF THE COMEDY OF MANNERS; THE FUTURE OF
THE THEATRE; STUDIES IN THE CONTEMPORARY
THEATRE; MOLIÈRE, ETC. ETC.

NEW YORK
THE VIKING PRESS
1934

Printed in Great Britain by Butler & Tanner Ltd., Frome and London

CONTENTS

v

LIST OF ILLUSTRATIONS

PREFACE

JONSON was not only an author of genius. He was perhaps the greatest of English worthies. By common consent he was accepted by a splendid generation as their most significant and representative figure. He gave to English comedy an unexpected turn. His tragedies were a grave majestic exercise. One or two of his lyrics are among the best in our treasury. His masks awed and diverted a King whose ambition it was to be taken for the most learned clerk in christendom.

But Jonson was even more important in life than in literature. He took it upon himself to stand for the vocation, and as the priest of Apollo he demanded and obtained a place of honour and esteem for English letters. For forty years the poets and dramatists of England looked to him as their leader. All were the " sons of Ben ". In him they were no longer trivial and outcast but laureates and the companions of princes. Jonson had a natural insolence of disposition —a contempt of prejudice and place which often made it difficult for the authorities to decide whether he should more appropriately be thrust into the pillory as a leveller or persuaded into the laureate's chair as the lord of a dangerous mystery. He finally came to rest in Westminster Abbey, but he might as easily have ended at Tyburn—and nearly did.

This acknowledged leader of a great company was remarkable for his literary achievements, even more remarkable for his size and energy as a human figure, most remarkable of all as an expression of a period which he outlived. Jonson represented the Renaissance in England as definitely as Milton represented the Reformation. He wrote for a generation which had still an unbounded confidence in the senses and faculties of man. England had not yet accepted the great negation, chequered with indignant rebellion or uneasy defiance, which is our present legacy from Geneva. He is the principal English figure in the European tragedy which ended in the defeat of the scholars, when the mediaeval mind, emerging into the sunlight, was thrust back into the shadows. He belonged to a generation which had listened to Erasmus. He survived into the generation of Praise-God-Barebones. Of that generation we are still essentially the heirs. England has not yet recovered her inheritance. Every now and then comes a period of the fidgets, but the superficial freedoms on which we pride ourselves to-day are little more than the perambulations of a hungry beast in a cage. We are still strangers in Bartholomew Fair.

Jonson's plays will hardly return to the stage in our time. His best comedies and his Roman tragedies find only a few readers from year to year. The forty-four masks, the hundred and thirty-three epigrams, the plays of his earlier and later years, the occasional poems which make up the bulk of his work are seldom scanned. For most of us Jonson is the author of *The Fox* and *The Alchemist*, of *Bartholomew Fair* and of *Every Man in His Humour*, the first poet laureate of England and the determined practitioner of a peculiar theory of comedy. The biographer who would make his genius familiar cannot, therefore, deal with his work by allusion. Frequent and full quotation is not only justified but necessary.

Jonson as a contemporary figure, child of the Renaissance, lover of life and learning, is writ warm and large in the pages of Eric Linklater's *Ben Jonson and King James*. No apology either to the author of that vivacious study or to the public is needed for presenting him again from a different angle. This biography, however, has a second intention. It is aimed not only at presenting the man but at giving the reader a fairly complete idea, by instance and example, of Jonson's achievement as poet and dramatist. There will be no attempt to impose on the reader general estimates or vague appreciations. The best and worst of Jonson shall be offered, and those who disagree with the views submitted will here find the material they need for a confutation.

BEN JONSON

CHAPTER I

The First Twenty-Five Years

BEN JONSON was born in 1573. Men lived quickly under Elizabeth. Jonson was a finished scholar at thirteen, a soldier at seventeen, married at nineteen, celebrated for his lost tragedies at twenty-three, convicted of homicide and the author of one of the most famous of English comedies at twenty-five. Incidentally, he had found time to collaborate and quarrel with a number of contemporary authors, to change his religion, to be suspected of a plot against the Government and, most notoriously of all, to be a bricklayer.—

Of Jonson's parentage not much is definitely known. Fuller, writing his *Worthies*, " could not find him in his cradle," but, he adds, " I could fetch him from his long coats ". Fuller, indeed, claims to have discovered Ben " as a little child in Hartshorn Lane near Charing Cross ", but he can tell us little else. Jonson himself, in the celebrated conversations at Hawthornden, told Drummond that his grandfather was a gentleman—in other words entitled to wear coat-armour, his coat being of three spindles or rhombi. He had come, so Jonson thought, originally from Annandale and thence to Carlisle. Thereafter he had served under Henry VIII. Jonson's father, imprisoned and forfeited under Mary, turned

B

minister upon his release and so remained till his death in 1572 or 1573. Benjamin was born a month later, probably in Westminster. Neither the exact date of his birth nor the name of his mother has been ascertained.

The rest is gossip or conjecture. We may reasonably infer that a modest gentleman from the Border, taken into the service of the King at a time when the throne looked for support to the ability and good sense of the yeoman classes, was a person of character and intelligence. So much for the grandfather. Jonson's father comes a little nearer. Imprisonment and forfeiture under Mary point to firm convictions, and the fact that, after his release, he became a minister shows that he was of the stuff to be hardened rather than shaken by persecution. Jonson's mother is ambiguous. Antony Wood, the Oxford antiquary, says she was a silly woman, but her son tells a story to Drummond which leaves quite a different impression. In 1604, in circumstances to be hereafter described, Jonson was imprisoned with his friend and collaborator, Chapman, for his part in the writing of *Eastward Ho*, in which the odious Sir James Murray had discovered an attack upon the King's accent. There was some talk of the two companions having their noses cut for this offence, but James was a better and wiser man than the Scottish gawks surrounding him who misliked all forms of humour but their own. The storm passed and the friends were released. Jonson gave a feast, and to the feast came his mother —her first and last appearance on any stage. She drank to her son and showed him a paper which, if the sentence had taken execution, she had intended, says Jonson, as ungrammatically reported in the conversations, " to mix in the prison among his drink, which was full of a strong lusty poison, and that she was no churl, she told she minded first to have drunk of it herself ". Such stories, whether we believe them or not, are not told of a silly woman. We may infer that the old lady was a person of character and that the description applied to her by Antony Wood is but another illustration of his genius for misleading epithets.

Two years after the death of Jonson's father his mother married again. This time it was a master-bricklayer. But she respected, and persuaded her new lord to respect, the wishes of her first husband, who, being a minister, had doubtless desired his son to be well found in Latin. Young Benjamin was to look higher than the hod and, despite his poor condition, was put to school as soon as he was of age to take a pen between his fingers.

The education secured for Benjamin could hardly have been bettered even in that age when infant prodigies of learning were turned loose upon a brilliant world to stagger and confound posterity. He went to a school within the church of St. Martin-in-the-Fields, and thence, through the liberality of a friend, to Westminster. William Camden was then second master and seems to have taken a personal and special interest in his pupil.

> Camden, most reverend head, to whom I owe
> All that I am in arts, all that I know,

wrote Jonson in an epigram, and dedicated his first great comedy to his most learned and honoured friend, declaring that he was " not one of those who could suffer the benefits conferred upon his youth to perish with his age ". Tradition adorns the relationship of master and pupil by affirming, not on very good authority, that it was Camden who, passing by while Ben was helping his stepfather to build a wall and

3

hearing him repeating Latin verses as he wielded, presumably, the trowel, used his influence to get him admitted to the school. To Camden, at any rate, Jonson was indebted for his scholarship and, on his own confession, for a method of composition to which he remained faithful to the last. It was his habit, he told Drummond, to write first in prose and then to versify the result, adding that " so his master Camden had learned him ". Whether or not Jonson went on to Cambridge, as Fuller and Aubrey affirm, is doubtful; but it is clear that he owed nothing to the University and everything to his school. Possibly he was at Cambridge for a few months. Perhaps he was granted an exhibition for the purpose. But his serious education began and ended at Westminster.

Camden had done his work too well for the master-bricklayer. Young Jonson already had a notion that there were better things in life than building a wall. The usual war was in progress in the Low Countries and fighting was more to the taste of a scholar. Jonson broke away from his home and enlisted as a soldier. Of his performances in that capacity we have no record but his own. In the sight of both the camps, Drummond records him as saying, he engaged an enemy champion, slew him and stripped him of his armour. Doubts have been expressed whether Jonson was not complacently exaggerating a warlike achievement which a sedentary man of peace would naturally wish to remember with advantages. This, however, is carrying distrust too far. There can be no mistake about Jonson being all through life incorrigibly a fighter, with sword, cudgel or pen. If, as the custom was, a challenge was issued in a friendly spirit between armies tired of sitting still for months at a time, Jonson at eighteen years of age would not be the last to take it up.

He returned to London, probably in 1592, and immediately married a wife. " A shrew yet honest," he declared in after life. For the word honest, in the mouth of an Elizabethan, read chaste. Thus, she had two qualities which not unseldom go together. Of Jonson's married life we know nothing directly or in detail, but its general tenor may be inferred. There were three children, but for five years in the early thirties he lived apart from his wife in the household of Lord d'Aubigny, and there is cause to suspect that he was only very seldom at home. There is no reason, however, to doubt that he was sincerely attached to his wife. It is significant that she was a Catholic and that Jonson, in peril of his neck, was, as we shall see, persuaded to adopt that religion, to which he remained faithful for twelve years. He had no strong sectarian convictions, but he was large-hearted and susceptible. That he should have been attracted from the religion for which his father had suffered imprisonment and forfeiture to the faith professed by his wife declares a sympathy that extended beyond procreation and the household budget.

Jonson, says Fuller, was not happy in his children —which probably means no more than that he loved them dearly and lost them young. Not one of them survived him. His daughter Mary died in infancy.

Here lies, to each her parent's ruth,
Mary, the daughter of their youth.

Thus Jonson commemorates her in his epigrams. His first son died, at seven years, of the plague. This was the " child of his right hand and joy " of whom he told, both to Camden and to Drummond, a strange tale which points to more than an ordinary affection. He was staying at the time, along with Camden, at the house of Sir Robert Cotton in the country. There he " saw in a vision his eldest son, then a child and at London, appear unto him with the mark of a bloody cross on his forehead, as if it had been cutted with a sword, at which, amazed, he prayed unto God ; and in the morning he came unto Mr. Camden's chamber to tell him, who persuaded him it was but an apprehension of his phantasy, at which he should not be dejected. In the meantime came three letters from his wife of the death of that boy in the plague." The bearing of this story on the temperament and character of Jonson, poet of sound sense, never in his work a visionary, who made all his first drafts in prose, will be considered later. Here it is introduced as a clue to his family relationships. That he failed to be present at his son's death of the plague is not of great significance. There was always plague in London in those days, and it struck more swiftly than the posts would travel. Jonson loved his son and mourned him sturdily :

> Rest in soft peace and, asked, say here doth lie
> Ben Jonson his best piece of poetry.

Jonson outlived his second son by two years. Of him we know nothing except that his father made efforts in later life to obtain for him the reversion of a place at Court. We do not know when Jonson lost his wife, but clearly she was dead when he visited Drummond in 1618. Jonson was then forty-five years of age.

Jonson, home from the wars and having married a wife, must find at once a means of living. For a poor scholar, as yet without influence, there was little choice. Young men without prospects or friends under Elizabeth went inevitably to the stage. There were examples to encourage and deter. William Shakespeare, Richard Burbage and Edward Alleyn were making a modest fortune out of the theatre. It could be done with talent and circumspection. There were, on the other hand, a crowd of actors and authors uncertain of the morrow, spending or pledging their little money before it was earned. Let us look for a moment at these stages of London as a possible career in the middle of the last decade of the sixteenth century.

Robert Greene described the successful actor in 1592 as a man who had once travelled on foot, carrying his properties on his back, but his share in the playhouse wardrobe alone " was now worth £200 and he was able at his proper cost to build a windmill ", while Gamaliel Ratsey within a few years was referring to the flaunting actors who " by penny sparing and long practice of playing are grown so wealthy that they have expected to be knighted or at least to be conjunct in authority and to sit with men of great worship on the bench of justice ". The moralists had here much matter for indignation. " The very hirelings," said Gosson nine years before the Armada, " sit under the gentlemen's noses in suits of silk . . . scoffing when they come abroad, where they look askance over the shoulder at every man of whom the Sunday before they begged an alms." These same hirelings, however, or salaried actors, who begged an alms the Sunday before, were likely to be again begging an alms the Sunday following. The stable fortunes were made only by a few men who were able to invest capital in the established playhouses, the " housekeepers " or " sharers " who had a financial interest in their several theatres. Richard Burbage died worth £300 a year in land. Alleyn was able to retire at forty, and to buy the manor of Dulwich for £10,000, where he lived at the good rate of £1,700 a year. John Hemming was described by a contemporary as " of great living wealth and power ". Shakespeare was able to buy New Place and spend his last years in acquiring a coat-of-arms. But these were the exceptions.

The theatrical industry, in England as in France, inherited an organisation which went far back in its traditions. A dramatic company under the Tudors was a partnership to which were admitted only such as could pay their footing in money or in kind. Each admitted member had a " share " in the company. Play books, properties and wardrobe were held in common. Expenditure was jointly incurred and the profits divided—one of the items of expenditure being the salaries paid to hireling members of the troop. " Sharers " were under definite obligations in return for their privileges. They might not abandon the company without the consent of their fellows during the period for which they were bound. Otherwise they forfeited their interest. Those who retired with consent, however, were paid for the shares which they abandoned. The good conduct of the sharers was enforced by penalties. Those who came drunk to the stage, or missed rehearsals, or removed apparel or common property, might be fined or asked to withdraw. The sharers were admitted, even by the Puritans, to be honest and commendable folk. Gosson allowed that some among the quality were " sober, discreet, properly learned, honest householders and citizens, well thought on among their neighbours at home ".

Profit-sharing on an equal basis was the traditional arrangement. But when was equality of wealth maintained in any group of men for more than a day ? Improvident members were driven to sell or pledge their shares to their colleagues or men outside the company. There was soon a market in shares and a field was opened to the speculator, who, without himself being an actor or author, thus acquired a footing in the theatre and very soon tended to transform his footing into a control.

Of these industrial speculators the most celebrated was Philip Henslowe. Henslowe began as a speculator in small, unsavoury properties upon the bank called stews, whence my lord Bishop of Winchester had in previous generations drawn much good rent for pious purposes. Henslowe began his career by marrying a widow richly left. At one time he was a dyer but, more congenially, in the early nineties, a pawnbroker. Most of all he believed in real estate. His respectability, like the Bishop's, was beyond impeachment. He contrived, among other things, to be a Gentleman Sewer of the Chamber to King James, a vestryman, a churchwarden, and a governor of the free grammar school of Southwark. What is more to our purpose, he kept a diary or note-book of his transactions into which one day he was to enter the name of " Bengemenes Johnsones ".

Henslowe's first theatre was the Rose, built by himself on Bankside. Here he settled down in 1594 with Edward Alleyn as his principal actor and a company under the protection of Lord Howard, known therefore as the Admiral's Men. Thence in 1600 he moved to the Fortune. Henslowe's papers show us the under side of the life of an actor or dramatic author of the day. It had been the custom of the sharers in a company to allow the " housekeeper ", in other words the owner of the theatre, the whole of the payments made for admission to the galleries. The Burbages, at the Globe, however, being wise masters, admitted the sharers to these profits of the house, so that a " sharer " at the Globe might also be a " housekeeper ". The site of the theatre was conveyed by lease in two equal parts. The Burbages retained one of them; the other was divided among the five principal actors. The new system was intended to secure the greater comfort, permanence and prosperity of the company. In practice, however, it merely added to the opportunities of the speculator. The new shares of the housekeepers, like those of the primitive sharers in a company, might be pledged or transferred by inheritance or marriage—an arrangement which afforded a fine opportunity not only for the more provident members of the company itself, but for the capitalists from outside who sought to get control of the industry. To the former class belonged Shakespeare's editors, Hemming and Condell, who bought up by degrees all the housekeeping shares of their colleagues. To the latter class belonged speculators like Henslowe who had no interest in the theatre except as an investment and source of profit.

The results may be studied in detail in the famous diary. Henslowe, following the example of the Burbages, first took half of the galleries as principal landlord. But he was always at hand to accommodate his players and authors in their frequent emergencies. Inevitably, sooner or later, they came upon his books for money advanced on the security of their shares or, in some cases, of their personal talent or utility. Always he was ready to pay their poets, tradesmen or contractors. Soon, as a regular system, he was settling all accounts and charging them to the members of the company, who ceased to be an association of profit sharers and became his dependants. The process was easy and quick. In July, 1598, the very year in which we find Jonson marked as one of Henslowe's retainers, we read : " Here I begin to receive the whole galleries." A system of collective agreements between partners in a company had thus been superseded by a system of individual contracts made by the sharers and hirelings with the capitalist. The old association between members of a mystery had given place to an industrial exploitation of the theatre by a man of means. That nothing should be wanting to complete this substitution of the modern for the ancient system we find Henslowe at one moment in agreement with a certain John Cholmley who was a grocer and had a monopoly of the right to sell drink on the premises.

Thus Jonson, looking round upon the stages on his return from the wars, had to beckon him the example of Shakespeare in receipt of profits as a sharer and a housekeeper, not to mention small but gratifying payments received for occasional plays and for his services as an actor. But there stood also the awful warning of poor players and dramatists appealing to the tried courtesy and great love of " Father Hinchlow " for small advances to keep them in bread and sack.

Jonson, without capital and in urgent need of money, fell inevitably into the grip of the waiting capitalist, and his feelings, when he felt the grip closing upon him, can be inferred from the resolute efforts he made to be received into more kindly and respectable houses. But it was not so easy to escape. A significant entry concerning Jonson in Henslowe's diary reveals an arrangement typical of the capitalist's methods. Henslowe advanced to Jonson the money necessary to bring him into the company as a sharer and subsequently paid himself back by appropriating the proceeds of the share as they fell due. The poor sharer was thus securely tied. Most of the entries in the diary, however, refer to mere loans from day to day—made, in Jonson's case, to the author for account of work received or promised. From these entries and from the diary at large it may be inferred that even a successful author was lucky to get as much as ten pounds for the sale outright of an original play. Authorship alone was clearly not enough, especially as the dramatists were more often employed in collaborating with one another or in revising old work than in writing new and original comedies and tragedies by a single hand.

It is difficult to estimate Jonson's early contributions to dramatic art. Prior to the production of *Every Man in His Humour* in 1598, none of his achievements can be determined with precision. Clearly, however, he was not successful in these early years either as actor or author. " Although at first he could not hit the bore "—he writes of himself some forty years later in his prologue to *The Sad Shepherd*. Equally clearly he did not take at all kindly to the popular theatre. The prologue to *Every Man in His Humour*, his first significant personal utterance, is explicit.

> Though need make many poets, and some such
> As art and nature have not bettered much,
> Yet our's for want hath not so loved the stage,
> As he dare serve th' ill customs of the age,
> Or purchase your delight at such a rate
> As, for it, he himself must justly hate.

This was a difficult fellow from the outset, declaring in crabbed numbers that there were limits to the concessions which he was prepared to make to a public for whom he had no great respect.

Henslowe in 1597, as we have seen, was in partnership with Alleyn, financing the Admiral's Men at the Rose. We read in his diary that on July 28th of that year Jonson received an advance of four pounds. On December 3rd Jonson made proposals for a new play and, promising to complete it by Christmas, was given a further advance of twenty shillings. In August of the following year he is named as joint author, with Chettle and Porter, of a lost comedy, *Hot Anger Soon*

The First Twenty-five Years

Cold. With such flickering lights as these must we be satisfied.

Of Jonson as an actor almost nothing is known. A legend that he followed the cart as a strolling player has no more solid foundation than the fact that the London companies at this time often found it necessary to go on tour when plague compelled them to close their houses in the city. A tradition that he played the part of Jeronymo in *The Spanish Tragedy* is hardly more respectable. There were two popular plays of the period in which Jeronymo was the principal figure. In the first of them, by an author unknown, emphasis was constantly laid on the hero's diminutive stature. It was in fact a stage tradition that Jeronymo was a small man. Kydd, in *The Spanish Tragedy*, does not stress the point, but a big sturdy man like Jonson would hardly be cast for the part unless he were a good enough actor to live down the physical disclaimer. It is true that Richard Burbage, who was large and stout, played Jeronymo, but Burbage also played Hamlet; his physique counted for little because his acting counted for much. That Jonson, an indifferent actor, and a novice in the company, should be cast for a character for which he was physically unsuited rests on no better authority in the last resort than certain contemporary allusions to Jonson's connection with the play which are sufficiently well explained by the fact that he wrote some additions to it on the occasion of its revival in 1601. None of these references requires that he should have acted in it.

Of Jonson's acting, in fact, all that we can safely affirm is that he was not a success. Antony Wood, who rejects the story of his " ambling after a waggon ", states that he made his first appearance at " an obscure playhouse, called the Green Curtain, but that his first

13

action and writing there were ill ". All authorities agree that Jonson was not anywhere taken for a star. His appearance was not that of an actor. A lean scrag is Thomas Dekker's description of him at that time and Jonson, putting himself on the stage in *Every Man out of His Humour*, describes himself as a raw-boned anatomy who " walks up and down like a charged musket ". His complexion, too, was bad. " Like a rotten russet apple when 'tis bruised "—is Dekker's description. Aubrey states that he was " never a good actor, but an excellent instructor ", and Aubrey, who according to Gifford " thought little, believed much and confused everything ", could, nevertheless, hardly go wrong on so plain an issue. Apparently all that could be said in Jonson's favour was that he read well and his noble patrons, in later years, would frequently employ him for that purpose. The Duchess of Newcastle records that her husband " never heard any man read well but Jonson, and yet he hath heard many in his time ".

Jonson first walked into the full blaze of recovered history in 1597, when he became somehow implicated in the sensational suppression of *The Isle of Dogs*. To what extent did he share in the writing of that unfortunate play ? The principal author was undoubtedly Thomas Nashe, pamphleteer and satirist, who, though new to the stage, would require but little help with the pen. His fluency of word and fancy were notorious. Possibly, however, he needed advice, constructive or otherwise, from a practical playwright. *The Isle of Dogs* was produced by a company playing at the Swan, in July, 1597, as the Earl of Pembroke's Men. It was a fatal venture for all concerned. The Privy Council, deeming *The Isle of Dogs* to be a scurrilous, lewd and treasonable performance, not only arrested all the responsible parties on whom it could lay hands, but ordered a general restraint of plays in all theatres till further notice. Nashe, expecting trouble, had fled to Yarmouth. Jonson remained and, together with two actors of the Swan Company, Robert Shaw and Gabriel Spencer, was committed to the Marshalsea prison, whence he was not released until the autumn.

The Isle of Dogs is unfortunately lost, so we are unable either to measure the offence or to decide how much of it was due to Jonson. Two circumstances, in the absence of the play, are to be noted. Jonson was henceforth a man marked by the authorities and he had made the acquaintance in prison of Gabriel Spencer.

Jonson was released on the third day of October. *The Isle of Dogs* had ruined the company at the Swan, and Henslowe hastened to secure several of its members for the Rose, including two who had deserted him for the Swan in February and Gabriel Spencer, who had spent eight weeks with Jonson in the Marshalsea. These events had left some bitterness behind and there was worse to follow. The actors who in October, 1597, returned to Henslowe or entered his service for the first time were pursued with suits and menaces by one Francis Langley, who had financed the venture at the Swan and with whom they had contracted to play for twelve months under a bond from each of them for a hundred pounds. Jonson's name does not appear in these transactions, but they are of importance for the light they throw on the sharp, stubborn and litigious spirit with which these playhouse rivalries were conducted.

The company at the Rose was now in effect an amalgamation of the Admiral's Men with those of the Earl of Pembroke, Gabriel Spencer being admitted as a sharer, to whom Henslowe, as in Jonson's case, apparently advanced the necessary capital. Jonson's status at the Rose, an indebted actor and writer of plays with an illusory share in the company, was profoundly unsatisfactory. He was, in fact, rapidly drifting into the position of many of his older colleagues, who had been driven to indenture themselves to a master who, however forthcoming, required them to work to a programme and in collaboration with men of very unequal merit and experience. To be articled to Henslowe as a regular hack for account of the Admiral's Men was not to be endured, and Jonson again began to look elsewhere. The venture at the Swan had failed, but over against the Admiral's Men at the Rose was the rival company of the Lord Chamberlain at the Curtain, whose principal author was Shakespeare, and the even more dangerous Children of the Chapel at Blackfriars. Jonson in the summer of 1598 had a play in hand of his own unaided composition. *The Case is Altered* was his first independent comedy, and he gave it, not to Henslowe, but to the Children of the Chapel, while *Every Man in His Humour*, already in his head and possibly up his sleeve, went in September to the Curtain. Tradition insists that it was Shakespeare who had first sight of the second comedy and secured its acceptance.

This secession of Jonson from the Rose was deeply resented, and the feeling against him was aggravated by the success of his two plays. *The Case is Altered* was so well received at Blackfriars that it was revived in the following year and successes scored by the Children of the Chapel were particularly galling to the adult companies. Hardly less provocative was the production in September of *Every Man in His Humour* at the Curtain where James and Richard Burbage were building up an immortal reputation for sound management and splendid acting. Jonson during these critical weeks would scarcely be popular with his colleagues at the Rose. Of these none considered himself more aggrieved than Gabriel Spencer, a man of violent temper whose record was already stained with a fatal brawl. Two years previously, in the house of Richard East, a barber, he had killed a man, James Feake, in a sudden altercation. It is not known how he evaded hanging on that occasion. Suffice it that, escaping in December, 1596, he very nearly brought another and a better man to the gallows in September, 1598.

The fatal incident occurred only two days after the production of *Every Man in His Humour* at the Curtain. There was a meeting between the two men in Hogsden fields near Shoreditch. The rights of the affair are not easily determined, but there is no reason to doubt Jonson's definite statement to Drummond that he was " appealed to the fields ". In other words, there was a formal challenge and a fair encounter. There was matter enough for dispute. An allusion from Spencer to base fellows who, eating the bread of their master, betrayed him to rival houses would be more than enough to bring Jonson to his feet.

Jonson killed his man and was committed at the Old Bailey for manslaughter. The sequel is oddly disconcerting. Jonson saved his neck, not by pleading justification or fair fight, but by claiming benefit of clergy as a man who could " read like a clerk ". A memorandum on the conclusion of the affair, discovered in the Middlesex Session Rolls, runs as follows :

Middlesex :—The jurors for the Lady the Queen present that Benjamin Johnson, late of London, yeoman, on the 22nd day of September, in the fortieth year of the reign of our Lady Elizabeth by God's grace Queen of England, France, and Ireland, Defender of the Faith, etc., with force and arms, etc., made an attack against and upon a certain Gabriel Spencer, being in God's and the said Lady the Queen's peace, at Shordiche in the aforesaid county of Middlesex, in the Fields there, and with a certain sword of iron and steel called a Rapiour, of the price of three shillings, which he then and there had and held drawn in his right hand, feloniously and wilfully beat and struck the same Gabriel, giving then and there to the same Gabriel Spencer with the aforesaid sword a mortal wound of the depth of six inches and of the breadth of one inch, in and upon the right side of the same Gabriel, of which mortal blow the same Gabriel Spencer at Shordiche aforesaid, in the aforesaid county, in the aforesaid Fields, then and there died instantly. And thus the aforesaid jurors say upon their oath, that the aforesaid Benjamin Johnson, at Shorediche aforesaid, in the aforesaid county of Middlesex, and in the aforesaid Fields, in the year and day aforesaid, feloniously and wilfully killed and slew the aforesaid Gabriel Spencer, against the peace of the said Lady the Queen, etc.

It seems at first sight difficult to reconcile this memorandum with Jonson's own account of the matter. If Spencer stood in " God's and the Lady the Queen's peace ", the inference would normally be that Jonson had made a mortal and unprovoked attack upon him. Jonson, moreover, confessed the indictment and admitted to Drummond that he was " almost at the gallows ". How does this agree with the statement that he was " appealed to the fields " ?

The issue is of such capital importance—all the difference between brutal murder and a social gesture —that it is hardly possible to leave it ambiguous. There is one vivid particular which helps us to reconstruct what in all probability occurred. Jonson mentioned to Drummond, quite incidentally, that Spencer's sword was a full ten inches longer than his own. His adversary, however, previous to the killing, had hurt him in the arm. The encounter does not, therefore, seem to have been a formal duel with witnesses. There is, to say the least, a notable absence of punctilio. Jonson, on being "appealed to the fields", presumably met Spencer by appointment. Neither of them was in the mood to stand on ceremony. Possibly a duel was intended ; but what actually occurred appears to have been a scuffle which ended in a mortal wound for the challenger. In such circumstances, Jonson, faced with an indictment difficult to avoid, though it did him no dishonour, preferred the safer course. By claiming benefit of clergy he at least made sure that he would not be hanged.

Jonson was condemned to lose his goods and to be branded on the thumb with the Tyburn "T". Loss of goods did not worry a poet who was living from hand-to-mouth on advances from Henslowe, and the branding was notoriously a formality, the iron being hot or cold according to the disposition of the gaoler. In Jonson's case it was presumably cold, for no brand was ever mentioned as being found on him. Jonson himself relates how, when his judges during the time of his close imprisonment " placed two damned vilains to take advantage of him ", he received a friendly warning from his keeper. Evidently he was more popular with the prison staff than with his examiners, who must have found his behaviour extremely exasperating. They could " get nothing of him to all their demands ", he tells us, " but Aye and No ".

It may be asked why the judges should thus lay traps for a person arrested on a charge of homicide in a private brawl ? Was this device of the " two damned vilains " a normal stage in the judicial procedure of the courts in dealing with subjects already entered in the bad books of the Privy Council ? Jonson had been in prison once already for " lewd words "—the description given in Star Chamber minutes to any published or reported utterance in disrespect of things politically or morally established. Thereafter he would always be suspect. What were these interrogations to which Jonson would answer only " Aye " and " No "? An ingenious modern critic has suggested, in the absence of any known reason why the poet should have been baited in this fashion, that he imagined the whole thing. But that is a difficult explanation of a really simple matter. The " two damned vilains " were doubtless real enough. There were good reasons, as reasons went in those days, for looking closely into the conduct and associations of a man who at twenty-five had shown himself, in word and deed, to be of a violent and dangerous disposition.

It is significant that Jonson, having narrowly escaped a hanging, not only suffered no loss of public esteem but within a few months was on friendly terms even with those who had pressed his undoing. Among the latter, Henslowe had not been inactive. Four days after the scuffle he had sought advice from Edward Alleyn over the loss of one of his company slain by the hands of Benjamin Jonson, bricklayer, " which hurteth me greatly ". It was intolerable that a man to whom he had paid good money for indifferent plays should not only be profiting his rivals with successful comedies but should actually have killed one of his own actors and sharers. The term *bricklayer* betrays a deep displeasure. It was to be a classic gibe in the battle of the stages. Henslowe was clearly in a bad temper. Yet it was not long before he and Jonson were friends again. It is even more remarkable that none of the enemies whom Jonson made for himself during the next four years ever raised against him this small matter of a homicide publicly confessed. Jonson's part in the affair could not have been one of which he was ashamed or which could be effectively used to discredit him.

Within the year Jonson, released from prison and enjoying the success of his two plays at the Curtain and at Blackfriars, was collaborating, for account of Henslowe, with Dekker in a tragedy and with Dekker and Chettle in an historical play. Both these plays have perished and their production is merely of interest as showing that in the picaresque days of Elizabeth it was not incongruous for a man to bring his servant to the gallows on a Friday and help him kindly on the way to fortune on the Monday following.

The success of *Every Man in His Humour* in 1598 brings to a close this first stage in the career of Jonson as a dramatist and public figure. Here, for a moment, we will pause to consider his dramatic achievements at twenty-five and his very definite views on the stage as an honourable employment.

CHAPTER II

The Comedy of Humours

JONSON, writing the comedy of humours, proclaimed himself to be a stubborn and systematic realist. He was undertaking to present men and things as he saw them. The things were all about him in the streets, houses and taverns of London. The men he saw as humours walking—this man greedy, that man vain, jealous, proud, artful or fond. He took the world as he found it. But this was a mad world and comedy required that he should discover method in it. His characters were taken from life, but, once they had entered his comedies, they must leave behind them all their human inconsistencies and run true to form. Henceforth they were in the hands of a master logician who would present them as studies in special types of behaviour. There was to be no room for romantic wilfulness or unexpected fun. All was to be hard, clear and persistent. Here was an author who would never wait for an inspiration, never lose or see things in flashes, but look into himself steadily for things noted and remembered.

Was Jonson by nature, or merely by design, the melancholy comedian? Was there ever a chance that, had he permitted his instincts to run loose, undisciplined by scholarly reflection or stout purpose, he might have remained a writer of tragedies, scattering warm blood and jolly horrors? Was this, perhaps, a romantic poet strangled with learning or irked with too strong a sense of reality to let himself go? It is a theory attractive to the modern critic who in matters of character prefers a paradox to a category. It is amusing to seek in Jonson, so hard of outline, for a mystic or a visionary, to suspect him of native charms inhibited or turned aside. Those who would play with this idea may remember how the wraith of his beloved son appeared to him at death, and how Drummond describes him in after life as " oppressed with phantasy, which hath ever mastered his reason, a general disease among poets ". There are, moreover, passages in his plays where phantasy for a moment assumes control, as when Volpone " hath consumed a whole night in lying looking at his great toe, about which he hath seen Tartars and Turks, Romans and Carthaginians, fight in his imagination ". Such indications might tempt us to regard Jonson's genius as of the romantic order, overlaid and diverted from its bias by a scholar's education and by definite theories of the poet's task.

It is, nevertheless, a temptation to be firmly rejected. That Jonson, both as a man and a poet, had his moods and flashes of fine feeling and second-sight is true enough. No living character in literature or life was ever all of a piece—a fact which he himself would have done well as a dramatist to remember. The abiding reality of Jonson, however, lies elsewhere than at the end of his great toe. His namesake a century later was also a visionary, who sweated constantly in a mortal fear of death, but he has rightly been accepted as the embodiment of the common sense of his time and people. As with Samuel so with Benjamin. The author of *Every Man in his Humour* was not one whose mind could ever have run into the romantic mould and not a line he has written suggests that he ever lost his way. The comedy of humours was the natural expression of his genius and all his later masterpieces were achieved by following consistently in middle life the lines which he laid down for himself in his youth.

Those who would see in Jonson a lost romantic have naturally wished that they could see his earliest work. Jonson himself, however, deprived them quite deliberately of that pleasure and thereby probably spared them a disappointment. That he began as a purveyor of romantic tragedies is true, but it is doubtful whether he ever wrote a complete tragedy himself during these early years. His work for Henslowe more likely consisted in bringing old texts up to date, adapting them to the immediate occasion, writing additional acts and scenes or helping his colleagues to find a beginning, middle or end to their endeavours. There exists, in fact, no serious work of Jonson which he cared to acknowledge prior to *The Case is Altered*. Attempts have been made to find in this comedy a romantic indication. The plot is romantic—a son and a brother lost and found, loves crossed, a noble prisoner, a miser's daughter. The language, too, is at times romantic.

> Some spark it is, kindled within the soul,
> Whose light yet breaks not to the outward sense.

But this is the dead matter of the play, made to form and measure. The living stuff, embedded here and there, is all shrewd satire and sound sense. The whole play points unmistakably to its successor. Even its figures of romance expressly ridicule the fine stage pieces in which there is nothing but kings and princes. " They would have me make such plays," says one of them, " but an they'll give me twenty pounds a play, I'll not raise my vein." Is it a coincidence that Jonson had himself just received twenty pounds from Henslowe for writing a tragedy which was either not delivered or has since been lost ?

The Comedy of Humours

The best speeches of the play are made by a miser
as he buries his gold, in lines which instantly call to
mind the magnificent orations of Volpone penned by
the poet of humours in his prime :

> In, my dear life ! sleep sweetly, my dear child !
> Scarce lawfully begotten, but yet gotten,
> And that's enough. Rot all hands that come near thee,
> Except mine own ! burn out all eyes that see thee,
> Except mine own ! all thoughts of thee be poison
> To their enamour'd hearts, except mine own !
> I'll take no leave, sweet prince, great emperor,
> But see thee every minute. King of kings,
> I'll not be rude to thee, and turn my back
> In going from thee, but go backward out.

Such passages point directly to Jonson's later manner
—similar qualities and similar defects. The author
approaches eloquence in these lines by the same means
and in the same vein as in his greater comedies, isolating
the point of character which he desires to emphasise,
hammering upon it with persistence, embroidering
upon it with ingenuity, till the reader cries for mercy
where there is none. The prose passages point just
as definitely to the manner and matter of his later
comedies. Juniper the cobbler, walking from *The
Case is Altered* into *The Alchemist*, would find himself
at home, and there is more than a foretaste of the topical
railing against follies, fashions and the public taste
which abound in all the later work.

It is even more significant that the language of high
romance is itself derided. Thus the euphuist takes
leave of his guest : " Till my regression, so please you,
your noble feet may measure this private, pleasant and
most princely walk." Or he begs of another : " Will
you do me the honour to confine this noble spirit
within the circle of your arms." Jonson here mocks
the romantic style as Molière mocked the exquisite
terminology of the blue salon.

Ben Jonson

Even more decisive are the romantic passages themselves. With no real passion to keep him true, Jonson, when he tries romance, helplessly commits enormities from which even the tragedians he subsequently chastised would instinctively have recoiled. None of the bombast he was shortly to deride in *The Poetaster* better deserves the lash than the appeal of his own fair Rachel to the gallant who would possess her :

> Away ! forbear, ungentle Angelo !
> Touch not my body with those impious hands,
> That, like hot irons, sear my trembling heart,
> *And make it hiss at your disloyalty.*

It is unlikely that many of the plays to be hereafter mentioned will ever again be read, even by those who may be tempted to open the page at *Volpone*, *The Alchemist*, or *Bartholomew Fair*. Allusions to the lesser plays, however, with quotations now and then of significant passages, are essential to an adequate review of Jonson's work and method. The reader will be asked to accept these allusions and quotations without inquiring too closely into their context or the progress of the play to which they refer. Jonson's plots are ingenious. They are extremely complicated and effective for their purpose. Yet of themselves they are of little consequence. The reader or spectator does not hang upon events. There is rarely an interest in the incident or story. Jonson asks nothing of his plots except that they shall serve to keep his characters coming and going. An anxious father keeps his vagrant son under observation ; a jealous husband looks constantly to the virtue of his wife ; a resourceful servant bears an active and ingenious part in these proceedings ; young people amuse themselves at the expense of a town gull and a country gull ; a swaggering soldier cudgels whom he can and accepts a drubbing when he must ; a crusty but kindly magistrate exercises

26

The Comedy of Humours

his authority; Downright, a plain squire, lives constantly up to his name. Of such is *Every Man in His Humour*. There is no more incident than suffices to bring these people together in situations which enable them to show their quality. The progress of the play is designed from first to last to permit its characters to unfold. The same is true of its successor. *Every Man out of His Humour* is equally intricate and ingenious, but the plot has no importance in itself. An envious poor man, a vain and singular knight, a profane jester, an affected courtier, a doting citizen, a proud wife, a light-witted lady, a misanthropical knave—these are provided in turn with just the encounters and situations needed for their display and for a consummation of the author's design which, in this comedy, is to show the major humours of his people indulged to the point of exhaustion, so that in the end they are purged and suffer a momentary conversion. It would be lost labour to spend time on a presentation or study of Jonson's plots. They are the mechanics of his art. Our interest will lie in the characters, moods and subjects of his plays. All that we need to note of his situations is that they are adequate for his purpose. Jonson was excellent in construction. Perhaps the hand of the master is too often visible, but his invention and craft were seldom unequal to the matter in hand.

Jonson himself in *Every Man out of His Humour* indicates the kind of interest which he wishes us to take in his situations. In that play he introduces a series of dialogues between two critics who comment on the characters and incidents of the piece. They have just witnessed a scene in which one of the characters, in accordance with the poet's scheme, has been purged of his humour by its excessive indulgence. One of the critics, referring to the author, observes:

" I wonder what engine he will use to bring the rest out of their humours." His companion retorts : " That will appear anon. Never preoccupy your imagination withal. Let your mind keep company with the scene still." The interest which we are invited to take in the plot is here very clearly indicated. We are naturally tempted to wonder how the author will contrive to display his characters to best advantage and induce them to conform to his design. Even so, the author chides our wandering and calls us back to attention. Never worry about the plot, he says in effect ; just follow the scene and leave these things to me.

The Case is Altered prepared us for Jonson's impending rejection of the fashionable romantic stage. This rejection is explicitly announced in the prologue to *Every Man in His Humour*. No more kings and princes (he declares) :

> But deeds and language such as men do use,
> And persons such as comedy would choose,
> When she would show an image of the times,
> And sport with human follies.

Jonson thus proclaimed his subject and intention. He would make an honest effort to hold up the mirror to his contemporaries. His resolution was taken and in that moment the comedy of humours was born.

The term " humour " had once had a definite meaning, but like the " complex " of to-day it had in 1598 passed from the doctors and psychologists into common speech and purists were staggered :

> Daily to see how the poor innocent word
> Was racked and tortured.

Any mood, condition, habit or eccentricity might be called a humour. Jonson took the popular term, but he used it correctly and constructed upon it a method

The Comedy of Humours

of characterisation which he applied with an impressive consistency. The clearest statement of what he intended is given in the introduction to the second of his plays in that kind. *Every Man out of His Humour* was not produced till 1599, but it may usefully be considered here in connection with its predecessor. In the induction we read :

> In every human body
> The choler, melancholy, phlegm and blood,
> By reason that they flow continually
> In some one part, and are not continent,
> Receive the name of humours. Now thus far
> It may, by metaphor, apply itself
> Unto the general disposition :
> As when some one peculiar quality
> Doth so possess a man that it doth draw
> All his affects, his spirits and his powers,
> In their confluctions, all to run one way,
> This may be truly said to be a humour.

Jonson, in this passage, bases his comic method on the old physiology. Four humours, corresponding with the four elements—moist, dry, hot, and cold— formed the constitution of a man, whose character was determined by their proportion and balance. If one of the humours was in excess he deviated to that extent from the normal and thereby became liable to rebuke. The physiology is mediaeval, but the underlying theory of comedy implicit in the idea of a balance and proportion between the humours is not, therefore, the less valid. It amounts to much the same thing as was expressed by Aristotle in his golden mean, or by Horace in his *decorum*, or by Bergson in his theory of laughter as a social gesture whose evolutionary purpose is to arrest mechanical excess and keep the individual intelligently sensitive to his environment. This same idea, moreover, is the basis and inspiration of the comedies of Molière, who contended that even

Ben Jonson

virtue and wisdom may be excessive and therefore ridiculous :

> La parfaite raison fuit toute extrémité
> Et veut que l'on soit sage avec sobriété.

There is, indeed, little that is original or peculiar in Jonson's humours or the theory of comedy which he constructed upon them. The important point is that his genius needed a system and applied it without mitigation or remorse. All his comic characters, in the last analysis, are helplessly in the grip of their humour or ruling passion. Some are constitutionally subject ; others temporarily enslaved. In some of his characters the humour is the result of a permanent lack of balance ; in others it may be the result of association, sympathy, persuasion or habit. The first are incorrigible, but the second may be cured. Both come under Dryden's famous paragraph on the comedy of Jonson :

> Among the English by humour is meant some extravagant habit, passion, or affection, particular to some one person, by the oddness of which he is immediately distinguished from the rest of men ; which, being lively and naturally represented, most frequently begets that malicious pleasure in the audience which is testified by laughter ; as all things which are deviations from custom are the aptest to produce it. The description of these humours, drawn from the knowledge and observation of particular persons, was the peculiar genius and talent of Ben Jonson.

From time immemorial comic dramatists have tended to insist on two fundamental laws of the theatre. Neither of them, however, applies to the greater comedies and both were in due course shattered by two dramatists of genius—Shakespeare in England and Molière in France. First there was the law that a comic character must necessarily be a type rather than an individual—columbine, pantaloon, pierrot or harlequin ; the resourceful valet, the impertinent maid, the sere and yellow amorist, the pedant in his kind. To this first law the theory of humours was dangerously kind, and it was Jonson's misfortune that he did not escape its consequences. Secondly, there was the law that all portraits on the stage must be larger than life. To this law even Congreve subscribed. The distance of the stage, he argued, required it—a fallacy which confuses merely physical considerations with the essential principles of dramatic art. If Congreve were right in his contention, it would follow that no refinement of characterisation or complexity of motive would be practicable on the stage and his own plays, among others, would be condemned as dramatically impossible. Admittedly this ancient fallacy still governs the practice and determines the achievement of the great majority of dramatists, but its acceptance as a valid canon would definitely put the theatre on a lower level than any other of the arts and it explains why the theatre is too often regarded as an inferior muse. Fortunately, however, it is a law which no dramatic genius has in practice accepted, and it is immediately ignored when, owing to some accident of history or state of the public mind, the theatre is thrust into prominence—as in the times of Pericles, Elizabeth or Louis XIV.

From the peril of enlargement Jonson escaped more easily than from the pitfall of standardisation. To the latter he was liable by temperament and education. His natural love of clarity and system, aggravated by a scholar's training, necessarily drove him to the comedy of humours, to a presentation of types, to characters logically constructed and all of a piece, to figures which insisted that they were miserly, amorous or vain till they became mere figures of avarice, eroticism or conceit. To the former peril he was, however, stoutly rebellious. He had the scholar's love of consistency which committed him to types, but he had also the scholar's dislike of immoderation and, what was an even more effective safeguard, he had the eye of a realist for the society in which he lived. Jonson may be criticised for applying a fantastic and merciless logic to the development of his plot and characters, which brings them often to the edge of farce, but he cannot be accused of deliberately presenting his people larger than life, of thickening his outlines and blunting his intentions, in the conviction that the theatre must of necessity be a gross medium making its effects from a distance.

The old contention that the theatre should present types rather than individuals has inspired nine-tenths of dramatic production in every age. The originality of Jonson's types lay in the fact that he made or found them for himself as the result of observing or sharing in the life about him. They were not traditional stage figures accepted and perpetuated. Jonson was a scholar but his scholarship did not move him, as some critics have suggested, to copy the braggarts and misers and gulls of Plautus and Terence. He claimed for himself, with justice, that his comedies were from life, not figures of the antique stage or of the old morality. He takes his characters from Tudor houses and taverns ; he exhibits them in their native environment ; their talk is racy of the slang and topics of the day. The odd quality of his plays is to be sought precisely in this application of an individual realism in detail to a standardisation of the types selected. The result is an odd blend of bustling actuality with formal abstraction. Human categories, compact and trimmed, move amid the common disorders of life. The author has met his men and women in the street ; he has removed them for a moment to his study ;

there he has submitted them to a process of inspection and analysis ; thence he brings them out again into the light of day. They do not come out quite so gaily as they entered. They know henceforth exactly how they are expected to conduct themselves. Their movements are a little stiff. They are no longer incalculable. It is not difficult to predict what they will say or do in any given situation. They have now the automatism which belongs to the comic character ; they are absurd because they have surrendered to a ruling passion or habit to the extent of indulging it reflexively without reference to its timeliness or propriety.

Two examples from *Every Man in His Humour* will suffice to show how carefully Jonson avoided the kind of exaggeration which is so often assumed to be necessary on the stage, and yet fell into another kind of excess by presenting his types too consistently. The elder Knowell is a comic figure, but he is drawn with such moderation that, like the *misanthrope* of Molière, he might easily be taken as a foil to the follies of the rest. He is a wise, kind, naturally considerate father and friend. His " humour " consists in his being excessively a parent, over-anxious for the welfare of his son, zealous to retain the respect due to his years and his office, prompt to take offence at the levity and wilfulness of the younger generation. Nothing could be more carefully restrained than his presentation. There is no exaggeration or concession to that law of enlargement accepted by Congreve. Knowell is an illustration of Jonson's method at its best. Any father to any son is his complete description.

He is clearly, however, a comic figure. His paternal " humour " has become a reflex and he spends his fatherly wisdom and advice unseasonably on the first comer, delivering his best speech to a fool, obviously incapable of profit :

> Learn to be wise and practise how to thrive.
> That would I have you do ; and not to spend
> Your coin on every bauble that you fancy,
> Or every foolish brain that humours you.
> I would not have you to invade each place,
> Nor thrust yourself on all societies,
> Till men's affections or your own desert
> Should worthily invite you to your rank.
> He that is so respectless in his courses
> Oft sells his reputation in cheap market.
> Nor would I you should melt away yourself
> In flashing bravery, lest, while you affect
> To make a blaze of gentry in the world,
> A little puff of scorn extinguish it,
> And you be left like an unsavoury snuff,
> Whose property is only to offend.
> I'd have you sober and contain yourself,
> Not that your sail be bigger than your boat;
> But moderate your expenses now, at first,
> As you may keep the same proportion still.
> Nor stand so much on your gentility,
> Which is an airy and mere borrow'd thing,
> From dead men's dust and bones ; and none of yours,
> Except you make or hold it.

It is a speech that inevitably recalls the advice of Polonius to Laertes and, comparing the two figures, we measure almost the whole difference between the method of Jonson and that of Shakespeare. Polonius is a complete human character. The mere thought of him utterly destroys the more systematic figure. Polonius can be both wise and foolish ; he can have dignity and yet be ludicrous ; he can be inconsistent because he is alive. There can be no inconsistency in a character by Jonson. Knowell must run true to his " humour " in every scene. He can have no holiday from being the anxious father, as Polonius when he listens to the players or discourses of the madness of Hamlet. There is, however, no exaggeration or improbability of feature. Knowell is comic merely because he is unseasonably consistent.

That Jonson, avoiding enlargement of motive, nevertheless fell into another kind of excess is more clearly shown in his presentation of characters whose humours are less engaging or definitely abnormal. Kitely, the jealous husband of the play, is a striking illustration. Kitely is first cousin to Master Ford, the jealous husband of Windsor. Ford, however, as presented by Shakespeare is more than a jealous " humour ". He is a normal human creature, mystified and stimulated into an abnormal passion. Kitely, on the contrary, is an automaton, mechanically suspicious from the start, and his suspicion is systematically developed till it passes all belief. In any logical process there is an element of farce, for logic leads the fancy to extremes where of necessity it loses touch with the normal world. He moves in a private solitude where his humour rules supreme. Poison is mentioned and instantly he is at the point of death :

> Now I remember,
> My wife drank to me last and chang'd the cup,
> And bade me wear this cursèd suit to-day ;
> I feel me ill ; give me some mithridate,
> Some mithridate oil, good sister, fetch me ;
> Oh I am sick at heart, I burn, I burn.

Such excess is a necessary consequence of Jonson's method. Jonson's characters, supremely rational in their follies, ignore or transgress all the laws of probability which are valid in an irrational world. Kitely is an extreme case, but the method which here raises a smile will shortly enable the author to produce scenes of real penetration and power in which he gives us terrifying glimpses of a comic world inhabited by highly rational automata constructed in a fierce derision of the vices and follies of men.

It is to be noted that, even in this early play, the

Ben Jonson

author's concentration—slow, brooding and devout—
produces a kind of dark heat in the style of his verse.
There is no flash or radiance—no lightning in the
collied night. Jonson's eloquence came by study. It
is hard-wrought. The author does not wait to be
moved. He takes a definite subject and hammers it
into shape. Kitely's jealousy is described in phrases
minted and applied ; they do not spring from the
subject or carry us beyond it. They have no pro-
longations. They are deliberately apt. There is
never a phrase to look beyond the lamplight. Jonson's
verse combines the formality of a scholar with the
familiar precision of a realist. Classic simile alternates
with metaphors picked from contemporary fashions.
Kitely, afraid to leave his wife unguarded and alone,
begins with the Hesperides :

> . . . What earthy spirit but will attempt
> To taste the fruit of beauty's golden tree,
> When leaden sleep seals up the dragon's eyes ?

But he ends, after much hard hammering at his theme,
on a household note :

> The dangers are too many ; and then the dressing
> Is a most main attractive ! Our great heads
> Within this city never were in safety
> Since our wives wore these little caps. I'll change 'em,
> I'll change 'em straight.

We have failed to find a lost romantic in Jonson.
It would be more profitable, perhaps, to look for
a realist defeated. Jonson's naturalism was strong
enough to save him from the worst consequences of
his method and it may pertinently be asked whether
it might not have saved him altogether. He held it
to be the function of comedy, hitherto a camp follower
of the muses, to reflect the common man, to present
his follies without exaggeration, to follow him in his
normal business and desires. Jonson's naturalistic

bent was fundamental. As a scholar he had trained his fancy to frequent the garden of the Hesperides, but, striding in Bankside, his eyes were caught by those little caps of Dame Kitely, and they, too, must find a place. Might his genius have taken another turn if he had never sat under Camden—if his capacious mind had remained sensitive to merely contemporary impressions? It is an interesting, but an idle speculation. For better or worse Jonson was marked in boyhood with the sign of the scholar, and his scholarship, as we shall realise more clearly later, was as natural and as ineradicable a part of the grown man as his observation.

Jonson, the realist, escapes now and then from his method. Bobadil, the braggart soldier of *Every Man in His Humour*, is more than a type. One can imagine Bobadil emerging from the situation in which his " humour " is displayed and continuing to live of his own motion. He is less obviously a category than the rest. Jonson conceived him as a " humour ", but there were too many of his sort in the taverns of London to allow of his remaining a mere abstraction. He illustrates the odd blend of erudition and direct observation which was Jonson's peculiar secret, but observation prevails and to that extent the character is nearer life. He is not altogether ridiculous. He can turn a good phrase and has an instinct for fine living. " I love a cleanly and quiet privacy above all the tumult and roar of fortune "—thus he makes excuse for his humble lodging. Bobadil's portrait of Squire Downright is both lively and fanciful : *By his discourse he should eat nothing but hay*. His praise of tobacco may stand comparison with Falstaff's eulogy of sherris-sack and the invention with which he embellishes a quarrel is only equalled by the ingenuity with which he avoids it. Bobadil is alive, various and unexpected.

It is significant that Jonson, writing *Every Man in*

His Humour, first set his comedy in Italy and gave Italian names to his characters. For a poet may study humours as well in Italy as in England. But the realist intervened. This was not only a comedy of humours but a play of London life. Therefore, in a second version, presented shortly after the first, the scene was transferred. Lorenzo became Knowell, Museo became Brainworm, Thorello became Kitely. Jonson began in Italy and ended in Shoreditch just as Kitely begins with the Hesperides and ends with the little caps of his wife.

The change was in keeping with the author's topical allusions to places, persons and fashions and his determination to relate his comedy to common folk and the life of every day. No more foreign plots and cities. No more kings and princes. Comedy should keep to the low or middle reaches. Even gentlemen are rare. Jonson, in after years, lived in fine houses and was not unacquainted with kings. But his mind was given to the types with whom he had been most intimately connected in his impressionable youth. Therefore his comedies are plays of the tavern and the fair. They are crowded with gamesters and swindlers, varlets and gulls. The scale may rise to simple citizens, proud merchants and justices, but polite society is mostly ignored.

Of the two plays under consideration, *Every Man in His Humour* and *Every Man out of His Humour*, the second is the more formal and consistent. Jonson's comedy of humours was an experiment. The experiment was successful and he took it a stage further in the sequel. He explained his system at length in an induction and put upon the stage a brace of critics who delivered a running commentary on the play as it proceeded. The two main features of his previous work were deliberately emphasised: namely the logical development of a prevailing humour in each of his characters, which in this play ultimately finds a remedy in its own excess, and a realism which insists upon an everyday setting and persons taken from life. The first feature is even more consistently pressed than in the previous comedy. Sordido, of a mean and envious humour, is ultimately driven to hang himself. A number of rustics enter and cut him down. No sooner does Sordido recover his breath than he must scold his saviours for wastefully cutting the rope instead of undoing the knot : " You threadbare, horse-bread-eating rascals, if you would needs be meddling, could you not have untied it ; but you must cut it, and in the middle, too." This is carrying a humour to the extreme of farce. It is an even more striking example of the excess to which Jonson's method was liable than Kitely's panic of the poison.

The realism of the second comedy is sustained in all its accidents, and Jonson insists continually on this aspect of his work. Might not the argument of his comedy, says one of his brace of critics, have been " of some other nature, as of a duke to be in love with a countess and that countess to be in love with the duke's son, and the son to love the lady's waiting-maid ; some such cross-wooing with a clown to their serving-man, better than to be thus near and familiarly allied to the time ". To which the other critic answers with a reference to Cicero's definition of comedy : " *imitatio vitae, speculum consuetudinis, imago veritatis* —a thing throughout pleasant and ridiculous and accommodated to the correction of manners ".

There, for the moment, we will leave the comedy of humours. With astonishing results Jonson picked up the thread again some six years later in *Volpone*. First, however, we must consider what was happening to him in the years between.

CHAPTER III

Poetomachia

THE poets' war or battle of the stages lasted for three years. It began with a manifesto and ended with an apology. Often it seems but a tiresome brawling between rival dramatists in which mean issues hide, not very successfully, behind high words and legendary names. Poetomachia is a sounding title. It arouses majestic expectations. It sets us looking for noble causes such as might appropriately divide the choice and master spirits of a great age, and it has encouraged biographers and critics to enlarge, even to transfigure, the argument.

What, in effect, was the trouble? Jonson derided the style and vocabulary of the romantic tragedians and in particular of John Marston. Marston resented the derision and accused his friend of arrogance, railing and filching by translation. For three years the public enjoyed the quarrel and for three hundred years critics have studiously reviewed every phase of it. Was it, in substance, worth while? Has it any historic value except as a stimulating revelation of the man who provoked it?

Jonson began his serious career as a dramatist with a declaration already noted. His comedies were to reflect a faithful image of the times. To this preliminary manifesto he was shortly to add another. The true poet should be not only a painter but a prophet. He must not confine himself to anatomising the world; he must cleanse and refine it. This

ST. PAULS AND BANKSIDE

Detail from Visscher's Map of London 1616

[face p. 40

double task, for a man with so generous a flow of poetic scorn, had a double consequence. First, it led him to mock the princes and heroes of fashionable tragedy, who to the immense delight of the public made milch the burning eyes of heaven. Secondly, it led him to express contempt and indignation for actors and authors who degraded their vocation with vulgar and licentious excursions. There was no personal malice in these attacks. It was *furor poeticus* : it is the cause, it is the cause, my soul. The heroic dramatists, however, who warmed their public with mighty lines naturally resented the suggestion that they wrote fustian and the comic dramatists who shook its sides with laughter, broad as ten thousand beeves at pasture, disliked being taxed with lewdness and brothelry. Still, there might have been no poets' war if Jonson had been a man of normal sensibilities and dimensions. Happily for us he was the most tactless man who ever lived and a man who must carry everything he touched to an extreme. Happily, too, his age was large enough to receive him. For three years it resented him, and the theatres shook with the clamour that he raised. It then decided to accept him as a character. He became a national institution to be cherished and endured. Jonson, with an apology so fierce that it could only be uttered once on any stage, retired from the field to write tragedies and masks against the day when his comic genius, taking another turn, might come back to his humours with all forgiven.

Jonson never realised why he should have made himself so unpopular. He seldom knew how another man would take him. His praise was as likely to provoke offence as his censure, for it was invariably qualified, and his admiration, even though acceptable, was irritating. He spoke from the chair—a literary

Jupiter dispensing bolts or blessings to mortal men.
To his literary insolence there was no circumference.
As the priest of Apollo he permitted himself the
utmost liberty of indignation and rebuke, and he
honestly expected the poets to be gratified and to
mend their ways.   There is something almost pathetic
in his surprise that anyone should be offended by his
censure.   Some years after the battle of the stages
had been fought to a finish we find him in his dedication of *Volpone* to the sister universities recording
his grieved amazement that, though he bears malice
to no man, he has not escaped " from some the
imputation of sharpness ".   There are people, he
complains, who believe him to " have taken a pride
or lust to be bitter ".   Protestingly he inquires what
nation, society or general order or State he has provoked ?   What public person ?   Has he not preserved
their dignity, as his own person, safe ?   What broad
reproofs has he used ?   Where has he been particular
or personal, except—he adds with a last savage fling
at his victims—to mimics, cheaters, bawds, buffoons
and creatures who, for their insolencies, are worthy
to be taxed ?

Jonson, in fact, regarded himself as Apollo's champion
against all comers.   Young Knowell of *Every Man in
His Humour* (first version) proclaimed the state of
poesy to be " blessed, eternal and most true divine ".
Though she may appear in many but poor and lame,
patched up in rags and remnants and starved for want
of her peculiar food, her true condition is otherwise.
Set high in spirit, graced in art and philosophy :

> Oh then, how proud a presence does she bear !
> Then she is like herself, fit to be seen
> Of none but grave and consecrated eyes.

To this insolence of the poet, with a literary conscience that never slept or left him long at peace,

went also the conscience of a man to whom virtue and moral excellence were equally precious. Jonson was a son of the renaissance, but, looking back to the ancients, he remembered that Epicurus was a comely and wise philosopher. Pleasure must be moderate and fair. Liberty is not licence. The moral test must ultimately be applied. Jonson was too English to believe in art for art's sake. Good poetry and sound ethics must go together. There must be a decorum even in fruits of the lighter muse which must not stir laughter in " sinful things, execrable rather than ridiculous ". Thus, in the dedication to *Volpone*, he declares the " impossibility of any man's being the good poet without first being a good man ". It is the poet's privilege, he urges, " to inform young men to all good disciplines, inflame grown men to all great virtues, keep old men in their best and supreme state ". He is the interpreter and arbiter of nature, a teacher of things divine no less than human, a master in manners. Unfortunately, however, in despite of this lofty mission, there is, in many writers of the day who usurp the poet's name, " nothing but ribaldry, profanation and blasphemy " :

> That all are embarked in this bold adventure for hell is a most uncharitable thought, and, uttered, a more malicious slander. For my particular, I can, and from a most clear conscience, affirm that I have ever trembled to think toward the least profaneness ; have loathed the use of such un- washed bawdry as is now made the food of the scene.

All liberal and learned souls, he continues, must abhor such lust in liberty with its " brothelry able to violate the ear of a pagan and blasphemy to turn the blood of a christian to water ". It is the office of a comic poet to " imitate justice and instruct to life, as well as purity of language, or stir up gentle affections ". In this adventure :

Ben Jonson

If my muses be true to me I shall raise the despised head of poetry again and, stripping her out of those rotten and base rags wherewith the times have adulterated her form, restore her to her primitive habit, feature and majesty and render her worthy to be embraced and kissed of all the great and master spirits of our world.

These are astonishing words from a man who had just escaped the gallows ; from one who fell foul of authority on all possible occasions, who declared to Drummond, as from experience, that the use of a maid was nothing in comparison with the wantonness of a wife, who loved his lyric feasts,

> Made at the Sun,
> The Dog, the Triple Tun ;

and whose verses " Outdid the meat, outdid the frolic wine." From his grave praises of the poet's function one might construct a Jonson after the Shorter Catechist. That, however, would be a false conclusion. Jonson was no puritan in words, works or deeds. He lived frankly and heartily after his desires. Life was no vale of tears but an inheritance to be enjoyed. It was a poet's conscience that troubled him. He would spoil no man's freedom and envy no man's pleasure. But brothelry was tedious and excess was unlovely. His dislike of immoderation was that of the wiser pagans and in no way inhibitive. Jonson was so truly a child of the renaissance that his plays can no longer be performed. He cheerfully and instinctively disregarded criteria which his successors had either to accept or deliberately to challenge.

Too much emphasis should not be laid upon Jonson, master in morality and reformer of the stage. The poet—especially if he write for the theatre—is invariably driven to plead in ethics. To all good citizens the moral issue is more obvious and vital than any of the considerations of fitness and sincerity whereby dramatic genius is ruled. Molière, defending his *Tartuffe*, written with no thought except to make men laugh, was driven to pretend that he had composed it as a tract against hypocrisy and was even compelled to write a second version in which his impostor, no longer left triumphant, suffered defeat and retribution. Even Wycherley, scandalising the polite world with *The Plain Dealer*, had the impertinence to claim that it was his mission to chastise his contemporaries into a better way of living. Jonson took the inevitable line and it happened, in his case, to be one which accorded very well with his instincts and education. Apollo was a gentleman. The muse must be good as well as beautiful. It is to be noted, however, that, off his guard, Jonson was less concerned with the sins of society than with its follies. He quarrelled with his poet contemporaries less because they encouraged men to wickedness than because in his view they wrote bad verses and degraded their vocation.

Jonson's summary of Marston's part in the affair is concise and crushing. He told Drummond that " he had many quarrels with Marston, beat him, took his pistol from him, and wrote his *Poetaster* on him ", affirming, as origin of the dispute, that Marston had represented him on the stage as given to venery.

Marston was of an uncertain, stormy and enthusiastic disposition—son of an Italian mother and an English father. He had ill digested a classic education and had further distorted his fanciful intelligence with reading for the bar. He was younger than Jonson, but already famous as a pamphleteer with an astonishing power of invective. He seems sincerely to have admired Jonson. He began in any case by praising him. In the Autumn of 1599 he was employed to furbish up an old play for the Children of St.

Paul's, a piece entitled *Histriomastix*, a satire upon
players, one of the musty fopperies of antiquity for
which he himself professes sound contempt in a later
comedy. Among its characters is one Chrysoganus, a
poet-soldier, who holds himself a little aloof from his
fellows. Marston, intending a compliment, allowed
it to be inferred that Chrysoganus was Jonson in disguise, and ventured to enliven his admiration with a
little friendly chaff:

> How, you translating scholar, you can make
> A stabbing satire or an epigram,
> And think you carry just Rhamnusia's whip
> To lash the patient; go, get you clothes.

Commending Jonson was a dangerous pastime, and
flattery conveyed in this familiar style, concluding
with a friendly glance at his shabby coat, was unlikely
to be well received.

Marston's efforts to claim Jonson publicly for a
friend and brother were snubbed with cruelty and
precision. Jonson had spent several weeks in New-
gate with a rope round his neck. The experience
had not improved his temper or increased his respect
for society, and it was clearly a dangerous mood in
which he sat down to write a sequel to the play which
had made him famous. There had been little or
nothing in *The Case is Altered* or *Every Man in His
Humour* to justify the accusation, with which the
London stages would shortly be ringing, that their
author was a grinning monster of arrogance. There
had been purpose and dignity in these earlier pieces
and a proud conviction. The tone of their immediate
successor was strikingly different. *Every Man in His
Humour* had laid the town at his feet. *Every Man
out of His Humour* brought it about his ears. The
poet, escaped from the prison-house, strides out upon
the stage and delivers himself point-blank:

> Who is so patient of this impious world
> That he can check his spirit or rein his tongue ?

The play was preceded by an induction in which the author, speaking in his own person under the name of Asper, thus uttered his mind :

> My soul
> Was never ground into such oily colours
> To flatter vice and daub iniquity ;
> But, with an armèd and resolvèd hand,
> I'll strip the raggèd follies of the time
> Naked as at their birth.

What follows is the railing of an angry man whose conceit of the poet's vocation is such that he thinks the world should be grateful for his chiding :

> Good men and virtuous spirits, that loathe their vices,
> Will cherish my free labours, love my lines,
> And with the fervour of their shining grace
> Make my brain fruitful to bring forth more objects,
> Worthy their serious and intentive eyes.

So much for himself and this, after bitter scolding, for a final fling at his public :

> If we fail,
> We must impute it to this only chance,
> Art hath an enemy called ignorance.

Though Asper be rightly identified with Jonson, it is essential to note that the author, nevertheless, has a comical eye upon himself. He is well aware that a man in his rages—though it be Jonson—is apt to be ridiculous, and he presents himself as a figure of fun along with the rest of his characters. He even apologises for his indignation :

> Why this is right *furor poeticus* !
> Kind gentlemen, we hope your patience
> Will yet conceive the best, and entertain
> This supposition, that a madman speaks.

The critics of Jonson have strangely neglected to notice that in Asper he deliberately exaggerated his

own " humour ". This, however, is a cardinal circumstance and there is stranger to follow. For Asper,
having introduced himself as the author of the play,
retires to transform himself into one of its principal
characters, who must also, it is generally agreed, be
accepted as Jonson in masquerade. This is Macilente,
a disagreeable and censorious personage who rails continually, and whose railings, laid to Jonson's account,
are quoted as a further proof of insolence. This,
however, is sheer misunderstanding. The humour of
Macilente is thus described : a man well-parted, a
sufficient scholar and travelled, " who, wanting that
place in the world's account which he thinks his merit
capable of, falls into such an envious apoplexy, with
which his judgment is so dazzled and distasted, that
he grows violently impatient of any opposite happiness
in another ". It is a description which, taken with
the conduct and speech of Macilente throughout the
play, proves the exact contrary of what is commonly
alleged. Doubtless Jonson used Macilente as a vehicle
of his own disappointment and wrath, but it is equally
doubtless that he presented him as a comic figure and
obnoxious to reproof. Macilente may be regarded
as an exercise in self-correction. Jonson presents
him with detachment as embodying the excesses to
which he knew himself to be liable. The comic
author, conscious of his gifts and feeling that they
have not procured him the recognition he deserves,
lashes in himself the " envious apoplexy " which he
cannot altogether overcome. His presentation of
Macilente, far from being a proof of insolence, points
to an odd, cantankerous humility. The lash which
he applies to others falls with equal severity upon
his own broad shoulders. The point is of some
importance. The satirist, with no eye for his own
deficiencies, has no right to a hearing. The comedian,

unaware that he, too, can be ridiculous, lacks the vision and humanity essential to his vocation. The author of *Every Man out of His Humour*, looking after Macilente with a stern smile, in effect declares : there, but for the grace of God, goes Ben Jonson. It is the spirit in which Molière, with a smile less bitter and a sense of comedy more delicate and profound, regarded his *misanthrope*.

There is yet another passage in the play which shows that Jonson does not claim exemption from the wit that strikes at others. He has made bitter fun of himself in the person of Macilente. Now, in a more genial vein, he sketches a lively but satirical portrait of himself living frugally at home, but emerging on occasion to eat hungrily out of doors :

> This is what our poet calls Castalian liquor, when he comes abroad now and then, once in a fortnight, and makes a good meal among players, where he has *caninum appetitum* ; marry, at home he keeps a good philosophical diet, beans and buttermilk ; an honest, pure rogue, he will take you off three, four, five of these one after another and look villainously when he has done, like a one-headed Cerberus. . . . And then, when his belly is well-ballaced, and his brain rigged a little, he sails away withal, as though he would work wonders when he comes home.

Every Man out of His Humour is not remarkable for sweetness and light, but it has been singularly mis-read to the detriment of its author. The intrusions of Asper have been used as a proof, without qualification, of his conceit and the excursions of Macilente as evidence of a naturally venomous disposition. The critics, in their eagerness to discover the author in his plays, have not, in fact, allowed him to be a dramatist. Jonson admittedly presents his disgruntled characters with zest, but to identify him with them completely is to go flatly against the text.

Ben Jonson

There remained enough, however, with all deductions made, to provoke resentment and retaliation. It was the firm opinion of the town that here was a satirical rogue who sadly needed a purge, and the person for this business was naturally the man who had been unkindly selected for explicit and singular punishment. Jonson's satire had been mostly general, but there was a passage in which he derided the devout and friendly Marston as a writer of fustian and as one who claimed without sufficient reason to be a scholar. Jonson had introduced into his comedy of humours a certain Clove, whose glory it was to invite players and make suppers. " Prithee," says Clove, " let's talk fustian a little and gull them ; make them believe we are great scholars." Whereupon, sad to relate, he selects flowers and treasures from the remarkable vocabulary of Marston and, lest the application should be missed, brings in an explicit reference to *Histriomastix*.

Marston was caught where most he was tender to reproof. He, too, was a man of parts, out of Oxford and the Middle Temple, and from one scholar to another such gibes as Jonson had permitted himself were hard to bear. Were they not brothers in learning and distress, men made for finer things than to be entered upon the books of Henslowe ? Yet here was a colleague, for whom he had expressed a notorious admiration, mocking his taste in epithets. The trained satirist, whose " *scourge of vilainy* " had only a year since alarmed the town, put a rod in pickle for an unkind friend. The result was *Jack Drum's Entertainment*. The piece was played by the Children of St. Paul's. Jonson is lampooned as a silly bombastic fellow who

Thinks God infusèd all perfection
Into his soul alone, and made the rest
For him to laugh at.

The castigation of his arrogance, of which the world had just received a notable example that same year in *Every Man out of His Humour*, was fair comment, but for Jonson there were only two possible courses. He took them both. First he beat the author. Secondly, he set himself seriously to the task of cleansing the public stage, where such things were permitted.

Thus was planned and written *The Poetaster or His Arraignment.*

Prior to *The Poetaster*, however, there was some hearty and confused skirmishing between the parties. Jonson had written a play which will have to be considered later in another connection. *Cynthia's Revels* or *The Fountain of Self Love* is more important as Jonson's first serious effort to attract the attention of the Court than as a contribution to the battle of the stages. Tradition insists, however, that two of the most unpleasant characters in the play are intended to represent Marston and Dekker. The only passage that lends any colour to this assumption is one in which the two characters express hatred and envy of the one just man in the piece, a certain Crites, said to be Jonson in disguise. But Crites is not in the least like Jonson, except that he has a great contempt for fools. He is described as a " creature of a most perfect and divine temper ". He is presented as Jonson's ideal man—all his humours balanced. " Nature ", it is affirmed, " went about some full work—she did more than make a man when she made him " ; while the god Mercury declares : " It is beyond my deity to give him his due praises ; I could leave my place in heaven to live among mortals, so I were sure to be no other than he." The legend that, in drawing Crites, Jonson was presenting himself—a legend strangely accepted by his admirers, though it was in truth invented by his enemies—has no historic basis. Marston naturally took it for granted as a further proof of Jonson's arrogance and conceit. Marston further took it for granted that, Crites being Jonson, the enemies of Crites must be himself and his friend. There is really no ground for this assumption. Admittedly Jonson, through the mouth of Crites, utters Jonsonian sentiments, and very naturally the persons who attack Crites resort to gibes from which Jonson may himself have suffered : " Foh ! he smells all lamp oil with studying by candlelight," or " get him in one night and make him pawn his wit for a supper ". But there are no definite strokes of portraiture which point to Jonson in Crites or to Marston and Dekker in his detractors. That Jonson intended Crites to be himself is usually offered as a natural sequel to the presentation of himself as Asper in *Every Man out of His Humour*. The sequel, however, is not natural but contradictory. Jonson presented Asper with a smile for his own bad " humour ", whereas he presented Crites as the perfect man. *Cynthia's Revels* as a battle piece is less important, in fact, for what it contains than for the constructions placed upon it. " Application is now grown a trade with many," Jonson complained in his preface to *Volpone*, " and there are that profess to have a key for the deciphering of everything." In the case of *Cynthia's Revels* the " applications " were made by the victims themselves. Here was a pretty quarrel. It was a pity to let it die for lack of nourishment. So Marston fitted the caps and meditated further profit and revenge.

The play, however—though it was not intended to be systematically personal—was fuel to the flames in that Jonson continued to lay about him regardless of whom he might offend. Authors in general are taxed as promoters of other men's jests, who farce their scenes with stale apothegms. They penuriously glean wit from every laundress or hackney man, or derive their best grace with servile imitation from common stages or observation of the company they frequent, as if their invention lived wholly upon another man's trencher. Then, lest the spectator, on top of all this, should be feeling complacent, Jonson turns suddenly upon the civet wit among them that knows no other learning than the price of satins and velvets and yet will censure as desperately as the most professed critic ; upon those who swear down all but the old Jeronymo as it was first acted ; upon him who " shakes his bottle head and out of his corky brain squeezeth out a pitiful learned face and is silent ". Such censures are freely interspersed, in the Jonsonian manner, with the customary declarations of his own independence, originality and disdain of the public taste :

> In this alone his Muse her sweetness hath,
> She shuns the print of any beaten path ;
> And proves new ways to come to learnèd ears.
> Pied ignorance she neither loves nor fears.
> Nor hunts she after popular applause,
> Or foamy praise, that drops from common jaws.

Here was enough to fortify the suspicion that Jonson thought well of his own work and had small respect for that of his rivals. It was doubtless the common view that he needed taking down and it was obviously good business to assume the lead in a popular enterprise. It was calculation, perhaps, rather than resentment which prompted Marston and Dekker to fit the caps in *Cynthia's Revels* so firmly on their heads. Marston would wish to convince the town that he had successfully provoked his rival and was more than a match for him. His reply, put forward on behalf of himself and his brethren, was produced early in 1601, probably by the Children of St. Paul's, under the title of *What you Will*.

Marston's attack was nimble, direct and, above all, exasperating. He had no altars to defend. He was burdened with no theory or cause. He had no concern with the dignity of his art or sacredness of his vocation. He desired only to earn applause by his bold challenging of a common nuisance and to feed fat a profitable grudge. Jonson is lampooned as one Lampatho Doria, a " fusty cask, devote to mouldy custom "—a description well calculated to irritate an author who was continually claiming that his methods were new and his plays unlike any before written. Lampatho is " a canker-eaten, rusty cur ", the " snaffle of free spirits ". Moreover, he is proud in his own estimation, " very nectar—if you but sip of his love you were immortal ".

Jonson retorted with the play which, according to his own confession to Drummond, he deliberately wrote " on Marston ". This was *The Poetaster*, in which the poets' war, to lend it dignity, was transferred to Rome under Augustus and the issues between Jonson and his contemporaries presented as issues between Horace and his rivals, ultimately brought to judgment in the high court of Vergil. *The Poetaster* requires, as it repays, careful reading. The secret of Jonson's annoyance is laid bare—its origin, its complexion, its qualifications. It is the one play of our author in which we find, now and then, a cry from the heart. The well-fitted prose of the scholar halts for a moment ; there is a break in that odd blend of fancy and observation, a pause in that sprightliness as of syllogisms out on holiday or conceits dancing like dust in the sunlight of an attic brain ; and there shoots forth a phrase in which personal experience and a private passion prevail for a moment over the measured wrath of the man with a cause and a reputation to defend.

There is, in particular, a picture of Homer, " poor blind, rhyming rascal, that lived obscurely up and down in booths and taphouses and scarce ever made a good meal in his sleep ". There is also this of poets in general : a " poor sort of starved rascals that are ever wrapt in foul linen and can boast of nothing but a lean visage peering out of a seam-rent suit, the very emblems of beggary ". Or read this of the hungry mummer : " Let's have good cheer to-morrow night at supper : good capon and plover do you hear, sirrah ? And do not bring your hungry player with you there ; I cannot away with him. He will eat a leg of mutton while I am in my porridge."

For a moment the poor scholar looks out from the robes of Apollo's priest. It is no idle speculation to look here for the cause of that arrogance which was all this poet had to keep him warm and valiant. Pride in his vocation and disdain of those whose service was less austere were necessary to sustain him. Jonson, vicar of the muses, elect champion of art, which " hath an enemy called ignorance ", must walk constantly larger than life beside poor Benjamin with his " lean visage peering out of a seam-rent suit ".

Most of what has been written of Jonson's conceit implies that he took to himself personally all that he claimed on principle for an honest poet. His arrogance, however, has no touch of private vanity. It is the arrogance of a prophet. His censures are addressed, without rancour and quite impersonally, to those who need correction. He deprecates " applications " and denies that he has hitherto desired to rebuke any man in person. The offences he chastises may have been noted in this or that individual, but the reproof is general :

> I used no name; my books have still been taught
> To spare the persons, and to speak the vices ;

and finally he takes leave of his *Poetaster* with an address to the reader : " for in these strifes and on such persons it were as wretched to affect a victory as it is unhappy to be committed with them ".

The Poetaster should be read less as a personal attack upon Marston—though it began that way— than as a generalised onslaught upon the poets who, in Jonson's opinion, were bringing the stage into discredit. The play derives a certain remote gravity from the fact that the scene is laid in Rome. Jonson deliberately intended to give to his rebuke a dignity such as could hardly have been achieved by means of a contemporary London satire. In an *Apologetical Dialogue* appended to the play he thus describes its inception :

> Three years
> They did provoke me with their petulant styles
> On every stage ; and I at last, unwilling,
> But weary, I confess, of so much trouble,
> Thought I would try if shame could win upon them ;
> And therefore chose Augustus Cæsar's times,
> When wit and arts were at their height in Rome ;
> To show that Vergil, Horace and the rest
> Of those great master-spirits, did not want
> Detractors then and practisers against them.

There are two themes to the play, held together by skilful plotting and unity of interest. Ovid makes classic and composed love to the daughter of Augustus in a fashion which the author conceives to be highly romantic and he is banished. These are the ardours of poesy. The second theme presents Horace and the rivals who conspire against his reputation. The conspiracy is denounced to Caesar, who invites Vergil to judge between the parties and to devise a punishment. Horace is the poet in society and his circumstances are those of Jonson himself—a poor man but the friend of all good spirits, independent and fearless, subject to the envy of small minds, impatient of folly and pretence, jealous for his art and for those who practise it fairly. The chief conspirator against his peace and fortune is one Crispinus, whose enmity has its origin in the rejection by Horace of his importunate advances. Crispinus, ultimately revealed as Marston, stands for all poets who degrade their quality by constant running after recognition and by exceeding in their work the limits of good sense. He affects a learned and unlovely jargon and will do anything to be received. With him is associated Demetrius, identified with Dekker. The association of Dekker with Marston in the battle of the stages does not seem to have been due to any real malice on the part of the genial and disreputable author of *The Shoemaker's Holiday*. He went into the fray for pickings. " His doublet is a little decayed ; he is otherwise a very simple honest fellow, Sir, one Demetrius, a dresser of plays about the town here. We have hired him to abuse Horace and bring him in, in a play, with his gallants." Demetrius arraigned before Vergil, is given a dunce's coat and cap to wear. The doom of Crispinus is more elaborate. Pills of hellebore are administered, a light vomit, to purge his brain and stomach. A basin is brought and up come some of his choicest epithets—glibbery, lubrical, magnificate, snotteries, turgidous, ventosity, oblatrant, prorumped, obstupefact and the like. He is advised in future to be more careful in his classic diet. He is to taste each morning a piece of Terence, to shun Plautus and Ennius as meats too harsh for a weak stomach. He is to physic himself with the best Greeks, but to beware of

Lycophron as " too dark and dangerous a dish ".
He is not to " hunt for wild outlandish terms " and
to leave out words when neither his understanding
nor his sense is able to receive them. This fair
abstinence, humbly followed, will render him more
sound and clear.

In parentheses we may observe a rather curious circumstance, a warning to all scholars, schoolmasters,
professors and academies. Many of the words vomited
by Marston and held up to derision by the author
of the first English grammar have passed into the
language, whereas many of the words which Jonson
himself used in his plays have not only died out but
seem to us now every whit as barbarous as the heavings
of Crispinus. The first words that come from the
bad poet in his agony—retrograde, reciprocal, incubus
—now fall from our lips quite easily. Among others
used to-day without difficulty we find defunct, spurious,
clumsy and strenuous. To Jonson these words were
outlandish and impossible, though he himself resorted
to expressions which within a generation were entirely
obsolete. In running through his plays we light
upon such words as redargue, statuminate, vively,
tentiginous and threaves. Those same little pills of
hellebore administered to the author of *The Poetaster*
would have filled a basin with phrases that the good
genius of English has since neglected.

The charges brought against Jonson by his enemies
are explicitly set forth in *The Poetaster*. Self-love,
arrogance, impudence, railing and filching by translation, such is the formal indictment. He is further
described as a mere sponge—nothing but humours and
observation. He goes up and down sucking from
every society, and when he comes home he squeezes
himself dry again. He will sooner lose his best friend
than his least jest. He is " all dog and scorpion ; he

carries poison in his teeth and a sting in his tail ".
He deserves tickling " for his arrogance and his impudence in commending his own things ". Vergil,
giving judgment, rules that a poet, if he be a " full
and well-digested man ", may think well of his own
works without being accused of " inflation ". " Erection ", a fair term, would be more appropriate. A true
use of translation is stoutly upheld. It is as deserv-
ing of commendation as is invention or creation. As
for the charge of railing :

> His sharpness—that is most excusable,
> As being forced out of a suffering virtue,
> Oppressèd with the licence of the time.

On the real motives of the quarrel Jonson is equally
explicit. He accuses Marston of attacking him from
pure envy—for " keeping himself in better acquaintance or enjoying better friends ". Dekker is made
to confess that he had no real cause of offence :
" No great cause, not I, I must confess ; but that he
kept better company, for the most part, than I ; and
that better men loved him than loved me ; and that
his writings thrived better than mine and were better
liked and graced." Another motive, more real perhaps, is frankly announced by one of the conspirators :
" Say no more, then, but do it ; 'tis the only way to
get thee a new suit." Jonson glances again at this
motive in the *Apologetical Dialogue* :

> What they have done 'gainst me,
> I am not moved with ; if it gave them meat,
> Or got them clothes, 'tis well ; that was their end.

Hitherto Jonson had laid about him promiscuously
as the spirit moved him. In his first plays he had
mocked the tragedians, derided the exquisites, dropped
scorn upon his audience, satirised citizens, soldiers,
farmer, justice and fop. In *Cynthia's Revels* he had

turned, as we shall see, with equal asperity upon the fashions and follies of the Court. It was this resolute anatomising of the time's deformity in every nerve and sinew that provoked the poet's war. Here was a bear that might be baited with advantage. But the bear, thus baited, turned in *The Poetaster* with a cumbrous dignity upon his assailants. Not only did he lay flat the leaders of the pack. He struck deliberately at all who misprized his noble art : worldlings and men of law, soldiers, players and critics.

We have yet to consider Dekker's personal contribution and the part which has been most dubiously assigned to Shakespeare.

Dekker, though invariably named with Marston as one of Jonson's principal detractors, was never more than a secondary figure. There was no malice in the man. All London was talking of *The Poetaster* and there was enough public resentment at Jonson's presentation of himself as the good poet to make him a popular subject. Dekker had written a play about William Rufus—a highly romantic, improbable and surprising piece, written, as Dekker wrote, with a grin that broadened as the thrills increased. Into this comical-tragedy of a maiden in peril, regal tyranny, simulated death and hearty remorse he introduced, in a splendid disregard of dramatic propriety, a group of characters from Jonson's comedy. In Dekker's play the case against the enemies of Horace is tried again and the appeal is successful. Horace is awarded a crown of nettles, Crispinus and Demetrius being presented as the kind, forbearing and reasonable witnesses of his discomfiture. Horace is further twitted with his slowness as an author : he breaks out like Christmas but once a year ; and he is charged with a notable preference for fashionable company. All this was clearly thrust into the story of William

Rufus at the eleventh hour, but the exact chronology is hard to determine.

No one would ever have thought of connecting Shakespeare with the poets' war but for an observation made in a Cambridge play in 1601–2, wherein William Kempe is presented as saying : " Why here's our fellow Shakespeare puts them all down, ay, and Ben Jonson, too. Ben Jonson is a pestilent fellow ; he brought up Horace giving the poets a pill but our fellow Shakespeare hath given him a purge that made him bewray his credit." Where is this same purge to be found in the plays of Shakespeare ? The most engaging contention is that Ajax in *Troilus and Cressida* was meant for Jonson and that Marston was pilloried as Thersites. It is a theory which discovers Shakespeare as impartially deploring the whole affair—as well he might, for, while the Children of St. Paul's and of the Queen's Chapel piped each other down in rival accents, the Lord Chamberlain's men, whose business it was to make Shakespeare's fortune at the Curtain or the Globe, were proportionately neglected. Nevertheless, the identification is extremely hazardous. *Troilus and Cressida*, scientifically dated, would seem to have been produced after and not before the allusion to Shakespeare's purge. Nor was it Shakespeare's way to medicine his friends. The most that can be said for the theory that Ajax is meant for Jonson is that the character can be made to fit, after a loose and genial fashion :

> This man, lady, hath robbed many beasts of their particular additions ; he is as valiant as the lion, churlish as the bear, slow as the elephant ; a man into whom nature hath so crowded humours that his valour is crushed into folly, his folly sauced with discretion ; there is no man hath a virtue that he hath not a glimpse of, nor any man an attaint but he carries some stain of it : he is melancholy without cause and merry against the hair : he hath the

joints of everything but everything so out of joint that he is a gouty Briareus, many hands and no use, or purblind Argus, all eyes and no sight.

Elaborate characters, drawn in antithesis, though not frequent in Shakespeare, were fashionable among his contemporaries—exercises of virtuosity in which most dramatists were expected to be proficient. Shakespeare, in *Troilus and Cressida*, seems merely bent on showing that he can, if he likes, do this sort of thing as well as another, and there is no call to suspect a personal intention. Those who identify Ajax with Jonson naturally presume that Jonson was glancing at Shakespeare in the *Apologetical Dialogue* :

> Only amongst them I am sorry for
> Some better natures, by the rest so drawn
> To run in that vile line.

Here again, the inference is attractive, but dubious. Was it, in any case, a vile line for Shakespeare to suggest that, though Jonson (Ajax) might be an odd fellow, Marston (Thersites) was a sheer deformity? The wise critic will reject the tradition altogether.

The *Apologetical Dialogue*, in which Jonson uttered his last word on the poets' war, was only spoken once on any stage. When it was first produced and why it was withdrawn is not known. Presumably it provoked either a riot or an inhibition. Our author, discovered in his lodgings and urged by his friends to carry on the good fight, protests that he will waste no more time upon his detractors. Let them say that he is hit, hurt, sorry and reduced to silence. He will sit henceforth above the battle. He expresses astonishment that *The Poetaster* should have ruffled any man :

> I can profess, I never writ that piece
> More innocent or empty of offence.
> Some salt it had, but neither tooth nor gall.

Poetomachia

He had never, for instance, meant to traduce the law or to attack the soldier. He had been a soldier himself and had not shamed the profession. True, he had taxed the players—and yet but some of them and those but sparingly. So far Jonson is plaintive, but he soon flies into a passion. He is not, he pleads, malicious, but, were he so minded, he could write iambics to make them hang themselves ; rhyme them to death, " as they do Irish rats in drumming times ", stamp their foreheads with deep and public brands so that his prints might still be read in their pale fronts when their own poor writings were wrapping tobacco or some cheaper drug. He was charged with being slow. Had he not, even in frenzy, taken fifteen weeks to write *The Poetaster* while normally he could produce no more than one play in a whole year? One play in a year, indeed ! He wishes he could say he had never done as much. Is it not enough to make a man destroy his pen and throw his labours on the fire to see how the base and beggarly conceits of common scribes prevail with the multitude against :

> Things that were born when none but the still night
> And his dumb candle saw his pinching throes.

Thus, with apologies to all, the author bade his comic muse a long farewell ! For five years he was not again to venture on a comedy. On a note, almost of rapture, he dedicates himself to another mistress. Comedy has proved so ominous to him that he will try whether her sad sister be not of a kinder aspect :

> I that spend half my nights and all my days,
> Here in a cell, to get a dark, pale face,
> To come forth worth the ivy or the bays,
> And in this age can hope no other grace—
> Leave me ! There's something come into my thought,
> That must and shall be sung, high and aloof,
> Safe from the wolf's black jaw and the dull ass's hoof.

So ended poetomachia. As a critical episode in Jonson's life and an example of stage manners under Elizabeth it is worth considering. It turned Jonson for a while to tragedy, and perhaps it helped to discourage Marston from further excesses in that kind. Its general significance, however, was small. Nor were its personal consequences either serious or enduring. The stage in those days was an arena where hard hitting was expected and bones not easily broken. Within a year Marston was contributing with Jonson, Chapman and Shakespeare to the *Phoenix and the Turtle*, and in 1604 he dedicated to Jonson his revised version of *The Malcontent*. A year later, moreover, Jonson wiped away all trivial fond records of all this hearty strife by taking a hand with Marston and Chapman in the writing of *Eastward Ho*. His part was small, but significant, for the play was prosecuted and Jonson, who insisted on taking his share of the responsibility, voluntarily sought his own arrest. Poets might quarrel among themselves but when it came to meeting authority all ranks were instantly closed and a firm front presented to the natural enemies of justice and reason.

CHAPTER IV

Elizabeth and James

JONSON, in forty years, made no more than two hundred pounds out of his plays. His livelihood was elsewhere. This was the age of the noble patron, and Jonson was to spend most of his life sitting at the tables of men on whom he depended largely for employment and support. Among them, fortunately, was King James himself—for this was also the age of the Court mask—a form of entertainment in which Jonson, for nearly twenty years, had no rival in the land. Henslowe paid ten pounds for a play, but the Lord High Treasurer might be required to disburse as much as forty pounds for a mask. Jonson, lacking the popular touch, was driven from the common stage and it was a sound instinct which prompted him almost from the outset to seek the approval of a more fastidious public. Even during the poets' war he had been twitted with having finer friends than his estate allowed. He did not deny it. On the contrary, he admitted that much of the hostility he aroused was provoked by envy of his better company. The young barristers of the Inns of Court, men from the sister universities, and such noble friends as d'Aubigny, Pembroke, Cotton, and Spencer were better able to appreciate his learning than the audiences which were crowding into the Globe and the Blackfriars. Noblemen were educated in those days, and Jonson was constantly driven to appeal from the crowd to the judgment of more

Ben Jonson

sophisticated spirits. He was drawn socially upwards by a process of attraction and sympathy.

His progress may be followed in his dedications. *Every Man in His Humour* was dedicated to the gentlemen of the Inns of Court, great names in learning and no less examples of living. Therein he boasted of having the friendship of divers in their societies and expressed his firm conviction that, when the gown and cap were off and freedom reigned, they might be glad to take his poem in their hands without detriment to their more noble and useful studies. All this simply meant that Jonson had found in the Inns of Court an appreciative audience for his plays among the young intellectuals who frequented these " noblest nurseries of humanity and liberty in the Kingdom ".

Jonson's assaults upon the fount of honour were impressively resolute. Queen Elizabeth, drawn by its fame, attended a performance of *Every Man out of His Humour*, and Jonson in respectful compliment wrote an epilogue. That Jonson would never succeed as a courtier was sufficiently clear. There were three subjects to avoid at that time in approaching Elizabeth. One was any reference to the passing years. Another was any suggestion that she might ever need a successor. The third was any allusion to my Lord of Essex. Jonson, with his genius for being inopportune, contrived in his brief epilogue to bring in all three of them. " Let death himself admire her," he exclaims,

> And may her virtues make him to forget
> The use of his inevitable hand.
> Fly from her, Age ; sleep, Time, before her throne.

As a poet's idea of what was likely to please his Queen upon a pleasant afternoon this was not felicitous, and the references to Essex—as sore a subject as death or

66

the passage of time—were as little likely to be well received, more especially as they were coupled with a hope that there might come a change in her admired and happy government.

Jonson made a more direct and massive bid for the royal favour in his next play. *Cynthia's Revels* begins excellently with a dedication to the Court as a bountiful and brave spring that waters all the noble plants of this island. The dedication, however, is signed characteristically by " thy servant *but not slave*, Ben Jonson ", and it contains a declaration to the effect that " it is not powdering, perfuming and every day smelling of the tailor that converteth to a beautiful object, but a mind shining through every suit which needs no false light either of riches or honours to help it ". This was odd language for a courtier, and the play was in keeping, for it presented a palace swarming with elaborate fools and water flies.

There was worse to follow. Was it an innocent blunder or a further proof of Jonson's matchless impertinence that we should find in this play a further reference to the Earl of Essex ? No one witnessing the comedy in 1600, could possibly miss the analogy between Diana justifying the death of Actaeon, who had been so unfortunate as to look too boldly upon her charms, and Elizabeth unseasonably surprised by Essex in her chamber, before she was ready to face the mirror, upon his sudden and disobedient return from Ireland.

> Seems it no crime to enter sacred bowers,
> And hallowed places with impure aspèct ?

Thus speaks Diana, defending her severity towards the rash young man who " by presuming far, did, to our grief, incur a fatal doom ". The blood of Essex, fresh on the block, smells aloud in this daring passage.

Ben Jonson

It is improbable that Elizabeth saw the play and, fortunately for Jonson, her Privy Council, which saw everything that happened in the land, decided not to notice it. Essex, in disgrace and done to death by his mistress, was a theme to be avoided by anyone who valued his own head or the Queen's peace, and the biographer must observe with amazement that the author of *Cynthia's Revels*, so often taxed with matters infinitely less remarkable, should on this occasion have been so happily ignored. Falkland, writing of Jonson, strangely affirms that Elizabeth

> With her judicious favours did infuse
> Courage and strength into his younger muse ;

but there is no evidence in support of this statement. Jonson had no favours from the Queen, judicious or otherwise. The wonder is that he escaped a whipping.

Jonson, unsuccessful with Elizabeth, must for the moment rest content with friends and supporters less distinguished. High on the list was Richard Martin, barrister-at-law, who soon had occasion to be of service. *The Poetaster* with its *Apologetical Dialogue*, only once uttered upon any stage, was equivalent to a breach of the peace. Someone, at any rate, was minded to make a Star Chamber matter of it and Jonson, indicted before the authorities, found himself in need of an advocate. Richard Martin intervened with the Court and was rewarded with a dedication. Jonson sent him the play on publication : " for whose innocence, as for the author's, you were once so noble and timely an undertaker to the greatest justice of this kingdom ". Posterity, he said, would owe to his virtuous and worthy friend the reading of a piece, " which so much ignorance and malice of the times then conspired to suppress ".

Jonson, in his friends, was already flying high.

There was Master Camden and the great Selden. There was John Donne, equally proud and more solitary in spirit, to prove that Ben could admire in others the qualities which he respected in himself. Donne, when Jonson first made his acquaintance, was Chief Secretary to the Lord Keeper. Then, too, there was Sir Robert Townshend, who regarded it as a privilege for men of means and discretion to feed and warm poor scholars ; Esmé, Lord d'Aubigny, in whose hospitable house Jonson lived for five years ; and Sir Robert Cotton with whom he was staying in 1603 when his eldest son died of the plague. From this time forward, in fact, for many years, Jonson seems rarely to have lived at home. He stayed with his patrons or was busy organising festivities at the noble houses of England—Althorp, Theobalds, or Connington. He needed books ; he was stimulated by fine society, and he liked a good table. In the fashion of the day he might obtain these things by hospitality.

It is an axiom that the surest way to lose a friend is to do him a service. Jonson survives this supreme test of a generous nature. To all his noble friends he is candidly and sincerely grateful. To none of his benefactors was he more indebted than to d'Aubigny, and to him there is an epigram, striking in its simple sincerity. The poet declares that, if he should fail in gratitude to this good friend, no hope remains that any man could ever be thankful for benefits received. Anything he may achieve has been rendered possible by help given and received in all affection, and the best he can do in return is to make his work worthy of these " timely succours ".

Meanwhile, there was a family to house and feed. From time to time Jonson must put aside such gentlemanly tasks as translating the *Ars Poetica* of Horace, receive again the overtures of Henslowe and be persuaded into writing some new scenes into *The Spanish Tragedy* for the Admiral's Men. This was the play which he had mocked in his first comedy, and which came inevitably to his mind whenever he was moved to attack the old romantic drama. Nevertheless, he consented. The price paid was ten pounds and the emissary who persuaded him to the contract was Edward Alleyn. Among the witnesses was one William Byrde who happened to be at hand with ballads to sell. He, too, must sing for his supper.

Elizabeth, unsuccessfully wooed with *Cynthia's Revels*, was now dead. James of Scotland had ridden south to be greeted as James I of England, and soon his queen was coming down to join him. On the list of houses where she would rest on the way was Althorp, where Lord Spencer of Wormleighton was waiting to receive her. Queen Anne was of a lively disposition and must be entertained. Why, with so many nimble pens at his call, Spencer should have sent for Jonson is uncertain. Presumably he had met the poet upon one of his country visits, heard him talk, sampled his wit and divined something of that inexhaustible store of fancy and invention, rooted in learning, which Jonson had at his command. If the poet would rest from satire, forget his theory of comedy and relax from the severity of the tragic line, who knew what would happen when that capacious mind, stuffed with curiosities, conceits and analogies, vestured with clean new-minted words, was free to be merely pleasing and ingenious?

Who would have thought it possible? The poet, attacked for his weight of learning, his slowness, the severity of his muse, his massive plundering of the ancients, drew lightly but seriously to the table and wrote, perhaps to his own grim surprise, a gracious trifle telling of Queen Mab and a mischievous satyr.

Jonson had found a new vocation and was thus committed to many years of profitable trifling.

Meanwhile, however, there had been a promise to fulfil. Jonson, bidding farewell to the comic muse, had undertaken to write a tragedy and the public was still waiting for that " something which had come into his thought ". It took form in *Sejanus his Fall* early in 1603, a composition too remote and grave for common folk and yet, by the peculiar fate which dogged him continually, charged before the Privy Council with riot and sedition and doomed to applications declared to be offensive to authority.

The play was produced by the Lord Chamberlain's Men at the Globe, with Shakespeare as one of the principal tragedians. It was hissed by the multitude and applauded by the nobility. Evidently the players themselves anticipated that Jonson's Castalian liquor would not easily be swallowed, for the version as acted contained easier verses by another hand. Possibly it was Chapman who put in a few direct and human touches. Almost certainly it was not, as some would like to believe, Shakespeare himself. The verses in any case are lost and their presence was only revealed to posterity owing to the fact that they were excised by Jonson when he came to publish the play in 1605 :

> Lastly I would inform you that this book in all numbers is not the same with that which was acted on the public stage ; wherein a second pen had good share ; in place of which I have rather chosen to put weaker and no doubt less pleasing of mine own than to defraud so happy a genius of his right by my loathèd usurpation.

It is unlikely that Jonson really considered his own lines to be weaker, though he was prepared to admit that they were less pleasing to a public whose noses he described on the same page as being " ever like swine, spoiling and rooting up the muses' garden ".

The prosecution of Jonson before the Privy Council is but another instance of the incomprehensible vagaries of censorship. *Sejanus* would seem incapable of local or contemporary application. It is a transcript from Tacitus and Suetonius done after the high Roman fashion. There is never a hint of English manners or mentality. It is a record of marble tyrannies, alabaster oppressions, liberties and rebellions in stone. There is no suggestion that the freedoms for which the victims of *Sejanus* died or the sinister divinity of Tiberius have the faintest analogy with anything to be observed in English contemporary laws, liberties or persons. But Jonson, for some unknown reason, had been making free again with his cudgel. " Northampton ", as he told Drummond, " was his mortal enemy for beating on St. George's day, one of his attenders " and Jonson went on to relate how he " was called before the Council for his *Sejanus* and accused both of popery and treason ". Lord Henry Howard, Earl of Northampton, son of the poet Surrey, was fortunately a person of little credit. " A dangerous, intelligencing man," said Lady Bacon, warning her sons against him as a " subtle serpent " who concealed his Catholic sympathies by ostentatiously denouncing popery in others. Jonson, in any case, seems to have had no difficulty in proving his innocence and discomfiting the informer.

It is significant, however, that Jonson, in the quarto edition of his play, added to his Argument in 1604, apparently in allusion to the gunpowder plot and to prove his loyalty, a postscript in which the fall of *Sejanus* is put forward as a warning to all conspirators : " Thus we do advance as a mark of terror to all traitors and treasons ; to show how just the heavens are in pouring and thundering down a weighty vengeance on their unnatural intents, even to the worst princes ;

much more to those for guard of whose piety and virtue the angels are in continual watch and God himself miraculously working."

Jonson, free of the Star Chamber, had to face the fact that with the public he had failed in tragedy as in comedy. Inevitably he was driven back to his fine friends. Queen Anne had smiled upon him and King James, as one scholar to another, was known to be partial to men of learning. It may seem odd that a dramatic author whose best plays are packed with characters from low life, whose spirit was so stubborn and unbending, who in his first attempts to attract notice in high quarters derided the affectations of society and expressed lively contempt for the supple flexure of a courtier's knee, whose imprisonments and appearances before the magistrates, Star Chamber and Privy Council stand like milestones along his career, should look as high as this for appreciation and support. Left to the public which had hissed *Sejanus* in 1603 he would, nevertheless, have starved untimely, and his main source of livelihood lay henceforth in the patronage of his noble friends. Jonson fully realised the situation. There was conviction and purpose in his resolute approach of the quality. The scale ascends by method from the gentlemen of the Inns of Court, through the learned universities and the peerage, to culminate in a royal master and the pension of a laureate.

It is admittedly a paradox. For Jonson was one of the most reflexively independent spirits who ever lived. He reacted violently against all forms of censure and control. " He never esteemed of a man for the name of a lord ", and " of all styles he loved most to be named honest ". So Drummond wrote of him, and related as a sample of his honesty how Jonson once had the audacity to tell the King, his master,

Ben Jonson

that the poet Buchanan had corrupted the royal ear when young and " learned him to sing verses when he should have read them ". Elsewhere, talking of preachers, Jonson is noted as saying that they flattered the great in their sermons and that " he hath a mind to be a churchman and, so he might have favour to make one sermon to the King, he careth not what thereafter should befall him, for he would not flatter, though he saw death ". These were not idle gestures. The same spirit breathes through all his dedications and petitions. He was often driven to beg a favour, but he never stooped for it. Nor had he any respect for social dignities, but only as they went with merit, learning or distinction of mind.

It was his failure to win popular applause from the ignorant that drove him to seek approval in quarters progressively higher. King James was a final stroke of good fortune—a prince of the late renaissance, a lover of learning and a full scholar. There was even an odd kinship of mind between the two men, outwardly so opposite in their disposition. Both had a love of logic and conceit. Both combined a liking for friendly discourse with a congenital tactlessness and a shrinking from indiscriminate company. Each could be humorous after his fashion and yet exquisitely ridiculous. Jonson climbed into the royal favour, as he had stepped into the good graces of Townshend and d'Aubigny—no ingratiating postures or deliberate art, but by feeling at ease in such society.

Jonson's progress in the polite world was helped, moreover, by his constant sense of the dignity of his vocation. He claimed respect as the poet or priest of Apollo. He sought his favours as rights due to a vicar of the muses, and resented slights as an offence to his high office. Drummond tells how, on one

JAMES I OF ENGLAND
By Van Somers (*Uffizi*)

[*face p.* 74

occasion, dining with Salisbury, he found himself at the foot of the table. Salisbury called down to him to know why he was not glad. Whereupon he bluntly answered : " My lord, you promised I should dine with you, but I do not." This was not the answer of a suitor but of a man in whom the dignity of letters was insulted. Such protests as these were from the ambassador of all the poets, not from the social pilgrim. Social distinction for himself he deliberately avoided. Thus in 1621 he was in peril of receiving a knight-hood on being named as reversionary to the office of Master of the Revels. In a letter written by Joseph Meade to Sir Martin Stuteville in that year we read : " Ben Jonson was not knighted, but scaped it narrowly ; for that his Majesty would have done it, had not means been made to avoid it," the writer emphasising, in a parenthesis, that the poet was himself opposed to the design. Jonson had no desire for a title which, at a time when the King was cannily exploiting the snobbery of his subjects for the benefit of the Exchequer, could scarcely be accepted as an honour by a representative of English letters.

Who would not be thy subject, James ? Jonson puts the question seasonably in the year following the King's accession when poets, counsellors and citizens still breathed more freely for the passing of Elizabeth. Jonson, before the throne, was submitted to the acid test. Even the great Chatham confessed that a peep into the royal closet intoxicated him. Jonson well survived the proof. He praises his sovereign, but urges him in the same breath to be a good King and make the most of his opportunities. There are three epigrams to King James. The first comes as near to flattery as Jonson ever allowed himself :

> How, best of Kings, dost thou a sceptre bear !
> How, best of poets, dost thou laurel wear !

But there are reservations. James in his youth had written some quite passable verse, which, Jonson handsomely allows, in lines drafted with more discretion than enthusiasm, was as good as any written in its own time and place. James as a King had not as yet made any serious mistakes. Jonson hopes that he will live up to his subjects' expectations. This, from our poet, was adulation. The second epigram was mild and formal. The King rules less by force than by example. His subjects have nothing to fear but their own offences and the just laws. Such sentiments, from a poet who stood in constant peril of Star Chamber, were optative rather than indicative. The third epigram was written in 1606 upon a false rumour of the King's death. A lucky chance, the poet observes, has enabled the King's subjects to show how much they value him:

> That we thy loss might know, and thou our love,
> Great heaven did well to give ill fame free way.

His Majesty is implored, however, to take better care of himself, and never again to play such an alarming trick upon his loyal subjects.

Meanwhile, it must not be forgotten that in 1603 Jonson, following his successful entertainment of Queen Anne on her way to London, had fallen back into disgrace. The authorities who had smiled on his fairies at Althorp were frowning upon *Sejanus* in Whitehall. It looked for a moment, indeed, as though Jonson's failure with Queen Elizabeth would be repeated with King James. For here was the Court organising the first big mask of the new reign and Jonson was laid by the heels for popery and treason. The splendid task of presenting *A Vision of Twelve Goddesses* at Hampton Court on Twelfth Night was entrusted to Samuel Daniel, one of the grooms of his Majesty's Most Honourable Privy Chamber and a poet whom Jonson notoriously held in slight esteem. Ingenious commentators find uncomplimentary references to Daniel in *Every Man in His Humour*. There is no evidence that Jonson had any feeling against Daniel except as a writer of bad verses, though he mentioned him later to Drummond as one who was " at jealousies with him ". Poor Daniel's jealousies were later to be only too well justified, for Jonson popped in between the succession and his hopes of being Master of the Revels and the first poet laureate of England. Daniel was a man of blameless life and of excellent temper, but *A Vision of Twelve Goddesses* invited ridicule. Whereby hangs a tale.

Jonson, though he was not allowed to undertake the mask at Hampton Court, was free of his trouble with the Privy Council in time to be present at its delivery. With him was Sir John Roe, a man, as he told Drummond, who loved him—an infinite spender, who was in the habit of saying that, when he had no more money in his purse, he would die—an undertaking which he shortly honoured by expiring of the plague in Jonson's arms and being buried at his friend's expense. Roe was one of four sons of a merchant adventurer of London. Jonson, writing his epitaph, commends his bravery with the sword and his piety. Elsewhere he refers in epigrams to Roe's habit of making many journeys, his two escapes from death in private quarrel and perils successfully met in the Netherlands, where the friends may first have become acquainted. Jonson declares that, should he meet death as Roe had done, no one need shed a tear upon his grave. To Roe he presented a commentary on Persius, celebrating him as a man " round within himself and straight ", who had bettered his trust to letters and taught himself to " tread " a worthy pen.

This sympathetic pair enjoyed *A Vision of Twelve Goddesses* to such good purpose that they were turned out by the Lord Chamberlain—"Ushered by my Lord Suffolk from a mask " was Jonson's description. Roe, in a quaint epistle on the incident, used a somewhat stronger expression :

> Forget we were *thrust out*. It is but thus :
> God threatens kings, kings lords, as lords do us.

Possibly the King was bored by *A Vision of Twelve Goddesses* and inquired who it was that had laughed. More probably his personal attention was not directed to Jonson until the following March when the poets of London were required to find for King James an entertainment on passing to his coronation. The King's tastes and habit of mind were notorious. Not yet known for the " wisest fool in Christendom ", he was already a terror for his learning. He loved classical allusions. He liked to air his familiarity with the ancients and his dexterity in reading symbols and analogies. The authorities, looking for someone upon whom the royal "wut " might be sharpened, could hardly miss a poet whose erudition was the wonder and despair of his generation. Jonson was commandeered for the occasion, and he has left for us in his collected works a minute description of this amazing bid for sovereign favour. Were ever such conundrums of learning so confidingly offered ? King James, passing through the City of Westminster, at every turn of his progress was met with riddles, insoluble to the profane, but such as might, in the opinion of the poet, " without cloud or obscurity declare themselves to the sharp and learnèd ". Among them, at Temple Bar, was a temple of Janus, presented

with overwhelming evidence for his four faces, and
an inscription from Ovid to signify that even four
faces were not enough to behold the glory of that
day.

The disposition of the new King had been well
studied. Nothing pleased him more than to be
hailed as a peacemaker and father of prosperity.
Accordingly, within the temple was Irene with her
silver dove and olive branch. Wealth, in the figure
of a little boy, his locks curled and spangled with
gold, stood beside her, while beneath his feet lay
Mars, grovelling, his armour scattered and sundry
sorts of weapons broken about him. Then, too, as
the King hated a noise, Esychia, or Quiet, stood as a
handmaid to Peace, with a nest of storks upon her
head to manifest a sweet repose, her feet upon a cube
to show stability and in her lap a perpendicular or
level as the ensign of evenness and rest. Tumult, in
a garment of divers and dark colours, with her hair
wild and disordered and a foul and troubled face, lay
prone. Other figures, too numerous to mention, but
all exceedingly apt, stood forth, appropriately backed
with inscriptions which invited and not seldom defied
the beholder to identify their sources in Claudian,
Pliny, Ovid, Varro and the rest—all tending to suggest
that the golden age was come, and that James had
been born to set right a world left out of joint by his
predecessors. Lines addressed to the King at Temple
Bar by the genius of the City and a speech made to
him by Electra, shyest of the seven lights of the
Pleiades, suggest, however, that, in celebrating the new
age, the poet is thinking resentfully of ancient or
present woes. Peace and Liberty are to come again
—perhaps. Avarice, Pride, Envy, Ambition and Flattery, rampant only yesterday, will vanish to-morrow
—as all good men must hope. Again the mood is

Ben Jonson

optative and it will soon again be necessary to lash the times in *Volpone* and to throw light into the dark places :

> Where men commit black incest with their faults,
> And snore supinely in the stall of sin.

Jonson, having gratified the King with these learned pastimes, did not allow the royal metal to grow cold. The King's coronation was quickly followed by the opening of his first high session of Parliament. A further tribute was required and Jonson wrote a *Panegyre on the Happy Entrance of James our Sovereign*. For the good of the land and to show that he is no flatterer, the poet's address reads in places more like an exhortation to virtue and humility than a celebration of divine right. Here was a fine opportunity to soothe the royal ear with sweet phrases and tributes unreserved. Characteristically Jonson preferred to point out clearly and firmly that kings are heavenly in their office but men in their persons ; that, since their acts are open to envy and inspection, they should be all the more careful in their public acts ; that there had been many bad kings in the past who had plundered the church, corrupted justice and been infamous in their pleasures ; that it was very necessary to avoid evil habits ; and, finally, that kings could do more by good example than by tyranny :

> He knew that those who would with love command
> Must with a tender, yet a stedfast, hand
> Sustain the reins, and in the check forbear
> To offer cause of injury or fear ;
> That kings by their example more do sway
> Than by their power ; and men do more obey
> When they are led than when they are compelled.

It is impossible to ascertain when Jonson first met his royal master face to face. At Althorp only the Queen had been present, and at Hampton Court

Jonson had been " ushered forth ". Most probably
Jonson was first presented to the King in 1604, on
May Day, when Sir William Cornwallis entertained
both King and Queen in his pleasant garden at Highgate. Sir William, remembering how Spencer had
induced the poet to unbend in a little mask of fairies,
invited him to devise an entertainment. Jonson put
on a May-time spirit. The royal pair were received
at the gate by the Penates of the house attired in the
antique manner, with javelins in their hands, standing on each side of the porch. The poet assures his
Queen that

> Every line of her divine
> Form is a beauteous story.

Beauteous is a vile phrase, but the sentiment was apt
and loyal. If Jonson could have brought himself to
say as much of Elizabeth he might have come more
speedily to favour. He was fortunate at last in having
a queen who might without perjury be praised as
good to look upon.

The royal guests passed thence into the house, and,
through it, into the garden where Aurora, Zephyrus
and Flora were waiting with a song in three parts.

> All birds their music bring ;
> Sweet robin, linnet, thrush,
> Record from every bush
>   The welcome of the King
>   And Queen ;
> Whose like were never seen,
>   For good, for fair ;
> Nor can be ; though fresh May
>   Should every day
> Invite a several pair,
> No, though she should invite a several pair.

A banquet followed and, after the banquet, Pan
waited in the garden beside a Bacchic spring whence
flowed a lusty liquor to expel sadness. The royal

company were served with much familiar chaff, and
Mercy at the last called down a blessing on the royal
visitors : " That your loves be ever flourishing as
May and your house as fruitful ; that your acts exceed
the best and your years the longest of your predecessors ; that no bad fortune touch you nor good
change you, but still that you triumph in this facility
over the ridiculous pride of other princes and for
ever live safe in the love rather than fear of your
subjects."

The familiarity and candour of the relations between
Ben Jonson and King James are clear from many
sources. The man who dared to tell his sovereign
that he had a bad habit of singing his verses must
have been very sure of his footing. Jonson wrote to
Drummond in May, 1619, recording, not as anything
to be specially noted but as a matter of course, that,
on his return from Scotland the King " professed
(thank God) some joy to see me ". How did Jonson
fare upon his first encounter ? Doubtless they quoted
copiously at one another, James singing his lines.
The King would want to air his appreciation of the
poet's learned riddles at Temple Bar, and perhaps
require elucidations here and there. The wistful
monarch had found a subject to appreciate his conviction that a King should be the best clerk in his
kingdom. Jonson doubtless agreed with his royal
master when it was honestly possible to do so, and
they were presumably ready to laugh in unison if
the jest were sufficiently recondite. The ice was
broken and Jonson might now be reasonably sure that,
when next the season came round for a mask at Court,
he would not be overlooked or his performances at
Althorp and Highgate be forgotten.

CHAPTER V

Star Chamber

THE position of Jonson as a purveyor of entertainments to the Court was made finally
secure in January, 1605, when by royal
invitation he wrote his first royal mask for the Queen.
Therein his erudition was taxed to satisfy an odd
persistent fancy that she had to be black as well as
comely. Jonson, beginning with Pliny and Solinus
and remembering a river in Aethiopia by the name
of Niger, brings a bevy of black beauties to Whitehall
and celebrates Britannia ruled by a sun,

> Whose beams shine day and night, and are of force
> To blanch an Aetheop and revive a corse.

The Mask of Blackness was performed at Whitehall
in the Banqueting Hall, ingeniously and splendidly
transformed by Inigo Jones at a cost of three thousand pounds. Its devices included waves which
seemed to move and billows to break, tritons and
sea-horses which writhed their heads, a great concave
shell for the maskers which moved upon the waters,
with six sea monsters swimming beside it, and the
main triumphant upon a silver throne in a blue sky
set with stars. The Queen remembered it for two
years and demanded a sequel which Jonson duly
provided in *The Mask of Beauty*.

Carleton, writing to Winwoode, describing the
Queen and her ladies in *The Mask of Blackness*,
declared that their apparel, though rich, was " too

light and curtizan-like for such great ones ". Nor was the Queen's fancy to be black commended. The rival ambassadors of France and Spain were invited to " come as private men to a private sport ". The Frenchman declined, but the Spanish Ambassador forgot his office and, coming to enjoy himself, was " taken out to dance and footed it like a lusty old gallant with his country woman. He took out the Queen and forgot not to kiss her hand, though there was danger it would have left a mark upon his lips. The night's work was concluded with a banquet in the great Chamber, which was so furiously assaulted that down went table and trestles before one bit was touched." Carleton thought that the black faces and hands, which were painted bare up to the elbows, were a " very loathsome sight ", and he was " sorry that strangers should see our Court so strangely disguised ". The press was so great that ladies complained of the " fury of the white staves ", and many got " shut up in several heaps betwixt doors and there stayed till all was ended ", while a lord's ransom was lost in chains, jewels and purses stolen or mislaid. Boisterous farce and solemn comedy went hand in hand, for the Spaniard's private invitation had been converted at the last minute into a public one and the French party was mortally aggrieved.

Similar scenes had occurred at another of Jonson's masks, no longer extant, given in December of the previous year in celebration of the wedding of Sir Philip Herbert to Lady Susan Vere. On that occasion also there had been " no small loss that night of chains and of jewels and many great ladies were made shorter by their skirts and were well enough served ". There again the dresses had been " rather costly than comely ", and there had been a diplomatic incident. The Venetian Ambassador, having been

placed at table in the seat which should have been
kept for the Queen's brother, had been lured into a
closet and forgotten until supper was safely begun.
James had been forced to apologise for this merry
solution of the problem, and in compensation he had
offered the Ambassador a stool in the royal box.
The Ambassador had accepted the stool, but had
preferred to stand for three hours rather than make
use of it. Of such tremendous issues is the foreign
policy of Sovereign States composed.

Jonson's part in these magnificent but clumsy
splendours was played behind the scenes, but they
gave him an insight into the disposition of King
James which stood him in good stead in cracks with
his royal master. Another misadventure was pre-
paring, however, and for a moment it looked as
though Jonson had been climbing for a fall. Chapman and Marston had written a play entitled *Eastward
Ho*, a comedy of London life, full of topical allusions
—none so popular as certain references to the hungry
Scots who had come flocking to London in the King's
train. To this play Jonson somehow contributed.
Chapman, eighteen years older than Ben, was a poet
whom Jonson loved, and Marston was already forgiven, the ink being scarcely dry on a handsome
dedication to Jonson of *The Malcontent* in which the
author of *Jack Drum's Entertainment* made amends
for his part in the poets' war with a tribute to his
most elegant and serious, his most candid and cordial
friend. Marston was extreme in apology as in quarrel,
being all modesty and admiration for the " learnèd
ears " of his late enemy, who must now be deemed
to have " art above nature, nature above art ", and
whose *Sejanus* would force applause from despairing
envy. Jonson's share in *Eastward Ho* was small and
would have defied detection by posterity had he not

insisted on sharing the disgrace it brought upon his friends. There is no trace anywhere of his style and the critics have been reduced to giving him a share in the plotting. The jokes against the Scots were harmless enough and have since become familiar on every stage. They are charged with little more than ubiquity and an ability to make hard bargains. There are Scots, it is reported, in Virginia and there is an allusion to a certain knight who bought his title for four pounds, the market price being thirty. This was mild teasing, but a certain Sir John Murray was, nevertheless, moved to visit the King and call for retribution when the play was printed in the Autumn of 1605. Chapman alone seems to have been arrested. Marston, probably the real culprit, had apparently escaped. There is no record of his having been committed and no appeals were made on his behalf. Jonson, hastening to join his colleagues, in any case, found only Chapman to keep him company. How, when they were to have had their ears and noses cut, Jonson's mother came to the prison prepared to mix in her son's drink a lusty strong poison has been related. Tweaking the Scots was clearly no light matter, and it would probably have gone hard with Chapman if Jonson had not stood by him and insisted on sharing his punishment.

Chapman and Jonson passed the time in prison writing letters to their friends and patrons. From Chapman we learn that " our chief offences are but two clauses and both of them not our own ". From Jonson we learn little more concerning the event, but a great deal about himself. The appeals he wrote to Suffolk, Salisbury and to the Countess of Bedford, excellentest of ladies, are as characteristic as his voluntary surrender. They deepen the impression made by his dedications.

Star Chamber

To Suffolk he writes :

MOST HONOURABLE LORD :

Although I cannot but know your Lordship to be busied with far greater and higher affairs than to have leisure to descend suddenly on an estate so low and removed as mine ; yet, since the cause is in us wholly mistaken (at least misconstrued) and that every noble and just man is bound to defend the innocent, I doubt not but to find your Lordship full of that wonted virtue and favour, wherewith you have ever abounded toward the truth. And though the imprisonment itself can not but grieve me (in respect of his Majesty's high displeasure, from whence it proceeds) yet the manner of it afflicts me more, being committed hither, unexamined, nay unheard (a right not commonly denied to the greatest offenders) and I made a guilty man, long before I am one, or ever thought to be : God, I call to testimony what my thoughts are and ever have been of his Majesty ; and so may I thrive when He comes to be my judge and my King's, as they are most sincere.

And I appeal to posterity that will hereafter read and judge my writings (though now neglected) whether it be possible I should speak of his Majesty as I have done, without the affection of a most zealous and good subject. . . .

It should be noted that this letter was written to the nobleman who had " ushered forth " its author with Sir John Roe from *A Vision of Twelve Goddesses* at Hampton Court. Observe, too, that God is invoked as a judge, not only of poets, but of kings and that there is an appeal to posterity which will " read and judge my writings though now neglected ".

The appeal to Lucy, Countess of Bedford, conveyed to her by a " worthy employed solicitor and equal adorer of her virtues ", is in courtlier terms :

EXCELLENTEST OF LADIES

And most honoured of the Graces, Muses, and me ; if it be not a sin to profane your free hand with prison-polluted paper, I would entreat some little of your aid to the defence of my innocence, which is as clear as this leaf was (before

I stained it) of any thing half-worthy this violent infliction. I am committed and with me a worthy friend, one Mr. Chapman, a man, I can not say how known to your Ladyship, but I am sure known to me to honour you. And our offence a play, so mistaken, so misconstrued, so misapplied, as I do wonder whether their ignorance or impudence be most, who are our adversaries. It is now not disputable, for we stand on uneven bases, and our cause so unequally carried as we are, without examining, without hearing, or without any proof but malicious rumour, hurried to bondage and fetters. The cause we understand to be the King's indignation, for which we are heartily sorry, and the more by how much the less we have deserved it. What our suit is, the worthy employed solicitor and equal adorer of your virtues can best inform you. . . .

Other letters were indited to the Lord d'Aubigny, the Earl of Pembroke and the Earl of Montgomery. The longest and most serious petition was addressed, however, to the Earl of Salisbury. It was discovered among the Hatfield State papers and is inscribed : " Ben Jonson to the Earl of Salisbury, praying his protection against some evil reports " :

MOST TRULY HONOURABLE,
It hath still been the tyranny of my fortune so to oppress my endeavours that, before I can show myself grateful in the least for former benefits, I am enforced to provoke your bounties for more. May it not seem grievous to your lordship that now my innocence calls upon you (next the deity) to her defence. God himself is not averted at just men's cries ; and you that approach the divine goodness and supply it here on earth in your places and honours cannot employ your aid more worthily than to the common succour of honesty and virtue, how humbly soever it be placed.

It is to be noticed that Jonson is already grateful for former benefits and he will allude later on to offences ingeniously discovered in previous plays. These references are probably to the incidents which had arisen in connection with the *Apologetical Dialogue* and *Sejanus*. The appeal continues :

> I am here, my most honoured lord, unexamined and un-heard, committed to a vile prison and with me a gentle-man, whose name may have come to your lordship, one Mr. George Chapman, a learned and honest man.

Follows a reluctant confession that the cause of this misfortune is a play and a vigorous complaint against those who have found in it more than was ever intended.

> My noble lord, they do not deal charitably who are witty in another man's work and utter sometimes their own malicious messages under our words. I protest to your honour and call God to testimony (since my first error, which yet is punished in me more with my shame than it was with my bondage) I have so attempered my style that I have given no cause to any good man of grief ; and if to any ill, by touching at any general vice, it hath always been with a regard and sparing of particular persons. I may be otherwise reported, but, if all that be accused should be presently guilty, there are few men would stand in the state of innocence.
> I beseech your most honourable lordship, suffer not other men's errors or faults to be made my crimes, but let me be examined by all my works, both past and this present, and not trust to rumour but my books (for she is an unjust deliverer both of great and small actions) whether I have ever (many things I have written both public and private) given offence to a nation, to a public order or state, or any person of honour or authority ; but have equally laboured to keep their dignity as mine own person safe.

The letter concludes with a definite petition that his lordship shall be either the " grateful means of our coming to answer " or the " most honoured cause of our liberty ".

Of the men in high places who befriended Jonson and employed him, Robert, Earl of Salisbury, was politically of most consequence. "Never cared for any man longer than he could use him," Jonson bluntly declared at Drummond's table; and at the table of Salisbury himself it will be remembered how, being at the foot of it with Inigo Jones and being demanded by my lord why he was not glad, he called back stoutly to his host: "You promised that I should dine with you, but I do not." But Salisbury at Theobalds was one of Jonson's first employers, and it is interesting to see how this most independent of good servants celebrates his lord. There are three epigrams to Salisbury. In the first our poet sadly inquires :

> What need hast thou of me or of my muse
> Whose actions so themselves do celebrate ?

There was a time when great men were glad of poets, but now the poets must needs be glad of great men. I cannot, says Jonson, hope to add to your fame, but it may add to mine with posterity :

> When men in my book read but Cecil's name,
> And what I write thereof find far and free
> From servile flattery, common poet's shame,
> As thou stands't clear of the necessity.

In plain terms it will add to the poet's reputation that he did not overpraise his master and to the master's reputation that he neither required nor exacted a eulogy. In the second epigram Salisbury is celebrated as a good servant of the State who seeks his reward not in public approval but in the conviction that he acts always for the best. The third was addressed to him when, in 1604, he became Lord Treasurer. It is again a characteristic performance. Jonson does not bring these early fruits of love to the Treasurer because he has any hopes or suits to prefer to his new office ; nor is he glad as a dependant rejoicing in the promotion of a master ; nor is he paying his tribute for fashion's sake ; nor is he moved by flattery to titles. But he rejoices that the wise king knows how to reward merit and to secure good talent for the public service :

> These, noblest Cecil, laboured in my thought,
> Wherein what wonder see thy name hath wrought !
> That whilst I meant but thine to gratulate,
> I have sung the greater fortunes of our State.

His lordship would read these tributes with a finer smile than he accorded to the celebrations of other men. This was an honest admiration of real gifts, warily employed.

Not only was Jonson set at liberty by the authorities ; he was almost immediately used by the Privy Council in some mysterious business that had to do with the gunpowder plot. The hand of Salisbury may be detected here, but the circumstances are obscure. Jonson started life as a Protestant, son of a grave minister and heir to a name that had suffered much for religion. We have seen how, almost at the gallows, he was converted to the Roman Catholic faith. " Then took he his religion by trust of a priest who visited him in prison "—is Drummond's note on the matter and, in summing up, Drummond declares his guest to be " for any religion as being versed in both ". For twelve years after his conversion Jonson remained a Papist, but was then reconciled with the Anglican Church and, ceasing to be a recusant, " at his first communion in token of true reconciliation he drank out all the full cup of wine ". All this points to an attitude typical of the Elizabethan settlement—no very deep convictions but an uneasy alternation between defiance and conformity. The point of present interest is that in 1605 Jonson was still a Papist and that the Government, seeking information, asked him to undertake a mission among his co-religionists. Somewhere hiding in London was a priest, name and address unknown, with valuable intelligence. Jonson's mission was to discover the priest and to induce him, under safe-conduct, to testify. Jonson found the priest, with the help of the chaplain of the Venetian Ambassador, but nothing would induce the man to leave his refuge or to speak a word. Jonson would seem, thereafter, to have prosecuted his inquiries elsewhere and to have reported the result to Salisbury, nothing very precise, but only a general conviction that a good many Catholics were in the plot. "All so enweaved in it," he declares, " as will make five hundred gentlemen less of the religion within this week." The report to Salisbury, to whom he had applied for delivery from the Privy Council a short while previously, is significant. It justifies the inference that Jonson's services were asked in this affair in return for Salisbury's intervention in the matter of *Eastward Ho.*

Jonson having shown his loyalty in an attempt to help the Government, continued to show it in after years by regular attendance at the parish church. This was a political and not a religious act, for he was not yet an Anglican. Not long after the conspiracy he was, in fact, summoned to appear with his wife before the Consistory Court of London on a charge of recusancy. Such charges were preferred as part of the normal routine of establishment. England was not made Anglican in a day. In Jonson's case, however, there seems to have been an enemy somewhere in the background, for he was also charged with being " by fame a seducer of youths to the popish religion ". He pleaded that the charge was doubly false : he was neither a seducer nor had anybody ever believed him to be one. The Court was evidently bothered, for Jonson appeared before it no less than three times, and divines were appointed to argue him into a better way of thinking. It is a tribute to the poet's reputation for dispute that for this purpose no less a person than the Dean of St. Paul's was chosen, assisted by the Chaplain of the Archbishop of Canterbury. Nevertheless, Jonson remained a Catholic for another six years to come. The outcome of these curious proceedings is not known, but the authorities would obviously not press the case too hard against a proven and loyal servant of the King and of my lord of Salisbury, particularly as Jonson was always ready to go to church and to see that his wife also attended according to the statutes.

Jonson's religion was that of any normal Englishman of the day to whom this world mattered more than the next. He hated a Puritan and, as a good pagan, had a natural sympathy with the old religion. As a loyal subject, however, he was prepared to render unto Caesar. He would go to church ; but he must think as he pleased, and not all the divines in Christendom could argue him out of a conviction until he was ready to change it of his own free will and intelligence.

CHAPTER VI

Maturity

SOME time during the summer or autumn of 1605 Jonson wrote *Volpone* or *The Fox*. The exact circumstances of his return to the comic stage are not known, but the dedication clearly indicates the mood in which he resumed pride of place among the poets of mirth and satire. The author who retired from comedy in 1601 returned in 1605 even prouder in spirit, but rather more cautious in his contempt of persons. While rebuking the licence and ignorance of the public stage he will not imitate those who " to make a name with the multitude or to draw their beastly claps care not whose living faces they intrench with their petulant styles ". But the amenities of the poets' war, if left behind, are not forgotten. " Petulant styles " was a phrase with a history, looking back to the scornful farewell of the *Apologetical Dialogue*.

The author's further references to the rotten and base rags wherewith the times had adulterated the form of poetry and his general scorn of the popular theatre indicated, moreover, very definitely that the more Jonson might apologise for past asperities, the less inclined he was to retract or modify his old habits and convictions. There were many who must have regarded the dedication of *Volpone* to the sister universities with a dubious eye. Marston who, in his preface to *The Malcontent*, had praised *Sejanus* glanced less kindly at Jonson in his *Wonder of Women or the Tragedy of Sophonisba. Volpone* had opened old wounds and Marston found it necessary to declare that " to transcribe authors, quote authorities and translate Latin prose orations into English blank verse hath, in this subject, been the least aim of my studies ". With this last fling at the " translating scholar " whom he had first provoked with his *Histriomastix* Marston forsook the stage and retired to a country vicarage in Hampshire.

The play was acted with the permission of the Master of the Revels by the King's Majesty's servants at the Globe. Richard Burbage played the Fox. Of its reception by the public there is no record. That it did not escape criticism is shown by the fact that Francis Beaumont, George Chapman and others were provoked to defend it.

> Thy bold and knowing muse
> Contemns all praise but such as thou would'st choose,

writes Beaumont in comfort and support ; while Chapman declares of the Fox,

> Before the best hounds thou dost still but play ;
> And for our whelps, alas, they yelp in vain.

Volpone continued on the stage till the theatres were closed in 1649, and was one of the first plays revived at the Restoration. Downes affirmed that it proved " very satisfactory to the town ", and Langbaine records that it was still popular a century later. The last public appearance of *Volpone* on an English stage was at the Haymarket before the death of the elder Colman. But those were already the dark ages of English comedy and there the Fox went finally to ground.

With the production of *Volpone* in 1605 Jonson entered upon a period of comparative ease and tranquillity. The next years were marked by the successive production of *Epicoene or the Silent Woman*

(1609), performed at Whitefriars by the Children of Her Majesty's Revels ; *The Alchemist* (1610), presented by the King's Men ; *Catiline* (1611), acted by the same company ; *Bartholomew Fair* (1614), put upon the stage by the Lady Elizabeth's Men at the Hope Theatre and *The Devil is an Ass*, again presented by the King's Men (1616). These were the years of maturity, in which Jonson wrote his best plays and passed, with *Bartholomew Fair*, beyond the summit of his achievement.

The biographical significance of the major plays is soon exhausted. *Epicoene or the Silent Woman* was not a conspicuous success. It pleased a few, but Jonson records against himself the gibe of a contemporary that " there was never one man to say *plaudite* to it ". As so often before, allusions were read or misread into the text which gave offence to some person or persons unknown. " My hope," writes the author in a dedication to Sir Francis Stuart, " is that this dumb piece should please you, because it hath pleased others before " and that " you find it worthy to have displeased none. . . . Read, therefore, I pray, and censure. There is not a line or syllable changed from the simplicity of the first copy. And when you shall consider, through the certain hatred of some, how much a man's innocency may be endangered by an uncertain accusation, you will, I doubt not, so begin to hate the iniquity of such natures as I shall love the contumely done me whose end was to be wiped off by your sentence." The character of the offence taken, if not given, in the play is indicated in the second of the two prologues which Jonson published in 1610, wherein he expostulates:

> They make a libel, which he made a play.

It was the old trouble. No man can be promiscuously

haughty without offending someone, and sensitive heads are ever ready to be misfitted with uncomely caps. Jonson was almost wistful in his protestations :

> The ends of all who for the scene do write,
> Are, or should be, to profit and delight.
> And still 't hath been the praise of all best times,
> *So persons were not touch'd,* to tax the crimes.

In a similar vein Francis Beaumont, in lines written on *The Silent Woman*, thus put the case for his friend and master :

> Where he that strongly writes, although he mean
> To scourge but vices in a labour'd scene,
> Yet private faults shall be so well exprest,
> As men do act 'em, that each private breast,
> That finds these errors in itself, shall say :
> He meant me, not my vices, in the play.

Epicoene, though it did not escape calumny, was nevertheless one of the most popular of Jonson's plays. It went rapidly through several editions and held the stage up to the Commonwealth. After the Restoration it was revived with applause, Wilkes and Booth often delighting the town in the part of Morose. Colman and Garrick both appeared in the play.

Jonson, on his production of *The Alchemist*, returned to the King's Men, and Richard Burbage was again his leading actor. Of its reception there is again no record, but the comedy was still in the repertory of the King's Men in 1612–13, when it was also played at Court. Still sore from " applications " found in his previous works, he insisted once again that his pen " did never aim to grieve, but better, men " ; that his wholesome remedies for the vices of the time were sweet ; that men's follies were shown in such a fashion that those who recognised them as natural need lay no claim to them as their own. In an address to the reader he complained parenthetically of the " concupiscence of dances and antics " which had so taken hold upon the stage that " the only way to tickle the spectators was to run away from nature and to be afraid of her ".

Jonson in *Sejanus* had taken to tragedy in a fit of spleen, and it was in a similar mood that he sat down to write *Catiline's Conspiracy*. The play was dedicated to the Earl of Pembroke, who had succeeded Lord Suffolk as Chamberlain. The author first bewails " so thick and dark an ignorance as now almost covers the age " and craves to stand near the light cast by his lordship who dares in these jig-given times to countenance a legitimate poem :

> I call it so against all noise of opinion ; from whose crude and airy reports I appeal to the great and singular faculty of judgment in your lordship, able to indicate truth from error.

There follows a plaintive declaration to the effect that his play " approacheth your censure cheerfully and with the same assurance that innocency would appear before a magistrate ".

In an address to the " Reader in Ordinary " the old insolence breaks forth and even passes all former bounds. The author professes indifference and contempt of the popular verdict. The praise of most men is based, not on judgment, but on their own ridiculous vanity and a secret feeling that they could, if they would, do the thing better themselves :

> For the most commend out of affection, self-tickling, an easiness or imitation ; but wise men judge out of knowledge. That is the *trying* faculty and to those works that will bear a judge nothing is more dangerous than a foolish praise. You will say, I shall not have yours, therefore ; but rather the contrary, all vexation of censure. If I were not above such molestations now, I had great cause to think unworthily of my studies, or they had so of me. But I leave you to your exercise. Begin.

Was ever public in this manner wooed ?

Maturity

Francis Beaumont and John Fletcher were among the dramatists who welcomed *Catiline* as a fine play, which should have been better received. Beaumont commended the author, who had not itched after the wild applause of common people :

> But thou hast squared thy rules by what is good,
> And art three ages yet from understood ;
> And (I dare say) in it there lies much wit,
> Lost, till the readers can grow up to it.

There is here a sly suggestion that even Beaumont himself found the play just a little beyond him. Fletcher, comparing it with the popular trash of the town, roundly declared that *Catiline* would outlive its author. Like gold it was stamped for continuance.

Three years passed before Jonson wrote another play for the common stage. *Bartholomew Fair*, presented by the Lady Elizabeth's Men at the Hope Theatre, was dedicated to the King and performed in his presence on November 1st, 1614. Aubrey states that " King James made him write against the Puritans who began to be troublesome in his time ". Jonson would need no prompting to the task. The Puritans were his enemies by religion, vocation and temperament and in Zeal-of-the-Land-Busy he gave to the stage his most convincing and vital character. This was no intent and careful study of a humour, dissected and anatomised, but a type faithfully observed and presented with a careless vigour. We shall make his better acquaintance. Meanwhile, it should be noted that, in his prologue to the King, Jonson explicitly glanced at the " faction " whose ways had long vexed his Majesty, being careful to add, however :

> These for your sport, without particular wrong
> Or just complaint of any private man.

Bartholomew Fair seems to have been the most

successful of Jonson's comedies. All to whom Merry England was dear in the seventeenth century naturally applauded it. It was revived with laughter after the Commonwealth, when Charles II frequently commanded its performance and is said to have enjoyed especially the portrayal of Cokes, the simpleton. It provoked neither insult nor apology, and there is a pleasant tradition that Milton, among the saints, commended the play for its satire and ranked it with *Volpone* and *The Alchemist*. Among other traditions connected with *Bartholomew Fair* must be noted the legend that it first provoked the exclamation put upon the author's tombstone in Westminster Abbey : " O rare Ben Jonson ! "

Last of the comedies, belonging to this period of maturity, but already touched with decline, came *The Devil is an Ass* produced at Blackfriars by the King's Men towards the end of 1616. There is no dedication and the usual explanations and tirades are omitted. Of its reception nothing is known. Jonson, however, sending a copy of it to Newcastle on publication, complains that " his devil has played the absolute knave with him ".

Jonson was now at the height of his fame. He was a poor man but a social figure—equally at home in the parlour and the tavern. This was no longer the lean, angular and ready man, who had killed Spencer in Hogsden Fields and beaten Marston for having traduced him on the stage. Nor was he yet the man of girth who would soon be jesting at his own unwieldiness. Physically he was still strong and active, and within a year or so was to walk on foot from London to Edinburgh. In fame and disposition he stood between a violent youth and his final status as the most sovereign of English worthies. Before going down with him in sickness, beggary and the decay of his powers, let us stay a moment among the friends of his prime.

Jonson was no great lover of women and we look vainly in the majority of his plays for female characters of any depth or significance. His confessions to Drummond show a man easily satisfied in his loves. He lived, when we discover his address, away from his wife. But there was no other abiding relationship. One of his grounds of quarrel with Marston was that the latter had " represented him on the stage in his youth as given to venerie ". This was a libel, but not entirely groundless. Drummond reports him as expressing the view from experience that " a maid was nothing in comparison to the wantonness of a wife ", and told of " strange accidents " that befell him in his casual pleasures :

> He saw a picture, painted by a bad painter, of Esther, Haman and Ahasuerus. Haman courting Esther in a bed, after the fashion of ours, was only seen by one leg. Ahasuerus' back was turned, with this verse over him : And wilt thou, Haman, be so malicious as to lye with mine own wife in mine house ?
> He himself, being once so taken, the goodman said : I would not believe ye would abuse my house so.

Such incidents, however, were of small importance and soon forgotten. Jonson was not the man to torment himself either for love or lack of it.

He had, nevertheless, some notable friendships with women, and there were many that he admired, disliked, praised, or offended for qualities that appealed to the poet without greatly disturbing the man. One of these was the Countess of Rutland. He was dining with her one day when " her husband, coming in, accused her that she kept table to poets ". It may be assumed that Jonson was not backward in defending his vocation, and the Countess found it necessary to write to him afterwards, presumably in excuse of her lord. Jonson answered the letter, which my lord intercepted. " But he did not dare to take me to task for it," Jonson declares. This lady was the daughter of Sir Philip Sidney, and married to an oaf. Jonson in an epitaph declares that her father, could he have seen her " rare and absolute numbers ", would either have burned or bettered his own. There has survived part of an epistle which Jonson wrote to her in verse. In form it is a compliment to her literary gift, but in substance it is an epistle in praise of poetry. Incidently it is a rich example of Jonson's stubborn honesty in compliment. It begins with a fine railing against mere place and riches, and the " noble ignorants " who turn their " quarter-face " upon the poets—a shrewd cut here at my lord, Roger Manners, fifth Earl of Rutland. It continues :

> With you, I know, my offering will find grace.
> For what a sin 'gainst your great father's spirit
> Were it to think that you should not inherit
> His love unto the Muses, when his skill
> Almost you have, or may have when you will ?

Was ever such a courtier ? Praising his lady he must yet slip in an " almost " for conscience' sake. It is further to be noted that the author passes almost at once to warm eulogy of a rival lady, Lucy the bright, of whom is more to follow.

The emotions inspired by Elizabeth, Countess of Rutland, were not all as abstract and cautious as those of Jonson. Overbury, we learn from Drummond, was in love with her and caused Jonson to read his *Wife* to her. Overbury's *Wife* is a dull play, but Jonson read it well and commended the author. The morning after Jonson " discorded with Overbury, who would have him intend a suit that was not lawful ". In other words, Overbury, having found a sponsor to the lady, was presumably hinting that my lord Pandarus was a useful fellow. Thereby Jonson lost a friend whom he had hitherto admired for his learning and proud spirit.

Bright Lucy, of the epistle to Elizabeth, was that same Lucy, Countess of Bedford, to whom Jonson wrote from the Marshalsea prison in 1605. To her he penned the most cordial and delicate of his epigrams. Here are no clumsy reservations or tactless digressions :

> This morning, timely rapt with holy fire,
> I thought to form unto my zealous muse
> What kind of creature I could most desire
> To honour, serve and love—as poets use.

She must be fair and free and wise ; she should be courteous, facile and sweet, more good than great, hating pride, full of the softer virtues ;

> Only a learnèd and a manly soul
> I purposed her, that should, with even powers
> The rock, the spindle and the sheers control
> Of Destiny, and spin her own free hours.

It was the fortune of bright Lucy to inspire much fine metaphysical passion in the poets of the time. She was the declared inspiration of John Donne in the days before his thoughts were in the dust with Jezebel and she is the likeliest candidate for Jonson's sole sequence of love songs—the poems to Charis, including the loveliest of all his lyrics :

> Have you seen but a bright lily grow
>   Before rude hands have touch'd it ?
> Have you mark'd but the fall of the snow,
>   Before the soil hath smutch'd it ?
> Have you felt the wool of bever,
>   Or swan's down ever ?
> Or have smelt o' the bud of the briar,
>   Or the nard in the fire ?
> Or have tasted the bag of the bee ?
> O so white, O so soft, O so sweet is she !

Ben Jonson

Lucy was not, like Elizabeth, a poetess; but she loved learning and good books. Jonson, sending her a copy of Donne's satires, observes that " rare poems ask rare friends ". It was not the least of her virtues that her purse was open—too freely, some said—to her admirers, and there is an epigram of Jonson which he was always ready to recite, thanking her for pressing upon him unasked the " buck " denied him, after solicitation, by a lord.

Bright Lucy had a cousin, Cecily Boulstred. Donne, writing her elegy, mourns her as young, beautiful and witty. Her wit on occasion seems to have been exercised at Jonson's expense with the result that, to be even with her privately, he wrote an epigram on the *Court Pucelle*. Mistress Cecily was given to habits that never failed to exasperate him. She was something of an exquisite—a lady euphuist, apt to labour a phrase rather than to inquire the sense of it. She was given also to dressing her person with the same fancy and elaboration as her thoughts. Jonson felt that correction was necessary. It should be salutary, but anonymous. Let her wear the cap if it fitted.

> What though her chamber be the very pit
> Where fight the prime cocks of the game for wit!

She had made fun of Apollo's priest and had dared him to retaliate. He would have none of her airs and affectations. " Farthest I am ", he declares, " from the idolatry of stuffs and laces." Let others admire her velvet gowns and spangled petticoats and be lip-thirsty for her conceits. He gets increasingly angry as he writes—not an unusual thing with poets; and, finally, becomes most ungallantly personal:

> Indeed her dressing some man might delight;
> Her face there's none can like by candle-light.

All was noted against her. She had twice contracted

to marry and twice repented. She had begun to prefer priests to poets. She was notoriously difficult of approach—hence the *Court Pucelle*. Yet there were men—Sir John Roe was one of them—who wrote verses to her, in secret, to which no true maid might appropriately listen.

This is the one really spiteful product of Jonson's muse. Certainly he would have torn it up when it had served its purpose, which was to relieve his feelings. Unfortunately, however, having composed the epigram, he allowed it, as he told Drummond, to be " stolen out of his pocket by a gentleman who drank him drowsy ", and this same gentleman, most ungentlemanly, took it at once to Mistress Cecily—which, says Jonson, " brought him great displeasure ". More interesting than the incident is the sequel. Cecily Boulstred died untimely of a fever some two years afterwards and set all the poets weeping. Jonson, in high remorse, wrote a respectful epitaph of which his wisest editors have affirmed that, though bearing his initials, it could not possibly have come from the same pen as the spiteful epigram. Those, however, who have followed him so far will find no inconsistency. He had been unkind—he had even been unjust—and his amends were as characteristic as his offence.

Of other women Jonson wrote ceremoniously as the times required, but always pertinently. Of Mary, Lady Wroth, author of *Urania*, he could say little more than that she was a Sidney :

> And, being named, how little doth that name
> Need any Muse's praise to give it fame ?

Or he must celebrate her as an epitome of classic graces—Ceres in a wheaten hat, Flora in a shepherd's tire, Diana in the chase, or Juno without a peacock

for formal occasions. In an epitaph to Susan, Countess of Montgomery, a lady of strict piety, he was driven,
for lack of other matter, to remember that there was
once a Susanna whose virtue confounded the elders.
Jonson's compliments are either studiously general or
carefully appropriate. To Katharine, wife to Lord
d'Aubigny, his host for five years, he wrote an epistle
in which, side-glancing, as was his custom, at the
follies and vices of the time, he celebrated her as a
good wife and expectant mother :

> How you love one, and him you should ; how still
> You are depending on his word and will ;
> Not fashioned for the court or strangers' eyes,
> But to please him, who is the dearer prize
> Unto himself, by being so dear to you.

In the many epigrams and epistles which Jonson
wrote to the women of his time he avoided irrelevant
flattery. Nor was there much in the nature of gallantry. Only in one epistle, written in later life, do
we find him confessing himself as personally smitten ;
and the confession, made to a certain Lady Covell,
was prudently turned—all hope of a more familiar
approach being carefully excluded :

> You won not verses, madam, you won me,
> When you would play so nobly and so free.
> So have you gained a servant and a muse,
> The first of which I fear you will refuse.

As well she may, he hastens to add, for he is a tardy,
cold, unprofitable chattel. He is fat and growing
old. He turns the scale at twenty stone within two
pounds, and approaches his friends only to break chairs
or crack a coach. His Muse, however, is another
matter. She is nimble, chaste and fair. She can
tread the air, stroke the water and sleep in a virgin's
bosom. She will serve to make his lady merry on

the dressing-stool o' mornings and at afternoons to keep away ill company.

Jonson grows old gracefully in spirit, though not in frame. This was no Falstaff in whom desire had outlived performance, but a man who accepted whimsically his decline and preferred to offer his mistress a nimble muse than to sigh heavily in vain. Jonson's many friendships with women of the time, formally preserved in his epigrams and epistles, reveal him socially as a good companion, a guest sure of his welcome, honest rather than tactful, not to be moved or corrupted into extravagance.

Jonson lived in the age of the tavern. The drink was canary—none other than the good sherris sack celebrated by Falstaff : " It ascends me into the brain ; dries there all the foolish and dull and cruddy vapours which environ it ; makes it apprehensive, quick, forgetive, full of nimble, fiery and delectable shapes." Of the Mermaid much has been written, but little is known. The legend of the Mermaid Club affirms that Raleigh founded it, but, when most it was frequented, Raleigh was in the Tower. The height of its fashion coincided, however, with the early years of Jonson's maturity, and these were the days to which the famous verses of Beaumont apply :

> For wit is like a rest
> Held up at tennis, where men do the best
> With the best gamesters. What things have we seen
> Done at the Mermaid ! heard words that have been
> So nimble, and so full of subtle flame,
> As if that everyone from whence they came
> Had meant to put his whole soul in a jest,
> And had resolved to live a fool the rest
> Of his dull life.

Tradition insists upon encounters between Jonson and Shakespeare. Sad chroniclers must not forget, however, that Fuller, who described these meetings, was only eight years old when Shakespeare died.

> Many were the wit-combats between Shakespeare and Ben Jonson. I behold them like a Spanish great galleon and an English man-of-war. Master Jonson, like the former, was built far higher in learning, solid but slow in his performances ; Shakespeare, like the latter, lesser in bulk but lighter in sailing, could turn with all tides, tack about and take advantage of all winds by the quickness of his wit and invention.

Fuller wrote like a modern biographer. Things seen in his mind's eye were bravely set down as history.

Here, nevertheless, were Shakespeare, Jonson and Beaumont. Who were the others ? We can do no more than fill in the blanks with eligible names : Chapman, Fletcher and Drayton among the playmakers, Donne among the poets, Sir John Roe among the good fellows, Selden among the scholars. But the Mermaid still stays remote—eluding us as a sanctuary where Shakespeare trod, as though fate had decreed that we should never meet him face to face or see him plain.

We come nearer to Jonson in the latter days of his supremacy, when a new generation, eager to be sealed of the tribe of Ben, gathered about him at the Old Devil Tavern at Temple Bar. There, in the Apollo Room, Jonson, the happy laureate, lorded it over his sons. Over the door was written :

> Wine it is the milk of Venus
> And the poets' horse accounted ;
> Ply it and you all are mounted.
> 'Tis the true Phoebean liquor,
> Cheers the brains, makes wit the quicker ;
> Pays all debts, cures all diseases,
> And at once three senses pleases.
> Welcome all who lead or follow
> To the Oracle of Apollo.

Maturity

The keeper of the tavern was one Simon Wadloe, Old Sim, Simon the King—as he was variously called. Above the black marble mantelpiece surmounting the hearth—where a fire must always be kept burning (*focus perennis esto*)—were engraved in gold letters the convivial laws drafted by Jonson himself in trenchant Latin :

> Idiota, insulsus, tristis, turpis, abesto ;
> Eruditi, urbani, hilares, honesti, adsciscuntor ;
> Nec lectae feminae repudiantor.

" Let the dull, stupid, sad and base fellow keep away. Let the learned, polite, merry and worthy fellow approach. Nor let women of merit be thrust out." Socially the qualifications were broad. The poor poet was admitted on the same footing as the wealthy man of law, and such noble lords as had no need, for lack of a better pedestal, to stand upon their dignity. The younger playwrights, Field, Browne and Marmion, were there ; Herrick brought in the younger poets ; Falkland, Sir Kenelm Digby and Sir John Suckling had several titles to be present ; Pembroke and d'Aubigny would almost certainly attend upon occasion. Apollo's laws were strict. It was forbidden to be either mute or garrulous. Members of the club were not allowed to read bad poems or pressed to write them. Fiddlers were not permitted to attend except by special invitation. There must be no publishing abroad of what was said or done within doors. Each member of the company must pay his footing. The dishes must be choice rather than costly. The service must be swift but silent. There was no quarter for noise, pugnacity or bad behaviour. The lawgiver lays it firmly down, in letters for all to read, that it shall be counted as an offence to throw cups, break glasses, smash windows or mishandle the furniture. Men were not limited in liquor, but must carry it to the pleasure and profit of the company.

Marmion, fresh from one of these assemblies, went home to write his comedy, *A Fine Companion*. He sat down to show Careless, young gallant of the piece, arriving drunk upon the stage, but more exalted with the vapours of Apollo than with the fumes of Bacchus. Whence come you, asks his lady ? From the Apollo, he answers :

> From the heaven
> Of my delight, where the boon Delphic god
> Drinks sack and keep his Bacchanalias,
> And has his incense and his altars smoking,
> And speaks in sparkling prophecies ; thence I come !
> My brains perfumed with the rich Indian vapour
> And heightened with conceits ; from tempting beauties,
> From dainty music and poetic strains,
> From bowls of nectar and ambrosiac dishes,
> And from a mighty continent of pleasure,
> Sails thy brave Careless.

Falkland, in his eclogue to the memory of Jonson, supplies some further touches :

> To him how daily flocked, what reverence gave,
> All that had wit or ever hoped to have ;
>
> . . . . . .
>
> How the wise, too, did with mere wits agree,
> As Pembroke, Portland and grave Aubigny,
> Nor thought the rigidest senator a shame
> To contribute to so deserved a fame.

There is extant an epistle written by Jonson to one that asked to be sealed of his tribe, wherein he sets forth the major qualifications. His sons must be safe and sure in all they do ; face hardship and prove themselves true gold, though they bear no official superscription ; they must not be such as merely talk and never think ; they must be ready to serve their king when required, but not for ever be talking policy ; they must be honest in their friendships and follow reason. Incidentally Ben will have none of those that " live in the wild anarchy of drink ", and grow quarrelsome, malicious or bawdy in their cups.

Heads were hard in those days and throats capacious. There is nothing but the shrinking of the fastidious and sober Drummond to indicate that Jonson was ever much the worse for the liquor whose virtues he so pleasantly extolled in his epigrams and epistles. Assuredly he disliked a man who could not carry his liquor well. He would have no drunkard at his tavern to spoil the feast of reason. He would put no enemy in his brain to steal away his wits. King Charles, many years later, confirming Jonson as the laureate of England, added a butt of canary to his yearly pension. This was the only jest Charles ever made ; but it was kindly meant and would never have been aimed at a sot. Jaspar Mayne, one of the sons of Ben, explicitly defended his master from the charge of excess, easily brought and easily believed of a poet who grew to twenty stone all but two pounds. Evil tongues gave out that, sober, the poet's wit worked slowly, as elephants brought forth ; that his plays were drawn at the Mermaid and that the King's yearly butt was the source and fountain of his inspiration. The loyal Jaspar explicitly repudiates the calumny.

A notable article of the Apollo covenant was that which provided : *nec lectae feminae repudiantor*. Who were these women who might attend ? How were they chosen ? Not bright Lucy or chaste Susannah. Even in disguise a lady of rank, not though she were a poetess, might enter a tavern. Nor were there any women yet to correspond with Mrs. Bracegirdle or Mrs. Barry, who a generation later brought such as Millamant to life. Doubtless the article should be read as a warning rather than an encouragement. Women were not absolutely excluded, but they must

Ben Jonson

be "chosen", and they were not allowed to spoil these essentially male proceedings.

For the principal events of his life Jonson is always his own best authority. His theatrical career must be recovered for the most part from the prefaces, prologues and inductions to his plays. His social progress may be followed through his masks. His friendships, apart from the conversations with Drummond, are in the same way revealed in his epigrams and occasional verse. His friends were now scattered up and down from Whitehall to Eastcheap. Three illustrious figures that belong to this period of his life call for special notice : Walter Raleigh, Francis Bacon and William Shakespeare.

It is an obstinate tradition that it was Raleigh who first made famous the Mermaid tavern as a resort of wits. There is no evidence that Jonson met Raleigh previous to his imprisonment ; but in 1613 Raleigh, from the Tower, appointed Jonson to go with his son as tutor into France. The office was no sinecure. The younger Raleigh had small respect for authority. Already at Oxford he had quarrelled with his masters to the fond delight of an indulgent mother and the considered indignation of his sire. The visit to Paris ended equally to the scandal of professor and pupil. Jonson himself related to Drummond the story of his disgrace :

> Sir Walter Raleigh sent him governor with his son, anno 1613, to France. This youth, being knavishly inclined, among other pastimes, caused him to be drunken, and dead drunk, so that he knew not where he was ; thereafter laid him on a car, which he made to be drawn by pioners through the streets, at every corner showing his governor stretched out and telling them that was a more lively image of the crucifix than any they had ; at which sport young Raleigh's mother delighted much (saying his father, young, was so inclined), though the father abhorred it.

Jonson, in his conversations with Drummond, said of Raleigh that he " esteemed more of fame than conscience ", adding that the best wits of England were employed in making his history of the world. Jonson himself contributed a chapter on the Punic wars, which Raleigh " altered and set in his book ". We find no epigrams or allusions to Raleigh in any of Jonson's verse, but this is not surprising. While Jonson was making his way with the Court, Raleigh was fast a prisoner of State and afterwards a licensed freebooter with dubious instructions. Raleigh was not a good subject for epigrams, though Jonson was not the man to have recoiled from public compliment if he had really admired the man. Evidence of any such warm or lasting admiration is to seek, however. Raleigh inspired fear, wonder and resentment rather than affection and one imagines that, if Sir Walter were ever on occasion at the Mermaid, Jonson, Shakespeare and the rest would sit mainly in corners and listen.

Of Jonson's journey to France one would like to know more. Donne was also in Paris at the time. So was a certain Daniel Featley—a Protestant minister, lately tutor to young Raleigh at Oxford. Featley was deep in the religious disputes of the Huguenots and Jonson attended a debate on the real presence. Jonson in France was inevitably restricted to clerical company. He could talk no French and so must meet his acquaintances in Latin. Among the famous people he encountered was Cardinal du Perron, first of the great clerical statesmen who were to fashion French history during the next fifty years, hammer of the Calvinists, whose political intrigues were delicately spread from Paris to Rome. Du Perron was a wit and a scholar who had translated part of the Aeneid. He had a prodigious memory, a vast knowledge of ecclesiastical and profane antiquity, a sharp wit, a pure and eloquent style and such readiness in dispute that few cared to engage him. Jonson, however, was ready. To the first scholar of France his judgment was conveyed in a single word. " He told Cardinal du Perron," Drummond notes, " at his being in France, anno 1613, who shewed him his translations of Vergil, that they were naught." Jonson had little French, but enough to perceive that the Cardinal's verses were an elegant paraphrase rather than a true bill. The devout conscience of the scholar was offended and he was brave enough and friendly enough with his Eminence to say so. Perhaps the most amusing sequel to Jonson's encounter with the Cardinal was the indignant comment of Gifford. In furious defence of Jonson against the whole world and in an equally furious hatred of papacy, Gifford declared that the Cardinal, engaged upon undermining the liberties of the Gallican Church, had " little leisure for poetry and that little was misemployed ".

The visit to France in 1613 is the only authentic event, apart from the procession of plays and masks, in the period between Jonson's imprisonment on account of *Eastward Ho* in 1605 and his production of *The Devil is an Ass* in 1616, the year which brings the second period of his life to a natural conclusion. These were the years of his great endeavour and Jonson himself marked them off from the years that followed by the preparation and publication in 1616 of the first folio edition of his collected works.

Of personal encounters between the greatest scholar of the age and the man who took all knowledge for his province there is no record. The one personal glimpse we get of their acquaintance is a saying of Francis Bacon reported to Drummond. Bacon had heard of Jonson's proposed journey to Scotland and he appears to have joined in the Mermaid chaff at Jonson's expense : " For at his hither coming Sir Francis Bacon said to him, He loved not to see poesy go on other feet than poetical dactylus and spondaeus." There are two references to Bacon in Jonson's verse and prose. One is an address to England's Lord Chancellor on his sixtieth birthday, which was celebrated by Bacon at York House with great splendour.

> Give me a deep-crowned bowl, that I may sing,
> In raising him, the wisdom of my King.

The second reference is more significant. Jonson, celebrating his mighty friend in 1621, was part only of a general chorus. Bacon was then at the summit of his fortune. Jonson can, therefore, commend him as one,

> Whose even thread the Fates spin round and full
> Out of their choicest and their whitest wool.

Within a year, however, the Lord Chancellor had fallen into disgrace, and none so good to do him reverence. Yet in Jonson's *Discoveries* we read the following noble words :

> My conceit of Lord Verulam's person was never increased by his place or honour ; but I have, and do, reverence him for the greatness that was only proper to himself, in that he seemed to me ever by his work one of the greatest men and most worthy of admiration that had been in many ages. In his adversity I ever prayed God would give him strength, for greatness he could not want. Neither could I condole, in a word or syllable, for him ; as knowing no accident could do harm to virtue, but rather help to make it manifest.

Jonson's opinion of Bacon's genius is further developed in a note on the *Novum Organum*, " which, though by the most superficial of men, who cannot get beyond the title of Nominals, is not penetrated nor understood, it really openeth all defects of learning whatsoever ". His appreciation of Bacon's oratory, to which he had obviously listened, is generous without reserve or qualification. He—

> performed that in our tongue which may be compared or preferred either to insolent Greece or haughty Rome . . . so that he may be named and stand as the mark and *acme* of our language . . . No man ever spake more neatly, more pressly, more weightily, or suffered less emptiness, less idleness, in what he uttered. No member of his speech but consisted of his own graces. His hearers could not cough or look aside from him without loss. He commanded where he spoke ; and had his judges angry and pleased at his devotion. No man had their affections more in his power. The fear of every man that heard him was lest he should make an end.

Jonson's estimate of Shakespeare, his feeling for the man and general attitude to his work, is so clearly expressed that those who read what he explicitly set down with his own hand can only wonder at the legend which Shakespeare's editors constructed and at the pains and passion which the biographers and apologists have expended in its destruction. Jonson's blunt assertion to Drummond that Shakespeare wanted art, taken with certain qualifications which seasoned his admiration as a critic for the greatest of all dramatists, started a fable which every commentator on the works of either of the two parties, prior to William Gifford, felt bound to fortify and embellish. The plays of Jonson were ransacked by the early editors of Shakespeare for spiteful allusions in support of the received opinion that Jonson was insensitive to the genius of his great contemporary and envious of his success. The childish ingenuity expended on this enterprise is perhaps the quaintest of many illustrations of the peculiar circumstance that the editing of Shakespeare's works has for the most been left to critics who appear to be as lacking in any just appreciation of human probabilities as in ordinary common sense or poetic sensibility. Morose, in *The Silent Woman*, hating all forms of noise, alludes with distaste to plays which are nothing but fights at sea. This is interpreted as a sneer against *Antony and Cleopatra*. Jonson in the prologue to *Every Man in His Humour* announces that he intends to write comedies of real life. It is not in his design,

> To make a child, now swaddled, to proceed
> Man and then shoot up, in one beard and weed,
> Past threescore years ; or, with three rusty swords,
> And help of some few foot and half-foot words,
> Fight over York and Lancaster's long jars,
> And in the tyring house bring wounds to scars.

This is a spiteful allusion to Shakespeare's chronicle plays, in which time flies and history is traduced. Jonson declares that he is loath to make nature afraid in his plays " like those that beget tales, tempests and such-like drolleries ". This is a malignant reference to Shakespeare's Prospero. Of such is the indictment composed. One of the more serious editors even suggests that Jonson, in mentioning as a cure for the scalded leg of Ursula the pig woman the application of the white of an egg, is expressing contempt for Shakespeare's *King Lear* in which the same remedy is prescribed for the eyes of Gloster. The most careful reading of Jonson's plays can find no better instances than this of Jonson's resolute and unsleeping malice. The state of mind of the commentators which made it possible for the legend to survive so long is illustrated by the fact that a harmless apocryphal jest of Shakespeare concerning Jonson has frequently been quoted in support of it by a whole succession of critics. Shakespeare is said to have stood godfather to Jonson's eldest son.

Ben Jonson

Asked what he would bring to the christening he is reported to have said : " Faith Ben, I think I'll e'en give him a dozen good lattin spoons and thou shalt translate 'em."   If the jest were authentic and proved anything at all, it would show conclusively that the two men understood one another well enough for it to be possible for Shakespeare to rally Jonson in all good humour on a point regarding which he was notoriously susceptible. Such jests can pass only between good friends.

There is not a line anywhere in the plays of Jonson which suggests that he was glancing contemptuously at Shakespeare. The two exceptions—the reference to Lancaster's long jars in the prologue to *Every Man in His Humour* and a reference to *Andronicus* in *Bartholomew Fair*—are exceptions which prove the rule, neither of the plays, as Jonson well knew, being authentic Shakespeare. In every other case where Jonson derides the romantic and historical drama the cap would better fit a dozen heads. The plays of the time were full of alarums, battles by sea and land, trumpets and creaking thrones, and there were many critics who, with Sir Philip Sidney, made merry at this woeful machinery of the common stage. Loudest of them all was Shakespeare himself. Shakespeare first apologised for his devices :

> But pardon gentles all
> The flat unraisèd spirits that have dared
> On this unworthy scaffold to bring forth
> So great an object. Can this cockpit hold
> The vasty fields of France ?

He then satirised them in terms more vehement than any Jonson or Sidney ever used :

> Where (O for pity !) we shall much disgrace,
> With four or five most vile and ragged foils,
> Right ill-disposed in brawl ridiculous,
> The name of Agincourt.

Maturity

Nevertheless, the legend grew and, till William Gifford in 1816 produced his admirable fighting edition of Jonson's works, their author was still regarded as an envious detractor of his friend. Gifford destroyed the legend but almost at the expense of his own sanity. His pages bristle with indignant confutations and his volumes leave a final impression that the principal reason for his undertaking them was that he might prove, once and for all, that Jonson was not filled with a consuming hatred and black envy of his rival.

The truth lies for all to read in a few lines easily digested. Jonson on Shakespeare is all contained in the small note recorded by Drummond, a passage of the *Discoveries*, his verses on the Droeshout portrait and his tribute " To the Memory of my Belovēd Master William Shakespeare and What he Hath Left Us ".

Drummond's note will be discussed elsewhere. Jonson's petulant observation during the conversations at Hawthornden that Shakespeare wanted art and wrecked a ship on the sea coast of Bohemia must be read in the light of the brief but reasoned estimate of his *Discoveries*. This shall be quoted in full :

> I remember, the players have often mentioned it as an honour to Shakespeare, that in his writing (whatsoever he penned) he never blotted out a line. My answer hath been, Would he had blotted a thousand. Which they thought a malevolent speech. I had not told posterity this, but for their ignorance, who choose that circumstance to commend their friend by wherein he most faulted, and to justify mine own candour ; for I loved the man, and do honour his memory on this side idolatry, as much as any. He was (indeed) honest, and of an open and free nature ; had an excellent fancy, brave notions and gentle expressions ; wherein he flowed with that facility, that sometimes it was necessary he should be stopped : *Sufflaminandus erat*, as Augustus said of Haterius. His wit was in his own power ; would the rule of it had been so too.

Ben Jonson

Many times he fell into those things could not escape laughter : as when he said in the person of Caesar, one speaking to him, " Caesar thou dost me wrong." He replied, " Caesar did never wrong but with just cause," and such like ;· which were ridiculous. But he redeemed his vices with his virtues. There was ever more in him to be praised than to be pardoned.

Comment is hardly necessary. Jonson was near enough to his sun of poets to discover spots and he had the eye of an eagle, to look unwinking on this splendour. Such criticism as he permitted himself was from his own point of view not only honest but inevitable, and he did not scruple to utter his mind. Jonson has explicitly declared it to be the office of a friend to be honest in censure :

> It is an act of tyranny, not love,
> In practised friendship wholly to approve.

Again :

> Little know they that profess amity,
> And seek to scant her comely liberty,
> How much they lame her in her property.

For I loved the man and do honour his memory, *on this side idolatry, as much as any*—there is here an honest warmth, qualified only by a characteristic refusal to pretermit his judgment. The famous reference to Caesar who did never wrong but with just cause is alone unfortunate. It puts Jonson oddly with the pedants and started them on a career which has yet to run its course.

The lines on the Droeshout portrait are formal—to be quoted more as an example of Jonson's lapidary style with an epigram than as a key to unlock his heart :

> This figure that thou here seest put,
> It was for gentle Shakespeare cut,
> Wherein the graver had a strife
> With nature, to out-do the life ;

Maturity

O could he but have drawn his wit
As well in brass, as he hath hit
His face ; the print would then surpass
All that was ever writ in brass ;
But since he cannot, Reader, look
Not on his picture, but his book.

The epitaph, written to the memory of my belovèd Master William Shakespeare, too long to be quoted in full, is a sufficient answer to all charges of envy or lack of understanding. Neither man nor muse can praise too much the writings of Shakespeare. They are even proof against the perilous commendations of ignorance, blind affection or malicious insincerity :

Soul of the age !
The Applause, delight, the wonder of our stage !
My Shakespeare rise ! I will not lodge thee by
Chaucer or Spenser, or bid Beaumont lie
A little further to make thee a room.
Thou art a monument without a tomb,
And art alive still while thy book doth live,
And we have wits to read and praise to give.

Shakespeare outshines the sporting Kyd and Marlowe's mighty line :

And though thou hadst small Latin and less Greek,
From thence to honour thee I would not seek
For names ; but call forth thund'ring Aeschylus,
Euripides and Sophocles to us.

His works might compare with all that Greece or Rome had produced or inspired :

Triumph, my Britain, thou hast one to show
To whom all scenes of Europe homage owe.
He was not of an age but for all time !

. . . .

Nature herself was proud of his designs
And joyed to wear the dressing of his lines.

. . . .

The merry Greek, tart Aristophanes,
Neat Terence, witty Plautus, now not please ;
But antiquated and deserted lie,
As they were not of nature's family.

Ben Jonson

This was an astonishing verdict—a comparison, in Shakespeare's favour, with the masters of antiquity. Jonson clearly had no doubt of Shakespeare's supremacy. All his criticism takes that supremacy for granted. Shakespeare, he definitely declared, stood quite alone.

Yet more surprising is what follows. Jonson had censured Shakespeare for a facility that often rode near to carelessness or indifference. Shakespeare wanted art. Would he had blotted a thousand! But Jonson, in this final judgment on his friend, takes a wider view of his achievement than in his ejaculation to Drummond or the note which he entered in the *Discoveries*. He realises on reflection that to charge the greatest poet of his time with lack of art was, in effect, treasonable to his own vocation. Therefore, he writes :

> Yet must I not give Nature all ; thy Art,
> My gentle Shakespeare, must enjoy a part.
> For though the poet's matter nature be,
> His art doth give the fashion.

The poet who writes a living line must sweat and strike upon the Muse's anvil :

> For a good poet's made as well as born,
> And such wert thou ! Look how the father's face
> Lives in his issue, even so the race
> Of Shakespeare's mind and manners brightly shines
> In his well-tornèd and true filèd lines,
> In each of which he seems to shake a lance
> As brandish'd in the eyes of ignorance.

The epitaph concludes in a choir of angels singing to his rest a dear friend and the greatest genius of his time and race. Sweet Swan of Avon, star of poets— the last phrases fall in a full concord of heart and mind. Is it not enough for those who may still incline to believe that Jonson was grudging either in his love or admiration of Shakespeare to be reminded that it was Jonson who first applied to him the endearing epithets which have become almost an echo of Shakespeare's name and a part of our national consciousness concerning him ? This epitaph of Jonson on Shakespeare is surely the most sincerely affectionate and generous tribute ever offered by one great poet to another. There is nothing formal. Nothing is withheld. It is no elegiac performance. There is no improving the occasion or taking the dead for a theme. Jonson in these lines brings Shakespeare nearer to posterity than anything that has ever been written or recorded concerning him.

CHAPTER VII

The Tragedies

MERES in 1598 named Jonson in his list of the nine poets who were " our best for tragedy ". We have no tragedies of Jonson but *Sejanus* (1603) and *Catiline* (1611). All others were destroyed by the author. Of the tragic work to which Meres alludes not a line remains. Only by accident does Jonson refer to the fact that he ever wrote a tragedy previous to *Sejanus*, when he lets slip in the preface that it was so far the best of his efforts in that kind.

Did Jonson, in fact, ever write a full tragedy single-handed except for the two which he acknowledged ? That he was employed by Henslowe to adapt, revise and amplify existing plays is clear. That he ever wrote complete and original tragedies of his own in these early years has no other support than Meres and his own fugitive allusion. He had at any rate no wish that they should survive him. He had written for a fee and he had written in the fashion. The lost plays, in fact, if any, were such as he had cruelly mocked in the induction to his first comedy.

Reference has already been made to his collaborations with Chapman, Marston and others. Of his work in this kind the only specimens that survive are the additions which he is credited with having composed for *The Spanish Tragedy* in 1602. He was paid for these additions and the additions are extant. The only ground for rejecting them is that they are quite unlike anything to be found in *Sejanus* or *Catiline*. To do so, however, would be unreasonable. It was precisely because this early tragic work of Jonson was completely different from anything which he wrote after his own manner and principles that he wished it to be forgotten. The additions to *The Spanish Tragedy* had necessarily to be in keeping with the original stuff of the play. The author's mood was that of Hamlet outfaced with Laertes: Nay, an thou'lt mouth I'll rant as well as thou:

> Night is a murderous slut,
> That would not have her treasons to be seen;
> And yonder pale-fac'd Hecate there, the moon,
> Doth give consent to all that's done in darkness;
> And all those stars that gaze upon her face,
> Are aglets on her sleeve, pins on her train.
>
> .   .   .   .   .   .
>
> Where was she that same night when my Horatio
> Was murdered? She should have shone. Search thou the book.
> Had the moon shone, in my boy's face, there was a kind of grace,
> That I know—nay, I do know—had the murderer seen him,
> His weapon would have fallen.

Such stuff as this was cheap. Henslowe might buy it wholesale, and Jonson could write it as well as another. But he would not wish to preserve it.

Edward Alleyn, ambassador of Henslowe in this affair, seems to have suggested that what the old play needed most was an amplification of the scenes in which Jeronymo was exhibited as mad for the death of his son. Madness was a commonplace of the Elizabethan theatre, and no author who was unable to produce a creditable mad scene at a moment's notice could be regarded as having mastered the elements of his craft. Jonson's additions are handled in the traditional manner:

> Let the clouds scowl, make the moon dark, the stars
> extinct, the winds blowing, the bells tolling, the owls
> shrieking, the toads croaking, the minutes jarring and the

clock striking twelve. And then at last, Sir, starting, behold a man hanging and tottering and tottering, as you know the wind will wave a man, and I with a trice to cut him down. And looking upon him by the advantage of my torch, find it to be my son, Horatio. There you may show a passion ! Draw me like old Priam of Troy crying : The house is afire, the house is afire ! make me curse, make me rave, make me cry, make me mad, make me well again, make me curse hell, invocate heaven and in the end leave me in a trance.

Famous critics—even such as Lamb and Coleridge—have strangely denied that Jonson wrote these additions, not on the ground that they were unlike his other work, but that they were beyond his range. Lamb suspected Webster and Coleridge found a spiritual " kinship to passages in some one or other of Shakespeare's great pieces ". With all respect, it is difficult to find anywhere in the scenes attributed to Jonson more than a superficial resemblance to anything in the greater tragedies of the period. The sound and fury is there ; there is the usual furnishing of owls, clocks, bells, toads, and corpses under the moon. All this, however, is no more than a competent inventory. Moreover, in the one really striking passage, where mad Jeronymo talks of sons in the abstract, adopting the Elizabethan trick, so marvellously used by Shakespeare in his greatest scenes, of elevating a particular woe into a cosmic indictment, there is just that obstinate concentration upon a main idea, and just that logical progression, whereby Jonson in his greater comedies was occasionally to achieve the effect of an imagination working at high pressure :

These slippers are not mine, they were my son Horatio's.
My son ? And what's a son ? A thing begot
Within a pair of minutes—thereabout.
A lump bred up in darkness, and doth serve
To ballace these light creatures we call women ;
And at nine months' end, it creeps forth to light.

What is there yet in a son,
To make a father dote, rave or run mad?
Being born, it pants, cries, and breeds teeth.
What is there yet in a son? Ay, or yet,
Why might not a man love a calf as well?
Or melt in passion o'er a frisking kid,
As for a son? Methinks a young bacon,
Or a fine little smooth horse colt,
Should move a man as much as doth a son.

This firm, persistent handling of an initial fancy is quite in the manner of Jonson, and it is significant that, as soon as the conceit is exhausted and will yield or suggest no more, the writer, driven back upon common form, falls flat. He can grow hot in logic, but in passion he is merely shrill:

Well heaven is heaven still,
And there is Nemesis, and Furies
And things called whips,
And they sometimes do meet with murderers.

Admittedly we are far removed from the "flat sanity" which Swinburne found in the Roman plays. These early exercises in tragedy are significant as showing the kind of drama which Jonson, under the rulings of a definite purpose, deliberately set aside. Though he consented to write additions to *The Spanish Tragedy*, he continued to deride the public which took it for a masterpiece, and in *Every Man out of His Humour* he mocked its most famous lines:

O eyes! no eyes, but fountains fraught with tears.
O life! no life, but lively form of death.
O world! no world, but mass of public wrongs,
Confus'd and fill'd with murder and misdeeds.

Concerning *Sejanus* and *Catiline* there have been some remarkable opinions. Hazlitt, in his lectures on the dramatic literature of the Age of Elizabeth, contends that Jonson's "serious productions are superior to his comic ones ". This is an impish judgment, defended with an argument which in effect denies that these " serious productions " are tragedies at all. " Sense and industry ", Hazlitt declares, " agree better with the grave and severe than with the light and gay," and he goes on to compare the author to a mole that burrows into his material and throws up soil upon the surface. Not thus are tragedies written. Coleridge also is high, but dubious, in compliment. He wishes we had " whole volumes of such plays ", and regards them as a " mode of relating great historical events in the liveliest and most interesting manner ". It was Dryden in his " Essay on Dramatic Poesy " who began praising Jonson's tragedies in this dangerous fashion. Jonson, he affirms, was the " greatest man of the last age ", but, " dressed in all the ornaments and colours of the ancients " it was his virtue to " give place to them in all things . . . You track him always in their snow. . . . He invades authors like a monarch, and what would be theft in other poets is only victory in him. . . . With the spoils of these writers he so represents old Rome to us, in its rites, ceremonies and customs, that, if one of their poets had written either of his tragedies, we had seen less of it than in him."

Dryden and the later critics, praising Jonson in this vein, were picking up the cue which the author had himself dropped in his preface to *Sejanus*. Therein Jonson claimed for his tragedy " truth of argument, dignity of persons, purity and height of elocution, fulness and frequency of sentence ". In straining after these qualities he declared himself to have discharged the offices of a tragic writer. To which it must be answered with all respect that, even though all these offices be discharged, the result is not necessarily a tragedy, and that Shakespeare, who wrote carelessly upon a hint from Thomas North, was happier than Jonson who based his work with elaborate care upon the texts of Sallust and Cicero, of Suetonius, Tacitus and Dion.

Young, the author of *Night Thoughts*, speaking later for the romantics, said generally of Jonson that he " was very learnèd, as Samson was very strong, to his own hurt ; blind to the nature of tragedy he pulled down all antiquity on his head and buried himself under it ". Must we then conclude that, if Jonson had been less of a scholar, he would have fared better as a writer of tragic plays ? It is too simple an inference. Jonson's learning was essential to his muse. All his finest and most individual passages are charged with it. That he allowed it to run to extremes is no justification for thinking that he might have done better without it. Webster allowed his imagination to run to extremes and Ford his sensibility. But neither would have done with less. Each had the defect of his qualities.

He invades authors like a monarch. These tragic texts are a mosaic, in which each fragment is a morsel from the ancients. Soon, however, we begin to be struck with a paradox that gives a clue to the whole process of the author's mind and method. Jonson is most himself in the passages which come nearest to his sources. His mind and pen follow naturally the drift of things read and remembered. These old authors have become part of his imaginative reaction to present life. They are woven into the texture of his thought. They condition his response, not merely to an historic theme, but to people and things of every day. They even determine to a large extent his feelings and beliefs about himself. He can light no fire till his passion strikes a spark into the dry tinder of his learning. Then there is pother enough :

often a thick smoke in which we perish, sometimes a fire to warm and cheer posterity, now and then a pure flame of poetry in which the ancient stuff goes up in a swift blaze and the poet seems to be shining by his own light.

The extent to which Jonson assimilated antiquity, to bring it forth again transformed and converted to his own use and experience, must be clearly appreciated before we can hope to understand not only his tragedies and comedies, but even his individual utterances and confessions. Some of the most amazing instances of this peculiar gift or process are to be found in the *Discoveries*. The *Discoveries* were a collection of notes or jottings in prose, published after Jonson's death in 1640. They are made, as he expresses it, " upon men and matters, as they have flowed out of his daily readings, or had their reflux to his peculiar notions of the times ". There are one hundred and thirty-seven sections, dealing with conduct, policy, literature and the habits of men.

The innocent reader would unguardedly accept them as a personal record of opinions, reflections and confessions, and later we shall insist on reading them as exercises in personal revelation. Here, however, we must face the paradox. There is hardly a paragraph—not even when Jonson is telling us about his own habits and inclinations or describing his contemporaries or expressing his personal and private views—in which the industrious scholar may not find that, though the hand be that of Jonson, the voice is that of Quintilian, Pliny, Plutarch, Plautus, Juvenal or Vitruvius. Jonson, when he tells us in so artless-seeming a style that poverty was ever his domestic and familiar, falls into the very words of Apuleius. The famous passages on Shakespeare and Bacon, though they read like pen-portraits directly inspired by sight and sound of their illustrious subjects, are in parts word-for-word reminiscences from Seneca's *Controversia*, while there are certain confiding admissions of the poet concerning his prodigious but failing memory which are delivered in phrases from the same source.

Thus Jonson, even when he is jotting down his thoughts and impressions of things nearest to hand and heart, falls naturally into the phrases of antiquity. This is more than transcription, more than imitation, more even than unconscious memory. Jonson, when he thought of his friend Shakespeare, or listened to Verulam, or surveyed his own career, set down his impressions quite naturally in the phrase and manner of his ancient masters, so that the *Discoveries*, his own personal record, which reads to the uninitiated as his most original and unprompted work, can be referred line by line to classic sources. A single leaf of the *Discoveries*, exclaimed Swinburne, enchanted at having found his poet so forthright and unbosoming, " is worth all his lyrics, tragedies, elegies and epigrams together ". Do but consider, he begs, its " fresh and vigorous spontaneity ". Alas ! the scholars on whom Swinburne thrust this " little golden book " with such enthusiasm soon reduced his contentions to an apparent absurdity. It was easy for them to show that these fresh, vigorous and intimate thoughts and confessions were little more than a series of excerpts and echoes from the classical writers. Nevertheless, Swinburne was substantially right, and the scholars were fundamentally wrong. Jonson, looking at Shakespeare, wrote : " many times he fell into those things which could not escape laughter ", or again : " but he redeemed his vices with his virtues ; there was ever more in him to be praised than pardoned ". Swinburne and the innocents who took this to be Jonson's voice are not to be laughed aside. What if the sentences fall according to Seneca? *Saepe incidebat in ea quae derisum effugere non possent.* Or again : *redimebat tamen vitia virtutibus et persaepe plus habebat quod laudares quam cui ignosceres.* The words had slept in his ear, with a prodigious company of others, for just this apt occasion. They fall from him as naturally as native wood notes. Jonson wrote quite naturally and involuntarily in quotations—not only in his tragedies, where the authorities are deliberately respected, but in notes and confessions where his speech would seem to be original and unconditioned. Jonson, in fact, not only wrote, he talked and sang in quotations. With him the word once uttered, whether of his own minting or another's, remained for ever with him, passed into his idiom and became part of his natural speech. These words, metaphors and phrases are points round which his thought condenses, so that, in speaking with the voice of Seneca in his *Discoveries* or of Cicero in his *Catiline*, he is not speaking less aptly or sincerely for himself. It may even be urged that he was never more natural and free, never nearer to the spontaneous utterance which he mistrusted because it so seldom came to him, than when he was speaking by the book.

In *Sejanus* the author's learning was more closely woven into the text, and was the result of a more thorough assimilation, than in the comedies or masks. The result is a lean, sober and smooth style, in which the ancients are uniformly covered and concealed. There are almost no outstanding passages, but a smooth progression, evenly apt and firm. Almost any speech will do as well as another to illustrate its quality. Take, for example, the lines in which Sejanus, informed

by Terentius of ill omens, defies augury and declares
that all his faith is in Fortune :

> What excellent fools
> Religion makes of men ! Believes Terentius,
> If these were dangers, as I shame to think them,
> The gods could change the certain course of fate ?
> Or, if they could, they would now, in a moment,
> For a beeve's fat, or less, be brib'd t'invert
> Those long decrees ? Then think the gods, like flies,
> Are to be taken with the steam of flesh
> Or blood, diffus'd about their altars ; think
> Their power as cheap as I esteem it small.
> Of all the throng that fill th' Olympian hall,
> And without pity lade poor Atlas' back,
> I know not that one deity, but Fortune,
> To whom I would throw up, in begging smoke,
> One grain of incense ; or whose ear I'd buy
> With thus much oil. Her I indeed adore,
> And keep her grateful image in my house.
>
> .   .   .   .
>
> To her I care not, if, for a satisfying
> Your scrupulous fancies, I go offer. Bid
> Our priest prepare us honey, milk and poppy,
> His masculine odours and night vestments. Say
> Our rites are instant ; which perform'd, you'll see
> How vain and worthy laughter your fears be.

The conduct of the tragedy is as regular as the
verse—the unfolding of a process rather than a passion.
Jonson's theme is the rise to greatness of a minion
and his sudden conspicuous ruin at the moment when
he grasps at a final supremacy. Every stage in his
evil progress is described with a minute but simple
fidelity. The appeal of the tragedy is to our sense of
an inevitable and just retribution. These are the
mills of God which grind slowly but exceeding small
and hard. We stand by the elbow of the climbing
minister as, stage by stage, he uncovers his design—
the removal of his competitors, the seduction to his
purpose of possible friends and allies, his manipulation
of the imperial favour. We hold all the threads in

our hands, but always we remain aloof from the passions of the play. We see farther, at every stage, than any of the protagonists and wait calmly for things inevitable. When the Emperor, seeing that his creature grows dangerous, cunningly prepares his fall, we follow every step in the counterplot that will bring down Sejanus as he touches the top of his fortune. We do not fear for him or pity him or even rejoice in the discomfiture of a bad man. We merely realise that in two moves or three checkmate is threatened. Similarly, in following the fortunes of the lesser characters, we are impressed as with an ordered calamity. We take sad note of the ruin and death of a free spirit and respond with a measured indignation :

> The coward and the valiant man must fall;
> Only the cause, and manner how, discerns them.
> Romans, if any here be in this senate
> Would know to mock Tiberius' tyranny,
> Look upon Silius and learn to die (*stabs himself*).

Such high and tranquil dying is only matched with the conduct of Livia, turning never a hair as she decides to remove her husband, the Lord Drusus :

> His designs,
> Are full of grudge and danger ; we must use
> More than a common speed.

Very typical are the smooth scenes in which Livia and Eudemus, her physician, allude to the small circumstance that for Sejanus' sake she is deserting her husband, and has, incidentally, agreed to poison him. Eudemus is painting her face, but she hardly needs it, for these promising designs have put life and colour into her cheeks.

> This change came timely, lady, for your health
> And the restoring your complexion.

Was ever villainy so abstract, so sedate ? Eudemus discovers all the secrets of the beauty-parlours of

The Tragedies

old Rome—the fucus, the ceruse, the white oil ; and,
as he makes up the face of Livia, he talks lightly and
pleasantly of Sejanus, his virtues and powers, her
high prudence in making so obviously a change for
the better in her loves.   Who would suspect that these
two were planning an assassination ?

> *Eudemus.*   When will you take some physic, lady ?
> *Livia.*   When I shall, Eudemus ; but let Drusus' drug
> Be first prepared.
> *Eudemus.*   I have it ready.   And, to-morrow morning,
> I'll send you a perfume, first to resolve
> And procure sweat, and then prepare a bath
> To cleanse and clear the cutis ; against when
> I'll have an excellent new fucus made,
> Resistive 'gainst the sun, the rain, or wind,
> Which you shall lay on with a breath or oil
> As you best like, and last some fourteen hours.

We are as remote from it all as gods in Olympus.
This is a tragedy cut in alabaster.   It has a grave
still beauty, which Hazlitt felt—a beauty that comes
of measure, avoidance and design.   There are less
faults in *Sejanus* than in any play of Jonson—not
excluding the masterpieces.   But genius does not
express itself by avoidance, and we shall find in the
great comedies a passion which is lacking in the
stately tragedy.   The power which went into the
writing of certain passages of *Volpone* would have
cracked the mould of *Sejanus*.

The author chastens himself in this grave and
formal exercise as in none other of his compositions.
The eloquence in *Sejanus*, when it comes, is simple,
lucid and dry :

> Methinks the genius of the Roman race
> Should not be so extinct, but that bright flame
> Of liberty might be reviv'd again ;
> And we not sit, like spent and patient fools,
> Still puffing in the dark at one poor coal.

Only now and then Sejanus in his pride is allowed
to be grandiloquent :

> My roof receives me not ; 'tis air I tread,
> And at each step I feel my advancèd head
> Knock out a star in heaven.

But such tall talk is rare. Even more rare are any
passionate or bitter intrusions of the author. The
vices of Tiberius and his rout,

> Masters of strange and new commented lusts,
> For which wise nature hath left not a name,

are recounted with little heat or colour. Nothing is
allowed to break the even progress of Sejanus to his
fall. Only now and then do we feel that the poet
may break the mood he has chosen, high and aloof
from his creatures, as when sight of the senators
crowding about Sejanus in his glory almost proves too
much for his self-control :

> See, see ! what troops of his officious friends
> Flock to salute my lord, and start before
> My great proud lord ! to get a lord-like nod !
> Attend my lord unto the senate-house !
> Bring back my lord ! like service ushers, make
> Way for my lord ! proclaim his idol lordship,
> More than ten criers, or six noise of trumpets !
> Make legs, kiss hands, and take a scatter'd hair
> From my lord's eminent shoulder.

There is one interesting and deliberate exception
to this general restraint. The dreadful end of Sejanus
and his children is recounted in the classic style by
messenger and, as in the antique tragedy, the author,
cheated of presenting his horrors directly to the
audience, allows himself a licence of expression beyond
all human measure. Jonson is always thorough in
applying a system or a method and, once we realise
that he has decided to follow the Greek model, we
anticipate the worst :

> These mounting at his head, these at his face,
> These digging out his eyes, those with his brain
> Sprinkling themselves, their houses and their friends ;
> Others are met have ravish'd hence an arm,
> And deal small pieces of the flesh for favours ;
> These with a thigh, this hath cut off his hands,
> And this his feet ; these fingers and these toes ;
> That hath his liver, he his heart. . . .
> The whole and all of what was great Sejanus,
> And, next to Caesar, did possess the world,
> Now torn and scattered ; as he needs no grave.
> Each little dust covers a little part.

This is Jonson of the comedies, carrying a fancy to excess, unable to cease until he has completely exhausted it.

Catiline is usually bracketed with *Sejanus*, as though the two tragedies were inevitably a pair. Yet there is a striking difference in the style, mood and conduct of the two plays. Flat sanity will do for *Sejanus*, but not for its successor. *Sejanus* is a quiet study in political manners. It is dry, level and unimpassioned. *Catiline* has other qualities. It presents a mood rather than a picture. It is uneven, adventurous and rich in suggestion. There are passages in which Jonson looks directly forward to Milton in the fall of his lines and his endeavour to convey supernormal dramatic issues.

The play, in spite of its faults, was well able to hold the stage. Admittedly, it was not received with general applause. So much is clear from Jonson's contemptuous dedication to the reader in ordinary and from his appeal against the thick and dark ignorance of the time to the more enlightened appreciation of my Lord Chamberlain. But the tragedy was frequently performed right up to the civil wars, and it was one of the first plays to be revived at the Restoration when, as Downes recorded, " it proved very satisfactory to the town ". Langbaine, moreover, noted that it continued " still in vogue on the stage and was always presented with success ".

Lord Dorset states that *Catiline* was Jonson's favourite work. Jonson, however, praised it for its faults rather than its virtues. He thought highly of the speeches of Cicero and esteemed poorly, in comparison, of the early scenes, which the public liked. " Though you commend the first two acts, with the people, because they are the worst "—thus he scolds the reader in ordinary—" and dislike the oration of Cicero, in regard you read some pieces of it at school and understand them not, yet I shall find the way to forgive you." But the reader in ordinary was right and no modern producer would allow Cicero to say more than was necessary to present him as a finished orator.

In *Catiline* Jonson now and then achieved a nobility of expression which he never approached elsewhere. Perilously—for it is perilous to speak so high without passion—he lifts his style to the level of a theme in which the defeated insolence of a proud and evil spirit sets itself to the spoiling of mighty Rome. It is a tragedy in the heroic vein. Catiline is more than life-size. From the moment when first he rises and comes forward, in the shadow of Sulla's ghost, he is an archangel of darkness :

> Was I a man bred great as Rome herself,
> One form'd for all her honours, all her glories,
> Equal to all her titles : that could stand
> Close up with Atlas, and sustain her name
> As strong as he doth heaven ! and was I,
> Of all her brood, mark'd out for the repulse
> By her no-voice, when I stood candidate
> To be commander in the Pontic war !
> I will hereafter call her step-dame ever.
> If she can lose her nature, I can lose
> My piety, and in her stony entrails
> Dig me a seat.

The actions of Catiline sustain his words. His

marshalling of the forces of evil in the commonwealth suggests Satan assembling his fallen angels. He will use all the arts of corruption. He will flatter the mortal wickedness in all his tools till they are ready to be used. Some are to be moved with vanity; others with their necessity and greed; others with fear of retribution for small crimes already committed. Even the frivolous shall be seduced—slight airlings to be won with dogs, horses or store and change of women. Orestilla, his wife, fit mate for Lucifer, will here be of comfort and assistance:

> Call all the great, the fair and spirited dames
> Of Rome about thee; and begin a fashion
> Of freedom and community. Some will thank thee,
> Though the sour senate frown, whose heads must ache
> In fear and feeling, too. We must not spare
> Or cost or modesty; it can but show
> Like one of Juno's or of Jove's disguises,
> In either thee or me; and will as soon,
> When things succeed, be thrown by, or let fall,
> As is a veil put off, a visor changed.

His speeches to the noble Romans, desperate and disappointed men, are strong in their force and colour. All the riches of the Empire are engrossed by the giants of the State. They swell with treasure. They amuse themselves with planing hills with valleys. They ransack the world for a witty meal. They cannot overcome their wealth, though they let in seas upon the land, wound the earth for marble and gold, plunder the East for Attic statues or Tyrian hangings or Corinthian plate.

> The rest,
> However great we are, honest and valiant,
> Are herded with the vulgar, and so kept
> As we were only bred to consume corn
> Or wear out wool, to drink the city's water;
> Ungrac'd, without authority or mark,
> Trembling beneath their rods; to whom, if all
> Were well in Rome, we should come forth bright axes.

For each of the conspirators he has an appropriate temptation. He feeds savage Cethegus with descriptions of the late cruelties of Sulla, like Iago feeding the jealous fancies of Othello, until his victim, taking fire, breaks into a rhapsody :

> The rugged Charon fainted
> And ask'd a navy rather than a boat,
> To ferry over the sad world that came.

To such a scene the legendary episode, in which Catiline invites his confederates to drink with him the blood of a slave, so that their conspiracy may be for all a sacrament of life and death, comes as an appropriate climax.

Oddly enough Jonson has introduced into *Catiline* a group of women more vividly and minutely drawn and more necessary to his design than any we find in his comedies. Fulvia lies warmly at the heart of the tragedy. Jonson was fortunate here in having for one of his principal sources perhaps the finest of all political romances. There was no call to improve upon Sallust : all Jonson had to do was to transpose him for the theatre. He brings the wanton Fulvia and Sempronia, pretentiously accomplished, upon the stage with entire success, and the scenes in which they figure are among the best he ever wrote. Fulvia's comments on Sempronia, the political lady, are as spirited and true to form as the comments of Sempronia on Cicero, her rival in Greek and policy. Both women live in their style of speech : Fulvia, sensual, greedy, inquisitive, frank with herself as with the first comer, a living picture of the woman who lived to become the wife of seamy Clodius and bright Antony ; Sempronia, profligate, elaborately accomplished, proud of her finger in any pie, clinging to her pleasures, but ruefully confessing that they come harder with the years. Jonson in these scenes wears his great learning as lightly as a bird flies. Not a line is without authority ; yet all seems spontaneous. Frankly these pagan scenes are not for a squeamish generation, but there is no attempt at emphasis. The sensuality is unforced and conveyed without offence. Fulvia on her lover is simplicity itself :

> The salt is gone
> That gave him season : his good gifts are done.
> He does not yield the crop that he was wont.
> And for the act I can have secret fellows,
> With backs worth ten of him.

Or again :

> I am not taken
> With a cob-swan or a high-mounting bull,
> As foolish Leda and Europa were,
> But the bright gold, with Danäe. For such price
> I would endure a rough, harsh Jupiter,
> Or ten such thund'ring gamesters, and refrain
> To laugh at 'em, till they were gone.

The scene between Fulvia and Quintus Curius, in which she draws from him the secret of the con-spiracy, is written with a surprising liveliness and charm :

> *Fulvia.* Shall I know your project ?
> *Curius.* Thou shalt if thou'lt be gracious.
> *Fulvia.* As I can be.
> *Curius.* And wilt thou kiss me then ?
> *Fulvia.* As close as shells
> Of cockles meet.
> *Curius.* And print them deep ?
> *Fulvia.* Quite through
> Our subtle lips.
> *Curius.* And often ?
> *Fulvia.* I will sow them
> Faster than you can reap. What is your plot ?

Did Jonson really believe that Cicero's oration was the summit of his tragedy, or was he here deliberately flying in the public face ? It is better, when in doubt, to believe him honest. There were good reasons for

his predilection.   Cicero was the first of the humanists.
He was also a man of humble origin who rose to high
office and might claim to be a saviour of society :

> I have no arms, no dusty monuments,
> No broken images of ancestors,
> Wanting an ear or nose ; no forgèd tables
> Of long descents, to boast false honours from,
> Or be my undertakers to your trust ;
> But a new man, as I am styled in Rome,
> Whom you have dignified ; and more, in whom
> You have cut a way, and left it ope, for virtue
> Hereafter to that place, which our great men
> Held, shut up with all ramparts, for themselves.

Cicero spoke excellent Latin which it was a pleasure
to " transcribe ". Moreover he did, so history had
insisted, deliver these same speeches against Catiline,
and Jonson had so great a reverence for historic truth
that it blinded him to the fact that the truth of history
and the truth of dramatic art are not coincident.
In allowing Cicero to deliver in full his great oration
against Catiline he allowed him in effect to suspend,
almost to destroy, the interest of his tragedy.   Perhaps
it is technically impossible to present a politician
successfully on the stage except, in effect, by ignoring
his politics. Jonson is too honest for such easy
courses. His exhibition of a statesman in action is
competent, accurate and complete. Cicero's discovery
of the plot ; his clever management of the spies who
keep him informed ; his subtle handling of the
moderates who, though innocent of the plot, were, as
he knew, ready to take full advantage of its success ;
his effective staging of the historic scene of denunciation ; his conduct of the final debate on the question
of exile or death for the confederates of Catiline—all
these things are admirable in their way ; but they are
never more than practical politics. In comparison
with the early scenes these later passages lack con-

viction and power. They fall, indeed, within the definition of Coleridge as a " mode of relating great historical events in the liveliest and most interesting manner ".

Jonson, whose sympathies were with civic virtue and good policy, was naturally indignant when his audience sighed for Catiline. Most readers, however, ordinary or extraordinary, also sighing, will regret his premature disappearance from the scene in a mist of evil rhetoric :

> Methinks I see Death and the Furies waiting
> What we will do, and all the heaven, at leisure
> For the great spectacle.

Nor can they feel anything but relief when Petreius, the Roman general, breaks into the conclave of the Senate—though it is Caesar and Cicero who speak on either side—to bring us the last news of Catiline and lift the tragedy once more to the heroic level :

> And, as in that rebellion 'gainst the gods,
> Minerva holding forth Medusa's head,
> One of the giant-brethren felt himself
> Grow marble at the killing sight, and now
> Almost made stone, began to enquire what flint,
> What rock it was that crept through all his limbs,
> And, ere he could think more, was that he feared ;
> So Catiline, at the sight of Rome in us,
> Became his tomb ; yet did his look retain
> Some of his fierceness, and his hands still moved,
> As if he laboured yet to grasp the State
> With those rebellious parts.

Can we reasonably regret with Coleridge that we have not whole volumes of such plays as *Catiline* ? Possibly, if Jonson had tried his hand again at tragedy he might have written a *Catiline* without a Cicero. Nevertheless, his instinct was right. Not in tragedy would he ever have found himself as in *Volpone* and *The Alchemist*. Not all his high purpose, fidelity and great range of expression could make up for the lack

in him of tragic passion and, though we praise his
Sejanus and his *Catiline*, it must be in terms which
acknowledge his wisdom in devoting a more serious
attention to the comic muse.

CHAPTER VIII

Whitehall

IT was all very well for Jonson to complain of " concupiscence and antics ", but, while he made only a handful of guineas from time to time out of the theatre, his livelihood depended upon his organising these same antics on a large scale for the nobility and the Court. The series of plays on which his fame rests with posterity were profitably interlarded with the series of masks whereby he secured maintenance and support.

The mask as practised by Jonson was no sudden invention, but the elaboration of a social custom rooted in old-English folklore. The mask or its equivalent can be traced in all its major conventions as far back as the chronicles extend. The features which were constant and which survived in all the masks of Jonson were the entry, the presentation, the mask itself and the revel. The entry was originally, by convention, a surprise visit of masked or disguised persons to the people of the house. They came with torchbearers and musicians and were introduced by the " presenters ". The mask itself was a ballet or pantomime performed before the company, and it was followed by the revel in which the company was invited to join the maskers in further dancing. Such was the framework. The " presentation " of the mask developed during the fifteenth century into a miniature play or dialogue introducing the visitors as allegorical or mythological men, women or monsters.

Ben Jonson

Another important feature of the mask, appearing later and considerably enlarged by Jonson himself, was a comic element which in earlier days took the form of a morris, but which Jonson introduced as an anti-mask or farcial interlude in contrast with the solemn splendours of the principal performance.

The characteristic of the mask which distinguished it from every other form of dramatic entertainment was the fact that in the revel with which it concluded the spectators, originally the people of the house, were expected to join the maskers, originally the visitors, in a final dance. This circumstance kept the mask true to its social origin as a compliment or pleasantry between friends. The mask, both in England, and later in France, thus inevitably remained an entertainment organised and performed by noble amateurs. Jonson wrote his masks for performers that included Prince Henry and Prince Charles, just as Molière wrote his ballets for a cast that might include on occasion even the " greatest king in all the world ". The mask never became a purely professional performance and, except in the rare hands of a poet, remained little more than an elaborate social diversion. Such poets as found it necessary to serve their masters in this kind had normally little opportunity for a profitable exercise of their talents. The misuse by Louis XIV of the comic genius of Molière was as scandalous as his later conversion of Racine into the tame historiographer of his glorious reign. Jonson's case was not so pitiful. The amateur status of the mask fitted his disposition and gave him a standing as Apollo's priest among the lords and ladies, while his intricate learning and the naturally ingenious bent of his mind found real recreation and relief in composing elaborate allegories and running to death the analogies and conceits in which he revelled. The mask was his salvation financially. Mentally it was just the solace he required.

To *The Mask of Blackness* given in 1605 succeeded *Hymenaei or the Solemnities of Mask and Barriers*, commonly known as *The Mask of Hymen*, given in the following year to celebrate the marriage of Robert, Earl of Essex, with Lady Frances, second daughter of the Earl of Suffolk. This was a wedding with a sequel that might have been devised by Webster or Ford or taken from the legendary annals of Florence of the cinquecento. Frances Howard, at thirteen, with a cloud of golden hair, lovely of form and face, slipped forth that night among the revellers with a youth who would one day be leading the Parliamentary armies against his king, while Frances herself was to come within seven years to the Tower for the murder of Sir Thomas Overbury.

The tale is in every history book and yet somehow the inferences are seldom drawn. The reign of James is commonly read as a preparation for the commonwealth. It was in truth a carnival, England's farewell to flesh in our time. The story of Frances Howard is a tale from Boccaccio, dark instead of merry. It is set in an environment of plague, feasting, of busy poetry and dead learning, of science coming to birth and discovery still beckoning the last of the adventurers to Eldorado. Jonson did his finest work by the light of these lurid years. *Volpone* and *The Alchemist* cannot otherwise be rightly measured or the genius of Beaumont. Exhalations from this splendid decay flicker even on Shakespeare's page.

Scarcely was the young maid married, afterwards to declare that she was never made a wife, than Essex went abroad. Drawn by the darling graces of Rochester she must then seek medicines to make him love her, and induce a magician to perform strange tricks with waxen images. And having won the love of Rochester, she needs must marry him, and therefore be rid of Essex.

These events came dangerously near to Jonson. He knew all the players in this evil tragedy. Overbury, the friend of Rochester, was the man, be it remembered, whose play he had read to Elizabeth of Rutland, and whose designs on that lady he had refused to forward. Overbury was opposed to the marriage of Frances with Rochester. He spoke and plotted against it on all occasions, till finally Frances persuaded her lover that, so long as Overbury was free to work against them, they would never succeed in their design. James could refuse nothing to his favourite, and Overbury, at the suit of Rochester, was committed to the Tower. A divorce or nullity suit was successfully arranged. Frances of Essex became Frances of Somerset, Rochester receiving, not only his bride, but a nobler title for her to wear.

The uttermost secrets of this horrible sequence will never be known. Overbury, still in the Tower, died shortly of poison, being attended for four months by an apothecary and the widow of a physician, both swearing, later, that they were in the pay of the Countess. But the Lady Frances, still uncharged with her crime, was married to my lord of Somerset in great splendour, dressed as a maid and carrying her dreadful secret. It is a tragedy dressed in velvet and pearls, with a great poet to celebrate its " solemn-ies ", with alchemists and apothecaries lurking in the shadows, with a beautiful white devil for its heroine and a king's favourite falling from favour at the close —a play of intricate motives and blazing passion. Was Rochester privy to the murder of his friend ? For what offence or cause ? That Overbury opposed the marriage was hardly reason enough. For what could he do against Lady Frances with her beauty, her wealth and her sly but powerful connections?

Jonson, who in 1605 composed *The Mask of Hymen* for the marriage of Essex, wrote for these more glittering nuptials, in 1613, *The Irish Mask* and *A Challenge at Tilt*. He had not the slightest suspicion of the truth. He saw nothing, but two friends, Somerset and Overbury, and a bride elect.

> May she, whom thou for spouse to-day dost take,
> Outbe that wife in worth thy friend did make.

Thus he wrote, in dreadful ignorance, to Somerset before the crime was whispered. Did Jonson stumble, here, in all innocence upon a clue to the tragedy? Somerset, perhaps, had loved his friend too well, and the Lady Frances was more jealous of the " wife in worth " than angry at him for opposing the match. Or had Overbury discovered some dark design against young Essex, who stood in the way of her felicity? These are conjectures, and history reveals no adequate motive for the crime. It records only that Overbury died; that Mrs. Turner, inventor of yellow starch, confessed to his murder and was hanged; that the Earl and Countess of Somerset were found guilty, but escaped execution for imprisonment; and that Jonson, editing his works in 1616, tore from *The Mask of Hymen* the name of Frances and from *A Challenge at Tilt* the name of Somerset.

The Mask of Hymen was published by Jonson in its final form without a name, as having been performed " at a marriage ". In a short introduction he declared his own peculiar office. His concern as a poet was not with crimes and policy, but with his standing and merit as an author. It is his part, he tells us, to furnish forth the things which are subjected

Ben Jonson

to understanding, which have the advantage over things objected to sense in that they are impressing and lasting, not merely momentary and taking. He supplies the immortal part of these solemnies, which else had gone out like a blaze, " so short lived are the bodies of all things in comparison of their souls ". Bodies may be sensually preferred, but, when souls still live, are utterly forgotten.

There follows a passage which shows that Jonson's masks, as may well be imagined, made difficult hearing for some of the spectators. He refers pugnaciously to those who " squeamishly cry out that all endeavour of learning and sharpness in these transitory devices, especially when it stops short of their little or no brain at all, is superfluous ". He is content that these fastidious stomachs should leave his full tables and " enjoy at home their clean and empty trenchers, fittest for such airy tastes ; where perhaps a few Italian herbs, picked up and made into a salad, may find a sweeter acceptance than all the most nourishing meats of the world ".

Nourishing, perhaps, but requiring a hard digestion. No one who reads these masks to-day can believe that the revellers who presented or witnessed them caught one-tenth of the author's meaning. Jonson, publishing them when their occasions were forgotten, provided abundant comments and references, rich and grave, with occasional allusions to the ignorants—in effect, all but himself—who were unable to perceive that every detail of his ritual and procedure had the superscription of antiquity. " Though here it be very clear," he suddenly exclaims in a footnote to *The Mask of Hymen*, " yet because there are some must complain of darkness that have but thick eyes I am contented to hold them this light." Such scolding falls unkindly upon such as cannot identify all these allusions to forgotten Roman authors or interpret correctly all these rites and symbols.

Jonson, presenting the souls or inward parts of these tinselled bodies, neglected to mention the musicians, painters, designers and choreographers who claimed a share in them. *The Mask of Hymen* was presented with music by Alphonse Ferrabosco, costumes by Inigo Jones, and dances by Thomas Giles. We look in vain for these names in Jonson's book. They were responsible only for the " outward celebration or show ", and had no claim to the " inward parts ". Jonson was later to insist with disastrous results that the name of Master Inigo Jones should not precede his own upon a title-page.

John Pory thus describes *The Mask of Hymen* in a letter to Sir Robert Cotton :

Both Inigo, Ben and the actors, men and women, did their parts with great commendation. The conceit or soul of the mask was Hymen bringing in a bride and Juno Pronuba's priest a bridegroom, proclaiming these two should be sacrificed to nuptial union, and here the poet made an apostrophe to the union of the Kingdoms. But before the sacrifice could be performed, Ben Jonson turned the globe of the earth, standing behind the altar, and within the concave, sat the eight men maskers, representing the four humours and four affections, which leaped forth to disturb the sacrifice to union ; but amidst their fury Reason that sat above them all, crowned with burning tapers, came down and silenced them. . . . Above the globe of earth hovered a middle region of clouds, in the centre whereof stood a grand consort of musicians and upon the cantons or horns sat the ladies, four at one corner and four at another, who descended upon the stage, not after the stale downright perpendicular fashion, like a bucket into a well ; but came sloping gently down. These eight, after the sacrifice was ended, represented the eight nuptial powers of Juno Pronuba, who came down to confirm the union. The men were clad in crimson and the women in white. They had every one a white plume of the richest heron feathers and were so rich in jewels upon their heads as was most glorious. I think they hired and borrowed all the principal jewels and ropes of pearl both in Court and city. The Spanish Ambassador seemed but poor to the meanest of them. They danced all variety of dances, both severally and promiscuously, and then the women took in men, as, namely, the Prince (who danced with as great perfection and as settled a Majesty as could be devised), the Spanish Ambassador, etc., and the men gleaned out the Queen, the bride and the greatest of the ladies.

It is a modest description. Jonson himself was so struck with the splendour and ingenuity of the costumes, scenery and devices that he recorded them in minute detail, not forgetting to observe that, though the ladies were clad in cloth of silver, laced with gold and full-gathered, there yet appeared through it all " some touch of their delicate lineaments ". He does not omit to praise the lords who sustained the nobler parts. *Nor do I court them*, he interjects, flinching from even the appearance of flattery.

On the following night, in *The Mask of Barriers*, Truth and Opinion wrangled upon the respective merits of marriage and virginity—an issue finally brought to a trial by battle between sixteen knights armed with pikes and swords. For this entertainment Jonson indited some shrewd verse on the doubtful blessings of either state :

> What griefs lie groaning on the nuptial bed !
> What dull society ! In what sheets of lead
> Tumble and toss the restless married pair,
> Each oft offended with the other's air ;

and for the maiden a crusty warning :

> So whilst a virgin doth untouch'd abide,
> All *unmanur'd*, she grows old with her pride.

It was not a pleasant dilemma with which to come before a wedding party. There were some pretty lines on both sides, but Jonson was slow in learning to be tactful.

All this was in January, 1606. In July, King Christian of Denmark came to England on a visit to his sister—a comely man, very like the Queen, not only in form and feature, but in appetite and disposition. He confirmed the tradition that there were no drinkers in the world like the Danes, and for nearly a month all good courtiers must precede him under the table. At Theobalds' on July 24th, 1606, the Queen of Sheba, in a pageant, bearing cream, cakes and jelly, fell into his lap and King Christian, rising to dance with her, all plastered with good things, fell down and was counted out.

It was a typical revel, showing the bright side of the shield which, being turned, showed darkly the smooth face of Frances and the curls of Rochester. We are fortunate in having a full account of it from Harrington :

One day a great feast was held, and, after dinner, the representation of Jonson, his Temple, and the coming of the Queen of Sheba was made, or (as I may better say) was intended to be made, before their Majesties, by device of the Earl of Salisbury and others. But alas ! as all earthly things do fail to poor mortals in enjoyment, so did prove our presentment thereof. The lady who did play the Queen's part did carry most precious gifts to both their Majesties ; but, forgetting the step rising to the canopy, overset her caskets into his Danish Majesty's lap and fell at his feet, though I rather think it was in his face. Much was the hurry and confusion ; cloths and napkins were at hand to make all clean. His Majesty then got up and would dance with the Queen of Sheba ; but he fell down and humbled himself before her, and was carried to an inner chamber and laid on a bed of state ; which was not a little defiled by the presents which the Queen had bestowed on his garments, such as wine, cream, jelly, beverage, cakes, spices and other good matters. The entertainment and

Ben Jonson

show went forward, and most of the presenters went backward, or fell down ; wine did so occupy their upper chambers. Now did appear, in rich dress, Hope, Faith and Charity. Hope did assay to speak, but wine rendered her endeavours so feeble that she withdrew and hoped the King would excuse her brevity. Faith was then all alone, for I am certain she was not joined with good works, and left the court in a staggering condition. Charity came to the King's feet and seemed to cover the multitude of sins her sisters had committed. In some sort she made obeisance and brought gifts, but said she would return home again, as there was no gift which heaven had not already given his Majesty. She then returned to Hope and Faith, who were both sick and spewing in the lower hall. Next came Victory in bright armour, and presenting a rich sword to the King, who did not accept it, but put it by with his hand, and, by a strange medley of versification, did endeavour to make suit to the King. But Victory did not triumph long ; for, after much lamentable utterance, she was led away a silly captive, and was laid to sleep in the outer steps of the antechamber. Now did Peace make entry and strive to get foremost to the King ; but I grieve to tell how great wrath she did discover unto those of her attendants ; and, much contrary to her semblance, most rudely made war with her olive branch and laid on the pates of those who did oppose her coming.

Jonson's part in this entertainment was to welcome the two Kings with appropriate lines in English or Latin and to write epigrams to be hung upon the walls. In May of the following year, however, he had more to do at Theobalds'. Salisbury, preferring Hatfield, had agreed to convey his home at Theobalds' to the Queen and Jonson was invited to write appropriate verses for the delivery. Performing this task, he was felicitous in allegory, but not yet entirely happy in his personal allusions. The King and Queen, on entering the gallery after dinner, discovered the Genius of the house in great dejection, having been informed that he must change his lord, who in the " twilight of sere age " was seeking another habitation. On learning who was to be his new mistress, however, his spirits rose. He must, nevertheless, ask some pertinent and possibly awkward questions :

> But is my patron with this lot content
> So to forsake his father's monument ?
> Or is it gain or else necessity,
> Or will to raise a house of better frame,
> That makes him shut forth his posterity ?

Jonson's next employment was *The Mask of Beauty*, written for the Queen as a sequel to *The Mask of Blackness*. " It was her highness' pleasure ", he tells us, " that I should think on some fit presentment, which should answer the former, still keeping the daughters of Niger, but their beauties varied according to promise." The maskers, in orange-tawny and silver and green, were accordingly the twelve daughters of Niger of *The Mask of Blackness*, now laved white, with four more ; the torchbearers were cupids ; the presenters were January, Boreas, Vulturnus and Thamesus ; the musicians being Echoes and Shades of old poets. The entertainment was presented in the new banqueting house at Whitehall and was given, as James informed the Venetian Ambassador, " to consecrate the birth of the Great Hall, which his predecessor had left him built merely in wood, but which he had converted to stone ". There were the usual diplomatic heartburnings and scandals, the Queen scattering invitations without regard to England's policy or the King's wishes. Among the many serious people whom it annoyed were the gentlemen of the Privy Council, called upon to find thirty thousand crowns for expenses. " One lady," a certain Chamberlain wrote to Carleton on January 8th, " and that under a baroness, is said to be furnished for better than a hundred thousand pounds. And the Lady Arabella goes beyond her ; and the Queen must not come behind."

No great lady could now feel herself decently married without a " solemnie ". Jonson's next mask, *The Hue and Cry after Cupid*, was composed, with nuptial songs, to celebrate the happy marriage of John, Lord Ramsey, Viscount Haddington with the Lady Elizabeth Ratcliffe, daughter of the Earl of Sussex. It was given in 1608 on Shrove Tuesday at a cost of three hundred pounds a man for each masker. Jonson has learned his business. There begins to be a lighter fancy and sweeter verse, with less learning. This is the mask from which Charles Lamb quoted extracts to show " the poetical fancy and elegance of mind of the supposed rugged old Bard ". Frankly, all should be quoted or nothing. The verse runs trippingly and to linger anywhere is unfair to the composer. It met a bright occasion with extreme felicity—a singular, brave mask, as Sir Henry Saville afterwards described it to his friend Sir Richard Beaumont.

Jonson, publishing it later, surprisingly records that even so light a trifle as this " laboured under censure." He " smiles at the tyrannous ignorance that will offer to slight me in these things ", and roundly complains of those who " give themselves a peremptory license to judge who have never touched so much as to the bark or utter shell of any knowledge ". It is not clear whether the poet is referring here to critics who blamed the masks themselves or Jonson for writing them. Peace be with them ; " they have found a place to pour out their follies and I a seat to sleep out the passage ".

The Mask of Queens, presented at Whitehall on February 2nd, 1609, again to music by Ferrabosco

THE MASQVE OF
QVEENES.

It encreasing, now, to the third time of my being vs'd
in those seruices to her Ma.tie personall presentations,
wth the Ladyes whome she pleaseth to honor; it was
my first, and speciall regard, to see that the Nobility
of the Intention should be answerable to theyr dig=
nity of theyr persons. For wch reason, I chose
the Argument, to be, *A Celebration of honorable, &*
true Fame, bred out of Vertue: obseruing that rule
of the best Artist, to suffer no object of delight to
passe wthout his mixture of profit, & example.
And because her Ma.tie (best knowing, that a prin=
cipall part of life in those Spectacles lay in theyr
variety) had commaunded mee to thinke on some Daunce,
or Show, that might praecede hers, and haue the place
of a foyle, or false-Masque; I was carefull to
decline not only from others, but mine owne steppes
in that kind, since the last yeare I had an Anti-Ma=
sque of Boyes: and therefore, now, deuis'd that twelue
Woomen, in the habite of Hagges, or Witches, sustayning
the persons of Ignorance, Suspicion, Credulity, &c.
the opposites to good Fame, should fill that part; not
as a Masque, but a spectacle of strangenesse, pro=
ducing multiplicity of Gesture, and not vnaptly
sorting wth the current, & whole fall of the Deuise.
First then, his Ma.tie being set, and the whole Com=
pany in full expectation, that wch presented it selfe
was an ougly Hell; wch flaming beneath, smoak'd vn=
to the top of the Roofe. And, in respect all Euills
are (morally) sayd to come from Hell; as also from
that obseruation of *Torrentius* vpon *Horace* his Cani-
dia.

Hor. in Art.
Poetic.

In the Masque
at my L. Hadding=
ton's wedding.

Humanitye. is not the least honor of yͤ Wreath. For,
if once the worthy Professors of these learnings, shall
come (as heretofore they were) to be the care of
Princes, the Crownes theyᵈ Soueraignes weare will
not more adorne theyᵈ Temples; nor theyᵈ stampes
liue longer in theyᵈ Medalls, than in such Subiects
labors. Poetry, my Lord, is not borne wᵗʰ euery man:
Nor euery day: And, in her generall right, it is now
my minute to thanke yͤ Highnesse, who not only
do honor her Wᵗʰ yͤ eare, but are curious to examine her Wᵗʰ yͤ eye, & inquire into her beauties,
& strengths. Where, though it hath proud a Worke
of some difficulty to mee to retriue the particular
authorities (according to yͤ gracious command, and a
desire borne out of iudgmᵗ) to those things, wᶜʰ
I writt ont of fulnesse, & memory of my former
readings; yet, now I haue ourcome it, the reward
that meetes mee is double to one act: Wᶜʰ is, that
thereby, yͤ excellent Vnderstanding will not only iusti=
fie mee to yͤ owne knowledge, but decline the
stiffnesse of others originall Ignorance, allready
armᵈ to censure. For wᶜʰ singular bounty, if my
Fate (most Excellent Prince, & only Delicacy of
mankind) shall reserue mee to the Age of yͤ Actions,
whether in the Campe, or the Councell=Chamber, yᵗ
I may write, at nights, the deedes of yͤ dayes; J
will then labor to bring forth some Workes as wor=
thy of yͤ fame, as my Ambition therin is of yͤ
pardon.

By the most trew admirer of yͤ Highnesse Vertues,

And most hearty Celebrater of them.

Ben: Jonson.

and scenery by Inigo Jones, brought Jonson into increasingly familiar touch with the royal household. The Queen, ordered by the King in November, 1608, to " meditate a mask for Christmas ", invited the poet to a conference. Jonson proposed that the argument should be a Celebration of Honourable and True Fame Bred out of Virtue. The Queen thereupon suggested that a mask of true fame might, for variety and contrast, be preceded by some dance or show to serve as a foil or false mask. Jonson, remembering the King's interest in daemonology, accordingly wrote an anti-mask of hags or witches for whom, though Jones devised the attire and the architecture, he himself prescribed " their properties of vipers, snakes, bones, herbs, roots, and other ensigns of their magic out of the authority of ancient and late writers ". Among the late writers was King James himself to whom Jonson, publishing his mask in 1616, alluded in one of his footnotes as an expert. More significant than these consultations and compliments was the interest taken in the mask by Prince Henry who, struck by the curious and minute particulars given by the poet of witches and their ways, asked him for chapter and verse. Jonson, on behalf of his vocation, made the most of this signal tribute of a prince's interest : " Your favour to letters and these gentler studies that go under the title of Humanity is not the least honour of your wreath. . . . Poetry, my lord, is not born with every man, nor every day ; and, in her general right, it is now my minute to thank your Highness, who not only do honour her with your care, but are curious to examine her with your eye and inquire into her beauties and strengths." Jonson protests that it is difficult for him to retrieve his particular authorities for things written out of the fullness and memory of his former readings, but he regards the time as well-spent, since it has enabled him to justify his work to the prince and meet the attacks of ignorance armed to censure. It was possibly this request of Prince Henry to be informed of his sources that induced Jonson, when he came to publish his masks, at a later date, to supply footnotes which have remained the wonder and despair of scholars in every generation. They are never more abundant or amusing than in *The Mask of Queens*. Not an authority is missed from Homer to King James. The MS. which Jonson wrote for Prince Henry is still extant, written in a fine hand ; the text floating in its commentary like Falstaff's halfpennyworth of bread in an ocean of sack.

Thus did Jonson annotate himself into the good graces of the royal household. Prince Henry was now the pride and hope of the nation. Even when we have discounted the praises of poets at Court and allowed that he died too young to have provoked an enemy or committed a mistake, enough remains to show that he had ability and the grace to wear it. In January, 1610, he had not yet appeared publicly in arms and he was eager to show his accomplishment. The King's consent was won with difficulty and Jonson was asked to write the verses. Jonson, for *Prince Henry's Barriers*, supplied a tale of Merlin, in which Henry was cast for the part of Meliadus, Lord of the Isles, who, in the tilting which followed, gave or received thirty-two pushes with the pike and three hundred and sixty sword strokes.

The speech of Merlin in *The Mask of Barriers* recalls the earlier exhortations to King James upon his coming into England. It was a grave summons to virtue and responsibility. Merlin ran rapidly forward and down the course of English history, dwelling on the abiding achievements of the greater Kings, emphasising in particular the victories of peace. Edward I was commended for an increase of " trades and tillage ", Edward III for erecting first the " trade of clothing ", of more value to his subjects than a golden fleece ; Henry VII for wisely filling his Exchequer.

> These, worthiest Prince, are set you near to read,
> That civil arts the martial must precede.

Naturally, however, a tribute must be paid to warlike prowess in a *Mask of Barriers*. The exploits of Coeur de Lion were remembered. Crécy, Poitiers, Agincourt and the great Armada were not forgotten. But Jonson consistently approved James' policy of peace, and in this surprising short history of the English people, he celebrates a process towards prosperity, union and stability. The seventh Henry but joined the two roses. King James has joined the rose with the thistle and the Prince, though he be strong in arms for defence of the Kingdoms thus united, is warned at the close to use his fortune with reverence and to remember that the King who in deeds of arms obeys his blood often tempts his destiny to no good purpose.

Henry was now a prince of pleasures, and in January, 1611, he decided to produce a mask at his own expense, with himself for the principal figure. Jonson in *The Mask of Oberon* returned to his lighter manner :

> Buzz, quoth the blue fly.
> Hum, quoth the bee.

It is a thing of satyrs and the lesser fays. The moon is twitted with Endymion. The satyrs in an anti-mask, waiting for Oberon, spend themselves in conjecture. He will build them larger caves, find them a better wine, gild their cloven feet, bind their crookèd limbs in hoops of shells and silver, tie fancy bracelets about their wrists, hang garlands upon their stubbed horns and trap their shaggy thighs with bells. Oberon enters in a chariot, drawn by two white bears and descends for his solemn rites, the maskers being encouraged by songs interspersed with their measures, till Phosphorus the day star calls them away and the splendid night draws reluctantly to an end :

> O yet how early, and before her time,
> The envious morning up doth climb,
>   Though she love not her bed !
> What haste the jealous sun doth make,
> His fiery horses up to take,
>   And once more show his head !
> Lest, taken with the brightness of this night,
> The world should wish it last and never miss his light.

Accounts signed by Suffolk and Worcester, Household officers, show that Jonson and Inigo Jones received forty pounds each from the Exchequer—a sum that compares handsomely with the ten pounds received by Jonson from Henslowe for a tragedy at the conclusion of the poets' war. Is it to be wondered at that Jonson should prefer to be as learned as he liked for forty pounds to serving a popular audience with plays above its head for just one-quarter of the sum ?

The winter mask had now become an established feature of the Court, and Jonson's livelihood was assured, until his fatal quarrel with Inigo Jones in 1630. *Love Freed from Ignorance and Folly* (February 3rd, 1611) was followed by *Love Restored* (January 6th, 1612). Then came *The Irish Mask* (December 29th, 1613), *Mercury Vindicated from the Alchemists* (January 6th, 1615) and *The Golden Age Restored* (January 1st, 1616).

Love Freed from Ignorance and Folly was a queen's mask, produced at Whitehall on February 3rd, 1611.

The maskers were twelve daughters of the moon led
by the Queen of the Orient. Cupid and Ignorance
presented them. This was an allegory which the
author carefully stressed in a footnote. Antiquity,
presenting Ignorance, gave her the upper parts and
face of a woman to entrap the unwary. But she has
the nether parts of a lion and the wings of an eagle
" to show her fierceness and swiftness to evil where
she hath power ". It is the nature of Ignorance to
hinder all noble actions and the monster " still covets
to enwrap itself in dark and obscure terms ", whereas
true love " affects to express itself with all clearness
and simplicity ". The mask is short, facile, courtly
and ingenious. Jonson and Inigo Jones again received
forty pounds apiece for it, and Ferrabosco twenty
pounds for the songs. The end is a hymn to the
beauty which not even Time can destroy :

> But he so greedy to devour
> His own, and all that he brings forth,
> Is eating every piece of hour
> Some object of the rarest worth.
> Yet this is rescued from his rage,
> As not to die by time or age :
> For beauty hath a living name,
> And will to heaven, from whence it came.

Love Restored, presented at Court on Twelfth Night,
January, 1612, is in a lighter vein. Robin Goodfellow
recounts in familiar prose the hazards he has run to
view the revels. It is a scene from life. Robin tells
how he has been beaten from the gate with a staff
and dropped from a ladder by one of the guard. He
then presents himself successively as an engineer or
scene-shifter, as a tire-woman, as a musician, as a
feather-maker, as a bombard man bringing meat and
drink to the country ladies who had fasted since seven
in the morning, as a citizen's wife, as a wineman or

chandler, and, finally, in his own shape as part of the device. The villain of the piece is one Plutus, god of money, who has stolen Love's ensigns, and " in his belied figure reigns over the world, making friendships, contracts, marriages—and almost religion ; begetting, breeding, and holding the nearest respects of mankind ; usurping all those offices in this age of gold which Love himself performed in the Golden Age ".

Incidentally there is some plain speaking against costly vanities in high places which are the " ruins of states ". It is suggested that certain ladies and their gentlewomen might be more housewifely employed in their chambers at home than in masking and revelling, and that their old nightgowns would become them better than their " flaunting wires and tires, laced gowns and embroidered petticoats ". It is Plutus that speaks, and Plutus is a villain ; but there were not a few of my sad lords of the Privy Council present who, had they dared, would have applauded the passage.

The Irish Mask, December, 1613, was one of the series given in honour of the wedding of Somerset with the daughter of Suffolk. Its most striking feature is its easy familiarity with the royal person. An Irish citizen, coming before the throne, blesses the King's sweet face, and the Queen's face, too, and behaves as stage Irishmen have always behaved from the beginning of stage time. The King liked the mask and had it repeated, being proud of his Irish policy. He had at least done better than Elizabeth. Ireland was comparatively quiet and James rose graciously to the compliment that he had loyal subjects in Ireland who were ready to run through fire and water. There were some, nevertheless, who doubted whether the entertainment was altogether politic.

Chamberlain wrote to Alice Carlton on January 5th, 1614 : " The maskers were so well liked at Court the last week that they were appointed to perform again on Monday. Yet their device, which was a mimical imitation of the Irish, was not pleasing to many, who think it no time, as the case stands, to exasperate that nation by making it ridiculous."

Mercury Vindicated from the Alchemists was presented on January 6th, 1615. The maskers were twelve Sons of Nature ; the first anti-maskers were alchemists and the second Imperfect Creatures in helms of limbecs, the presenters being Vulcan, Cyclops, Mercury, Nature and Prometheus, with a chorus of musicians. The purpose of the mask, according to Chamberlain, was " the gracing of young Villiers and to bring him on the stage ". The King contributed one thousand five hundred pounds to the expenses, though he could ill afford it. The learning of this mask, which is that of the alchemists, though obsolete, remains as evidence of Jonson's thorough and resolute grasp of any subject to which he was drawn. Mercury issues from the furnace of Vulcan, and, for his heels of quicksilver, cannot be recaptured. He breaks into a canter of light prose, making merry at the expense of the quacksalvers and of a public eager for strange knowledge and the miracles of the new science :

> They will calcine you a grave matron as it might be a mother o' the maids, and spring up a young virgin out of her ashes as fresh as a Phoenix ; lay you an old courtier on the coals like a sausage or a bloat herring and, after they have broiled him enough, blow a soul into him with a pair of bellows, till he start up into his galliard.

Now and then the author strikes a graver note :

> Sir, would you believe it should be come to that height of impudence in mankind that such a nest of fireworms as these are, because their patron Mulciber heretofore has

Ben Jonson

made stools stir and statues dance, a dog of brass to bark
and (which some will say was his worst act) a woman to
speak, should therefore with their heats . . . profess to
outwork the sun in virtue and contend to the great act
of generation, nay, almost creation ? It is so, though ; for
in yonder vessels, which you see in their laboratory, they
have enclosed materials to produce men, beyond the deeds
of Deucalion or Prometheus.

Whereupon the Imperfect Creatures issue from their
vessels, " sins against the excellence of sun and
nature, creatures more imperfect than the very flies
and insects that are her trespasses and scapes ".
They form a striking contrast to the Sons of Nature
brought in by Prometheus, in which the King was
invited to admire the graces of young Villiers and his
friends.

Extravagance gave way to simplicity in the following year with *The Golden Age Restored* presented at
Whitehall on New Year's Day, January 1st, 1616.
The maskers were sons of Phoebus, including as
representatives of English poetry, Chaucer, Gower,
Lydgate and Spenser. The anti-maskers were twelve
Evils, ultimately turned to stone with the gorgon
shield of Pallas. It was a great success and was
repeated by request on Twelfth Night, when it was
attended by the French, Venetian and Savoyard
Ambassadors in regard to whose invitations, exits and
entrances the usual genteel disputes and preliminaries
may be studied in the records of the higher diplomacy.
The mask is written in smooth idyllic verse, unusual
with Jonson :

> Then earth unploughed shall yield her crop,
> Pure honey from the oak shall drop,
>   The fountain shall run milk ;
> The thistle shall the lily bear,
> And every bramble roses wear,
>   And every worm make silk.

164

Whitehall

This was the last of the masks included in the first volume of Jonson's works, published in the year when Shakespeare died. It brings to a close, on an Arcadian note, a happy and successful period.

CHAPTER IX

The Masterpieces

JONSON reached the summit of his achievement in the three great comedies of his early prime : *Volpone or the Fox*, *The Silent Woman*, and *The Alchemist*. In matter, feeling, style and method, they express most faithfully his mind and temper. Jonson was a man of many moods. Readers who come upon his various achievements haphazard might well hesitate between them. Some have found in him a romantic poet who wilfully imprisoned his genius within the limits of a comic method artificially applied in and out of season. Others have preferred a sheaf of lyrics to all his tremendous output of tragedies, comedies and satires. Some linger by preference with his *Sad Shepherd* and treasure above all things his rare excursions into the pastoral manner. Others find him more appropriately embedded in the infinite variety of fanciful, erudite and ingenious masks. There is validity enough in their hesitations to make it necessary for anyone who gives supremacy to the three great comedies clearly to justify his election.

Jonson achieved excellence, no matter what his theme or purpose, by premeditation and design. He could not rely upon accidental felicities. His success came always by a consciously directed effort. He lived by the pen and yet, for him, words were stubborn, difficult and hard to fit. He must hammer his phases into shape like a smith. The heat of his inspiration is rarely of the blood. There is little radiance or light that shines by nature from his work. The warmth and glow of his greater pages is that of the forge. He is as deliberate and systematic in his lightest fancies as in his formal tragedies, in his delineation of a comic humour or exploitation of a dramatic situation. Paradoxically, it was exactly this intellectual concentration which enabled him to cover so wide a range. He would quite deliberately turn his brain to anything. With the same devout intensity of purpose he would write a mad scene for Jeronymo, particularise a passion, conduct an historic scene, walk in the meadows, linger with his rogues and gypsies, depict the London life of his time, dissect a character, exhaust a fancy or metaphor, indict an ode or epigram, construct a plot, invent incidents and surprises, satirise a fashion or a folly. In all these modes and manners his virtues, as also his defects, are due to the same peculiar quality of his mind. Always he exhausts the intellectual possibilities of his theme. He cannot bear to quit his lightest fancy till he has left no implication unexplored. When he succeeds, he is amazingly apt and full. Inevitably, on the other hand, he easily falls into complexity, an arduous elaboration, an obstinate harping—coming too near for our comfort to the metaphysical poets of the time. Secluded with a particular idea or special passion, he gets easily out of touch with the normal process of nature. It is a risk he runs in all that he undertakes. Whether he be presenting allegorical figures in a mask, a rogue in Shoreditch, or a tyrant in imperial Rome, he is equally exhaustive. Often he refines, dissects or complicates his material till nothing remains but a process applied in a vacuum.

Jonson is inevitably at his best when he is able to

Ben Jonson

concentrate upon permanent and observed aspects of human character. *Volpone* is not by accident his greatest play. Therein he took for a theme the most universal passion of mankind, susceptible of indefinite exploration, infinitely varied in its manifestations. It was a theme which not only called for the use at full pressure of his powerful intelligence but which aroused in him an impassioned but equable indignation, without exception or misgiving, which is the essential inspiration of great satire as distinguished from the lamentations of the defeated or the outcries of a wounded sensibility. The subject of *Volpone* is not, as is sometimes assumed, the narrow theme of avarice as presented in the masterpieces of Plautus and Molière. Jonson has a more spacious topic—the attraction and power of effective wealth. The Fox is no miser but magnificently a spendthrift, alike of his possessions and his faculties. Wealth is his instrument—a token of mastery. It is the bright minister of his strong lusts and gorgeous fancies. The splendid invocation with which the comedy begins is no crooning over a barren hoard. Volpone addresses his gold as one of the primaeval powers.

> Good morning to the day; and next, my gold!
> Open the shrine that I may see my saint.
> Hail the world's soul and mine! more glad than is
> The teeming earth to see the long'd for sun
> Peep through the horns of the celestial Ram
> Am I, to view thy splendour darkening his;
> That lying here, amongst my other hoards,
> Show'st like a flame by night, or like the day,
> Struck out of chaos, when all darkness fled
> Unto the centre.

It is a hymn to the golden calf. He continues:

> Dear saint,
> Riches, the dumb god, that giv'st all men tongues,
> That canst do nought, and yet mak'st men do all things;
> The price of souls; even hell, with thee to boot,

168

Is made worth heaven. Thou art virtue, fame,
Honour and all things else. Who can get thee,
He shall be noble, valiant, honest, wise.

Mere possession of wealth means nothing to Volpone. His relish is in the power it brings and in the manipulation of men for its acquisition. He rejoices in the exercise of a naughty intelligence alike in the getting and spending of his treasure and it is in this sense that he opens his heart to us in a preliminary discourse with Mosca, his parasite and master of his revels :

> Yet I glory
> More in the cunning purchase of my wealth,
> Than in the glad possession, since I gain
> No common way ; I use no trade, no venture ;
> I wound no earth with plough-shares ; fat no beasts
> To feed the shambles ; have no mills for iron,
> Oil, corn, or men to grind them into powder.
> I blow no subtle glass, expose no ships
> To threat'nings of the furrow-facèd sea ;
> I turn no monies in the public bank,
> Nor usure private.

Mosca, the parasite, prompt in confirmation, adds some further touches. Volpone has never afflicted the poor man, the widow or the orphan. Such courses he abhors. Nor has he grown rich by any stinting of his ways and means :

> You are not like the thresher, that doth stand
> With a huge flail, watching a heap of corn,
> And, hungry, dares not taste the smallest grain,
> But feeds on mallows and such bitter herbs ;
> Nor like the merchant, who hath filled his vaults
> With Romagnia and rich Candian wines,
> Yet drinks the lees of Lombard's vinegar.
> You will not lie in straw, whilst moths and worms
> Feed on your sumptuous hangings and soft beds ;
> You know the use of riches, and dare give now,
> From that bright heap, to me, your poor observer,
> Or to your dwarf or your hemaphrodite,
> Your eunuch or what other household trifle
> Your pleasure allows maintenance.

Volpone, smiling upon his parasite, promptly bestows upon him the alms so appropriately begged.

> Take of my hand ; thou strik'st on truth in all,
> And they are envious term thee parasite.
> Call forth my dwarf, my eunuch and my fool
> And let them make me sport. What should I do
> But cocker up my genius and live free
> To all delights my fortune calls me to.

He then lets us into the secret of his fortune and thereby indicates the argument and purpose of the play :

> I have no wife, no parent, child, ally,
> To give my substance to ; but whom I make
> Must be my heir, and this makes men observe me ;
> This draws new clients daily to my house,
> Women and men of every sex and age,
> That bring me presents, send me plate, coin, jewels,
> With hope that when I die (which they expect
> Each greedy minute) it shall then return
> Tenfold upon them ; whilst some, covetous
> Above the rest, seek to engross me whole,
> And counter work the one unto the other,
> Contend in gifts, as they would seem in love.
> All which I suffer, playing with their hopes,
> And am content to coin them into profit,
> And look upon their kindness and take more,
> And look on that, still bearing them in hand,
> Letting the cherry knock against the lips,
> And draw it by their mouths and back again.

The comedy may now begin. The suitors to Volpone are at hand and the Fox goes to bed to receive them. It is his habit to tantalise their hopes and stimulate their gifts and services by lying to all appearances at death's door. It is Mosca's part to receive them, to exact a tribute, to prick them into unspeakable confidences, while his master, behind the curtains of his bed, lies chuckling.

Voltore, the advocate, first comes knocking at the door :

The Masterpieces

> Fetch me my gown,
> My furs and nightcap ; say my couch is changing,
> And let him entertain himself awhile
> Without i' the gallery. Now, now my clients
> Begin their visitation. Vulture, kite,
> Raven and gorcrow, all my birds of prey,
> That think me turning carcase, now they come.
> I am not for them yet.

The first act of the comedy is a rising carnival of infamy. Voltore, the advocate, bribing his way into favour, sustained in bringing his gift by the hope that it will be the last, gives place to Corbaccio, himself upon the edge of the grave but joyfully ticking off the symptoms whereby Mosca convinces him that Volpone has hardly another day on earth :

> Excellent, excellent ! Sure I shall outlast him ;
> This makes me young again, a score of years.

Corbaccio has brought with him an opiate—one that would put the Fox to sleep for ever. Mosca gravely protests that his master has no faith in drugs and is, in any case, too far gone to need or profit from them. Mosca then persuades Corbaccio to prove his devotion to the Fox by making a will in Volpone's favour. Such a gesture will certainly secure him the succession, and the Fox will be dead before the week is out. With the entrance of Corvino, third of the legacy hunters, the proceedings assume a fantastic horror. Mosca, demonstrating his master to be deaf, dins into Volpone's ear the most frightful imprecations and insults. Corvino joins merrily in the pastime, while Volpone, in appearance a compound of villainous diseases, lies inwardly chuckling. So bad begins, but worse remains behind. Corvino has a young and beautiful wife. She is his most cherished possession —kept from the world and privately enjoyed, existing for himself alone. To Mosca, as the comedy moves to a climax, occurs the idea, delicious to the Fox, of inducing Corvino, as an act of courtesy, to bring his wife to the bedside of Volpone. Corvino, torn between the two master passions of his life, shall make them double sport. The lady is modest and comely, and Volpone is enamoured. The Fox will at the same time enjoy her beauties and deride the dreadful posturing of her lord.

The plot of the comedy, as always with Jonson, is an intricate piece of invention. To summarise it would be tedious. Its turns and surprises, clear upon the stage, are not easily or briefly recounted. Here we are concerned with the essential theme and broad effect of the play. Every scene is designed to exhibit the consequences of wealth, the insolence which it breeds and the infamies which are committed for lack or love of it. In Volpone himself we find the last results of possession. His chief delight is in a malicious exercise of his power for mischief and, as the play develops, we find him seeking mischief for its own sake, even though it be accompanied with risk and offer no prospect of profit or satisfaction. He loves to turn men's wits the seamy side without, and takes a curiously indignant pleasure in the process—a bitter and dark figure of retribution, tormenting the greedy souls about him and mocking their futility.

Mosca, infected with the spirit of his master, thus expresses the delight of this merry pair in their contrivances :

I fear I shall begin to grow in love
With my dear self and my most prosperous parts,
They do so spring and burgeon ; I can feel
A whimsy in my blood. I know not how,
Success hath made me wanton. I could skip
Out of my skin now, like a subtle snake.
I am so limber.

This is the mood which drives them into excesses which ultimately destroy them both, as when Mosca, having persuaded old Corbaccio to disinherit his son in favour of Volpone, arranges for the young man to be secretly present, with the result that the eavesdropper discovers Volpone's maladies to be feigned and is able to interrupt, not a moment too soon, the Fox's vigorous seduction of Corvino's wife. Mosca successfully extricates his master from the consequences of this disaster, but the Fox's passion for mischief, not easily corrected, undoes him completely at the last. Fey with the triumph of his escape from this first adventure, he pushes his comedy to the limit, feigning to die, and leaving all his wealth to Mosca, so that he may enjoy the disappointment of his expectant heirs.

Volpone confesses frankly to his ruling passion. His delight at avoiding the consequences of his vain attempt upon Corvino's wife—the means whereby Mosca deceives the fathers of Venice and makes all his dupes a party to the conspiracy is an astonishing feat of invention—is admittedly greater than if he had succeeded in his design :

> O more than if I had enjoyed the wench !
> The pleasure of all womankind's not like it.

This, agrees Mosca, is our masterpiece ; we cannot think to go beyond it. They proceed to comment, in a significant passage, on the blind obsession of their victims and then, with a supreme stroke of irony, Volpone, equally possessed, is made to prepare his own defeat in an imperious desire for yet " another meal of laughter ". What follows is the classic nemesis. The Fox has made a snare and put his head into it wilfully. No one appreciates the irony

of the final catastrophe more clearly than Volpone
himself :

> These are my fine conceits !
> I must be merry, with a mischief to me !
> What a vile wretch was I that could not bear
> My fortune soberly. I must have my crotchets
> And my conundrums.

Volpone is undoubtedly the fullest and finest of
Jonson's plays. There are passages in which the
faults inseparable from his peculiar genius are manifest,
but they are comparatively few and of small account.
There is a subordinate plot, introducing Sir Politic
Would-be and his wife, a travelled Englishman and
a blue stocking of the Renaissance, which is in parts
tedious and never indispensable ; there are scenes in
which Jonson's trick of exhausting his topic or carrying his moods and expressions beyond the human
limit is disconcertingly introduced—as in the scolding
by Corvino of his pretty wife for looking out of the
window ; there are passages in which the fanciful
author of masks impertinently intrudes, as in the
interludes wherein the dwarf, eunuch and fool are
required to amuse their master ; it may even be
urged that the plotting and counter-plotting of the
last two Acts calls for more attention and quickness
of apprehension than can be reasonably required of a
normal audience. But these blemishes are lost in the
force and splendour of the comedy as a whole. Jonson
was working on a subject near his heart, and the
comedy gains more than it loses by the concentration
of mind which he inevitably brought to bear on anything he undertook. All the important characters in
the play are creatures driven and possessed—precisely
the characters which Jonson, with his system of
humours and habit of intensity, was best qualified to
present with conviction and effect. There is no play

in any language in which the passion for wealth and the power it brings has been so completely expressed and dissected.

In the figure of Volpone Jonson presents the splendours of his theme. Was ever woman so magnificently wooed as the wife of Corvino ?

> Thy baths shall be the juice of July flowers,
> Spirit of roses and of violets,
> The milk of unicorns and panthers' breath,
> Gathered in bags and mixed with Cretan wines.

The remote jewels and curious luxuries of old Rome and new Italy are spread before the affrighted lady, who is invited to enact with her suitor all the fables of antiquity :

> Thou, like Europa now, and I like Jove,
> Then I like Mars and thou like Erycine.
> So of the rest till we have quite run through
> And wearied all the fables of the gods.

Nor are more modern forms of approach to be overlooked. He will have his mistress :

> Attired like some sprightly dame of France,
> Brave Tuscan lady or proud Spanish beauty ;
> Or the grand signor's mistress ; and, for change,
> To one of our most artful courtezans,
> Or some quick negro or cold Russian ;
> And I will meet thee in as many shapes,
> Where we may so transfuse our wandering souls
> Out at our lips, and score up sums of pleasures,
> *(Sings)* That the curious
> Shall not know
> How to tell them
> As they flow.

So much for the splendours, though these passages may be matched with a dozen others equally effective. For the infamies, as exhibited in the scrambling of the suitors for the Fox's inheritance, we may range at pleasure from scene to scene, finding every character true to its type and purpose. Peerless above them all stands Corvino. Is there another passage in English comedy where depravity under temptation is more searchingly portrayed than in the scene in which Corvino entreats his wife to be gentle with Volpone?

> What, is my gold
> The worse for touching, clothes for being looked on?
> This is no more?

The iniquity of the scene is sharpened by the fact that we still have ringing in our ears Corvino's denunciation of his wife for being too free of her innocent presence at an open window.

Epicoene or the Silent Woman is a comedy of a different colour. There are no intensities and the moralist is silent. Jonson, upon a conceit as trifling as ever served the purpose of a comic dramatist, has constructed a plot which enables him to present a series of amusing characters and divertingly to parade their follies. Admit the premiss of the play and its complications follow with ease and necessity. The whole composition is in tune with the fancy on which it is based. There is none of the satire which in Volpone bites into the substance of human nature, but a merry confounding of imposture and eccentricity. It is the most genial of the works of Jonson,—the freak of a happy mood; and he writes in prose, with a lighter pen and a looser spirit, allowing his theme to develop of its own motion. There is less of the deliberate exploration of ideas and metaphors which so often takes him farther than we can humanly follow without misgiving, and his invention is less elaborate. The possibilities of his plot are all implicit in the original conception, so that the incidents of the play seem to flow by a natural process. Dryden preferred *The Silent Woman* to all other plays of the period. For him it was the perfect example of a composition in which classic form and the essential requirements of the theatre were equally well met. It observes the unities of time, place and subject; the connection of scene with scene is inevitable and yet surprising ; each incident adds to the complication of events and leads to the final catastrophe. The resulting confusion is swiftly and easily unravelled by a timely disclosure which, far from being a merely arbitrary stroke of the author, is implicit in the main device of the play and throws into brighter relief the characters who are thereby disconcerted. To the free flow of incident and plot corresponds an unusual facility of expression. The persons of the play are in manner and conversation the most natural to be found in any of Jonson's comedies. Dryden, in praising the classic elegance of the play, noted also its rare quality of easiness, observing that Jonson " has here described the conversation of gentlemen with more gaiety, air and freedom than in the rest of his comedies ".

The play is based upon so light a fancy that a reader unfamiliar with Jonson's habit of deriving infinite conclusions from the smallest premiss might well fear that the comedy must soon break down for lack of argument. The principal character is one Morose, victim of a misanthropy which declares itself in a somewhat peculiar fashion. He has a horror of any form of noise. He has indulged his tender ears till the avoidance of clamour is the chief preoccupation of his life. He wears a huge turban of nightcaps buckled about his ears ; he has treaties with the fishwives, orange women and chimney-sweepers to avoid him ; no smith or armourer is suffered to dwell in the parish ; the waits of the city have a pension not to come near his ward ; any clatter within earshot of his house brings him out with a sword.

He has chosen a street to live in so narrow at both ends that it will receive no coaches, carts, nor any of the common noises. His foible is notorious. It has become a sport of the town to plague him, so that showmen are bribed to ring their bells or fencers to beat their drums under his window. He has devised a room in his house with double walls and treble ceilings, the windows closed and caulked ; he is known to have turned away a man for having a pair of shoes that creaked ; while his servants are taught to respond to his orders and inquiries by dumb-show.

Morose is a man of fortune. He has a nephew, Dauphine, to whom he churlishly refuses an allowance and who, partly from a natural resentment and partly with a view to exacting better treatment, sets forth ingeniously to entrap and plague his uncle. Morose, at the start of the play, heartily disliking his nephew, has resolved to defeat the young man's expectations by marrying and getting an heir to his estate. His problem is to find a wife who will permit him to live in silence, and never talk or make a noise. Dauphine, hearing of his uncle's intention, arranges that Epicoene, his page, dressed as a woman, shall be lodged near his uncle's house, and he ensures that the lady shall be swiftly famous for her silence and discretion. Not even his accomplices, who are parties to the plot, know that Epicoene is in reality a boy and the secret is kept as jealously from the audience. The sport of the play, previous to the discovery of the sex of Epicoene, all turns upon the dreadful plight in which Morose finds himself on discovering that his Silent Woman is a perpetual fount of clamour and that her friends, under frequent instigation from Dauphine, are ready to fill his house with every form of brawl and revelry. Seeking release from his pre-dicament, he turns for help to his nephew who only

leads him deeper into the maze. Finally, after
Morose's efforts to escape have involved all the minor
characters in comical pretences and exposed them all
alike to a sweet derision, the knot is cut by the revelation, for which Morose is required to pay the price
demanded by his nephew, that Epicoene is less a
woman than she seems.

Jonson, in *The Silent Woman*, comes as near to the
comedy of manners as any dramatist prior to Etherege.
Its fools are the fools of fashion ; Sir John Daw,
aspiring to be taken for a gentleman of the town ;
Thomas Otter, ruled by a termagant wife and driven
for refuge and self-respect to his bulls, horses and
bears ; and the collegiate ladies, whose pretensions to
emancipation are more truly expressed in their affected
profligacy than in their equally affected wit. The
style of the play is admirably appropriate to its lighter
substance. The conversation in the third Act between
the gentlemen, Truewit and Clerimonde, may be
quoted as a typical performance. The theme is
nature versus artifice in the adornment of women.
Clerimonde has made a song on the subject :

> Still to be neat, still to be drest,
> As you were going to a feast ;
> Still to be powdered, still perfumed :
> Lady, it is to be presumed,
> Though art's hid causes are not found,
> All is not sweet, all is not sound.
>
> Give me a look, give me a face,
> That makes simplicity a grace :
> Robes loosely flowing, hair as free.
> Such sweet neglect more taketh me,
> Than all the adulteries of art ;
> They strike mine eyes, but not my heart.

Truewit, his friend, is of a different persuasion :

> I love a good dressing before any beauty of the world.
> O, a woman is then like a delicate garden ; nor is there

one kind of it ; she may vary every hour ; take often counsel of her glass and choose the best. If she have good ears, show them ; good hair, lay it out ; good legs, wear short clothes ; a good hand, discover it often ; practise any act to mend breath, cleanse teeth, repair eyebrows ; paint and profess it.

There are several scenes in the play which would inevitably appear in any anthology of Jonson's work. Such, for example, is the scene in which Truewit endeavours to dissuade Morose from his design to marry Epicoene, all the possible pitfalls and disasters of marriage being recounted in the liveliest fashion ; the scene between Clerimonde and Truewit in which Morose's infirmity is described ; the scenes in which Morose makes his suit to Epicoene ; the scene in which Truewit expounds to Clerimonde the whole art of courtship. Of these scenes the first and last are perhaps the best examples of Jonson's virtuosity in composing variations upon a given theme. The first is written with an astonishing vivacity and bears comparison with the best of Congreve :

If she be fair, young and vegetous, no sweetmeats ever drew more flies ; all the yellow doublets and great roses in the town will be there. If foul or crooked, she'll be with them and buy those doublets and roses, Sir. If rich, and that you marry her dowry, not her, she'll reign in your house as imperious as a widow. If noble, all her kindred will be your tyrants. If fruitful, proud as May and humorous as April ; she must have her doctors, her midwives, her nurses, her longings every hour, though it be for the dearest morsel of man. If learned, there was never such a parrot ; all your patrimony will be too little for the guests that must be invited to hear her speak Latin and Greek and you must lie with her in those languages too, if you will please her. If precise, you must feast all the silenced brethren once in three days, salute the sisters, entertain the whole family or wood of them, and hear long-winded exercises, singings and catechisings, which you are not given to and yet must give for, to please the zealous matron your wife, who, for the holy cause, will cozen you over and above.

This is but a prologue and the rest of the tale is packed with ruin and discomfort.

Truewit is as ingeniously eloquent upon the art of courtship as on the perils of matrimony. All women are not to be taken all ways ; the various manners of approach are wittily enjoined, the assault being varied according as the object loves wit, valour, money or good clothes. These scenes are written with a genial felicity, and we find in them a broader observation of life and a greater humanity than in the later dramatists of the Restoration, who achieved a sterile perfection in this type of play.

Jonson is careful to ensure that we should have no misgivings concerning his principal jest. The baiting of Morose, if it were no more than the tormenting of an old man with a physical affliction, would be poor sport ; but the victim's dislike of noise—any noise, be it noted, except his own—is the physical expression of a sullen and unlovely disposition. " All discourses but mine own afflict me," he ingenuously confesses upon his first appearance, and the silence he exacts from others by no means precludes an abundant eloquence in himself. His hatred of others' noise is a symptom of a disagreeable complacency and legitimately we delight in its violation. " Of all sounds," he fatuously observes to his bride-elect, " only the sweet voice of a fair lady has the just length of mine ears." He would have her speak just suffici-ently for his pleasure. " I must have mine ears banqueted with pleasant and witty conferences, pretty girds and scoffs and dalliance." Concentration upon himself has, as its natural reverse, a hearty dislike of

Ben Jonson

those whom he suspects of designs upon his comfort. His hatred of Dauphine, which brings disaster upon him, has no just motive and is expressed with a feeble malice which calls for ridicule and retribution. On being accepted of Epicoene he exclaims : " Go thy ways and get me a minister presently *with a soft low voice*, to marry us. O my felicity *how I shall be revenged on my insolent kinsman*. This night I will get an heir and thrust him out of my blood like a stranger." We are reminded in the same breath of his physical affliction and of his malice, the two things being naturally connected and symptoms of the same obliquity. The author is even at pains to suggest how first his strange infirmity arose. The old man, in his final pleadings for peace, relates how his father had fostered in him the habit of thinking too closely upon himself : " My father, in my education, was wont to advise me that I should always contain and collect my mind, not suffering it to flow loosely ; that I should look to what things were necessary to the carriage of my life, and what not, embracing the one and eschewing the other ; in short, that I should endear myself to rest and avoid turmoil—which now is grown to be another nature to me." In a word, he was trained in early youth to look priggishly to his own comfort and advantage, and has now reached the condition to be observed in old gentlemen who sit in quiet corners and spend their days in creating for themselves islands of comfort in a troubled world.

The Alchemist is undoubtedly the most astonishing product of Jonson's genius, and there are critics who rank it as a finer achievement than *Volpone* or *The Silent Woman*. As a permanent contribution to English dramatic literature, however, it hardly ranks with its predecessors. Jonson, in taking for his background a contemporary superstition, inevitably forfeited to a large extent the comprehension of posterity. It is true that the grotesque apparatus of alchemy, with its fabulous elixir and philosophers' stone, is accidental to the play, and that the main interest of the comedy, unaffected by time or fashion, lies elsewhere. But Jonson, ridiculing the popular tricks and fallacies of the alchemist, becomes so deeply involved in their complexities that the general appeal of the satire is frequently obscured. His passion for extreme realism in detail and his extraordinary virtuosity of performance upon any given theme, which makes the play so remarkable a contemporary document, mars it as a permanent achievement, and the modern reader is teased with doctrines, allusions and paraphernalia to which he must remain very largely indifferent. Jonson is describing forms of imposture which will continue, in their essentials, to flourish as long as men are credulous and there are mysteries of nature to be exploited by rogues for their profit. But though the substance of the play is immortal, it comes before us in so strange a habit that it requires from audience or reader to-day a serious effort of imagination and a real ability to distinguish between accidents and essentials.

When Jonson in 1610 took the alchemists for a theme their claims were still respected by the Courts of Europe. Dreams of transmutation and eternal youth still haunted the imaginations of wise and ignorant alike. There was a contemporary of Jonson, one Simon Forman, who made a fortune from the black art and his name was legion. Queen Elizabeth had her tame alchemist and astrologer, Dr. John Dee, and the Emperor Rudolf II was a practitioner. The new science, far from displacing these mystifications, had for the moment endowed them with a more impressive terminology and given them a wider range. Beside the respectable dealers in magic, prevision and chemical experiment flourished a horde of sharpers who deliberately exploited the credulity of their victims. Jonson had read all the books, digested them and he set out to use his complete knowledge of the subject in his usual lavish and exhaustive fashion. The result is a detailed presentation and exposure in its divers branches of arts which to-day are as obsolete as the quackeries of our psychic parlours presumably will be a hundred years from now.

The Alchemist, moreover, besides having a background that has lost its colour, has not the extreme tension of *The Fox*. Jonson, in *The Alchemist*, rebukes imposture and satirises desires and follies which make it possible for the knaves of this world to prey upon its fools. The composition is in a lighter vein. There is not the same extremity of evil, active and unashamed, which gives to *Volpone* its wicked splendour and indignant sense of retribution. Volpone, playing upon his dupes for love of the game, is a moral portent. The rogues whom we meet in *The Alchemist* have no such significance. Livelihood is the beginning and end of their endeavour, and the play ends merrily with the ablest villain of the pack successfully outwitting the rest and making his peace with authority.

In only one respect is *The Alchemist* a better play than *Volpone*. For all its diversity of characters and incidents, it is surprisingly simple in construction. Master Lovewit has left his London house in the care of a servant, Jeremy Face. Face, during his master's absence, goes into partnership with Subtle, who lives by his wits, and with Doll, who is more than match for both of them and a handsome woman to boot. All three inhabit the empty mansion. Subtle, in velvet cap and gown, sets up as quack-of-all-trades. He is alchemist, astrologer, physician, phrenologist, palmist, philosopher and sage. Face brings in the victims and assists Subtle within the house as his assistant druggist, publicity agent and general utility-man. A variety of eager creatures come falling into the net—Dapper, a silly clerk who hopes to secure a familiar spirit to bring him luck and make him a successful gamester ; Drugger, a tobacconist, who is building a new shop and wants to know how he should appoint and plan it so that he may be lucky in his trade ; Tribulation and Ananias, Puritans from Amsterdam, who are prepared to traffic with the powers of darkness in the interests of their con-venticle ; Kastril, a country gentleman, looking for a nobleman to marry Dame Pliant, his sister, so that he may cut a figure in society. The play ends naturally and easily with the return of the master of the house and the discomfiture of the rogues and their victims.

Supreme among the dupes is Sir Epicure Mammon, already rich but drawn in quest of the philosophers' stone by dreams of wealth beyond mortal reckoning. He alone has something of the breadth and stature of Volpone ; but where Volpone is enormous in his love of power and the exercise of his intelligence, Sir Epicure is enormous only in his sensuality. Jonson presents this monster with a poetic licence whose only justification is that it succeeds. No city knight, with appetites so completely of the gullet and the groin, would ever have achieved the sumptuous fancies of which Sir Epicure is so gorgeously delivered. Jonson ransacked erotic Greece and sensual Rome in presenting this hyperbolical figure, thereby creating an effect which Charles Lamb found to be " equal to the greatest poetry ". Sir Epicure Mammon

Ben Jonson

epitomises the common man, drunk with the prospect of illimitable wealth and with visions of a youth perpetual and immune :

> For I do mean
> To have a list of wives and concubines
> Equal with Solomon, who had the stone
> Alike with me ; and I will make me a back,
> With the elixir, that shall be as tough
> As Hercules. . . .

From this comparatively modest level he soars high upon fancies which are beyond the normal reach of such a man, yet marvellously fit him and express his quality :

> I will have all my beds blown up, not stuft ;
> Down is too hard ; and then, mine oval room
> Filled with such pictures as Tiberius took
> From Elephantis, and dull Aretine
> But coldly imitated ; then, my glasses
> Cut in more subtle angles, to disperse
> And multiply the figures as I walk
> Naked between my succubae. My mists
> I'll have of perfume, vapoured 'bout the room,
> To lose ourselves in ; and my baths, like pits
> To fall into ; from whence we will come forth,
> And roll us in dry gossamer and roses.

From being merely wanton he becomes perverse. He will have none but virtuous wives of the city to be his mistresses ; none but the gravest of divines to be his flatterers ; none but eloquent burgesses to be his fools. On the subject of food he is paramount :

> My meat shall all come in in Indian shells,
> Dishes of agat, set in gold and studded
> With emeralds, sapphires, hyacinths and rubies :
> The tongues of carps, dormice and camels' heels,
> Boiled in the spirit of sol and dissolved pearl,
> Apicius' diet 'gainst the epilepsy.
> And I will eat these broths with spoons of amber,
> Headed with diamond and carbuncle.

The Masterpieces

My footboy shall eat pheasants, calvered salmons,
Knots, godwits, lampreys. I myself will have
The beards of barbels served, instead of salads;
Oiled mushrooms; and the swelling unctuous paps
Of a fat pregnant sow, newly cut off,
Drest with an exquisite and poignant sauce;
For which I'll say unto my cook, *There's gold,*
Go forth and be a knight.

On clothes he is not far behind:

My shirts
I'll have of taffeta-sarsnet, soft and light
As cobwebs; and for all my other raiment,
It shall be such as might provoke the Persian,
Were he to teach the world riot anew.
My gloves of fishes and birds' skins, perfumed
With gums of paradise.

Jonson, in *The Alchemist* as in *Volpone*, uses his
sharpers to whip the appetites and follies of their
victims. His satire falls more heavily upon the
cozened than upon the cozeners. His rogues perform rough justice upon their dupes, and the author
has a sneaking indulgence for these strange ministers
of retribution. The Fox comes as near to being a
hero as any character we shall find in Jonson's plays,
while in *The Alchemist* we watch the intrigues of
Face and Subtle in a pleasant mood of expectation
and take real delight in the discomfiture of Sir Epicure
Mammon, brought to account by the rogues themselves. It was a tenet among the alchemists that the
philosophers' stone might only be discovered and
employed by the pure of heart. Surly, his man,
warns Sir Epicure of this circumstance in the full
tide of his eloquence:

Why I have heard he must be *homo frugi,*
A pious, holy and religious man,
One free from mortal sin, a very virgin,

and the warning is repeated by Subtle, alchemist-in-chief, posing as the ascetic man of science :

> Take heed you do not let the blessing leave you,
> With your ungoverned haste. I should be sorry
> To see my labours, now even at perfection,
> Got by long watching and large patience,
> Not prosper where my love and zeal hath placed them;
> Which (heaven I call to witness, with yourself,
> To whom I have poured my thoughts) in all my ends
> Have look'd no way, but unto public good,
> To pious uses and dear charity,
> Now grown a prodigy with men. Wherein
> If you, my son, should now prevaricate,
> And to your own particular lusts employ
> So great and catholic a bliss, be sure
> A curse will follow, yea, and overtake
> Your subtle and most secret ways.

Sir Epicure foolishly thinks to deceive the holy man :

> I assure you,
> I shall employ it all in pious uses,
> Founding of colleges and grammar schools,
> Marrying young virgins, building hospitals,
> And now and then a church.

Face, however, has arranged that, while the great experiment is in progress, Sir Epicure shall be caught by the charms of Doll Common. The alchemist's failure to produce the stone will thus be explained and laid at the door of the sinner. This whole conspiracy is one of Jonson's happiest inventions. Diamond cuts diamond. The honest professional rogues are set to catch the amateur and prove the better men.

We are shortly to study in *Bartholomew Fair* the finished portrait of a Puritan. Tribulation Wholesome and Ananias, pastor and deacon from Amsterdam, may be regarded as preliminary sketches in that kind. They come seeking the stone as a weapon to be used on behalf of the saints. It will bring to the cause ships, armies, and powerful friends. The two men are well contrasted. Ananias is a difficult fellow and needs persuasion before he will consent to deal with the ungodly. Tribulation, the casuist, however, is more than equal to the occasion and the precious pair are induced by Subtle to put their purses, and even certain goods which they hold in trust for orphans of the sect, at his disposal. Subtle takes a special pleasure in plucking these unsavoury fowl and contrives at the same time to twit them shrewdly for their railing against bells, popish traditions and profane plays. In the cozening of Tribulation, as in the undoing of Sir Epicure, Subtle and his confederates win our sympathy by the zest and ingenuity of their proceedings and by the just retribution which they bring down upon their victims.

A critic who, in approaching *The Alchemist*, begins with reservations, concludes inevitably on a note of admiration. It is not surprising that, in spite of its having a more difficult background and less intensity of mood and purpose than *Volpone*, this play should be accorded first place by many excellent judges. The liveliness and colour with which Jonson has presented his thieves' kitchen, the simplicity of the action and the meditated justice of his composition place it firmly among the great plays of the English theatre. No single episode in our comic literature, outside the plays of Shakespeare, outshines the presentation and discomfiture of Sir Epicure Mammon. That huge glistening figure of greed is unforgettable and, though he bulks larger than life, his temptations are commensurate. These rogues spread nets of silk and gold ; the world, the flesh and the devil were never painted with so engaging a candour :

> Sweet Dol,
> You must go tune your virginal, no losing
> O' the least time ; and, do you hear ? good action !
> Firk like a flounder ; kiss, like a scallop, close,
> And tickle him with thy mother tongue.

Ben Jonson

Or again :

> He shall be brought here fettered
> With thy fair looks, before he sees thee ; and thrown
> In a down bed as dark as any dungeon ;
> Where thou shalt keep him waking with thy drum,
> Thy drum, my Dol, thy drum ; till he be tame
> As the poor blackbirds were in the great frost,
> Or bees are with a basin ; and so hive him
> In the swan-skin coverlid and cambric sheets,
> Till he work honey and wax, my little God's-gift.

When rogues present their wares so effectively it is small wonder that their victims fall into commensurate ecstasies. The play throughout is hyperbolical ; all the details are proportionate. There is no falsehood. Its exaggerations are not partial. It has the dimensions of a great fresco broadly executed by the resolute hand of a master.

CHAPTER X

Bartholomew Fair

JONSON, last of the English humanists, only just missed the full effects of the Puritan disaster. He outlived a generation which had fought a losing battle against the assemblies, corporations and conventicles. It was more than a contest of persons and sects. It raised the most important issue with which England was ever confronted, dividing not only parties and professions, but the minds of those who participated. Many of the most ferocious enemies of humanism were renegade poets, actors and dramatists. Donne, who began as a humanist, climbed at last into the pulpit as a prophet of doom. Corbet took orders and became a preacher. Marston forsook the stage for a country rectory. Pamphleteers like Munday and Gosson, who lashed the poets in a frenzy of indignation, addressed the pious world as brands snatched from the burning. Even the Protestant party and ministers of the Crown were not always sure of their attitude. There was a time when it looked as though the Reformation itself might encourage and use the play of free minds in its struggle with the Papists. The first Cromwell made a serious effort to mobilise the forces of merriment against the Catholic Church, while under Elizabeth cardinals, bishops and abbots were mocked in anti-clerical plays. There were masked revelries in the streets of London with the connivance of such pillars of authority as Sir William Cecil. This was a generation caught between the possibilities of a positive humanism and the moral forces which culminated in the negative ecstasies of the Fifth Monarchy.

It was a bitter struggle between fundamental human issues hiding behind contentions which may present themselves too easily to a modern mind as superficial and absurd. Jonson lived to see the saints triumphant and the humanities rejected. The godly chorus, preluding with diffidence while Erasmus and Sidney were still at hand to defend the new learning against the new morality, swelled to a deafening clamour as the reign of Elizabeth advanced, and by the time Jonson came to the theatre the cause of the stages was lost. Thereafter the humanists might be tolerated, but the few who still pleaded for freedom and learning were driven to meet the Puritans on their own ground. Even Jonson, who stood like a rock for the classic ideal, was compelled to apply the moral test, defending his plays not as the free expression of his mind but as a corrective of social error and human wickedness.

The more superficial absurdities of the Puritan indictment are easily mocked. Calvin's famous Argument based on solemn references to Deuteronomy xxii. 5, which prohibits the wearing of men's apparel by women and women's apparel by men, or the contention of Gosson that acting, being a simulation, is by its very nature " within the compass of a lie ", merely scratch the surface. Nor do the moral and social arguments, of which the controversy is mostly composed, go really to the heart of the matter, though there was much legitimate complaint, urged not only by the Puritans but the humanists themselves, against the vulgarity and licence of the popular theatre and against the disorders for which it served as a background and an opportunity. There was admittedly a certain propriety in the erection of playhouses on Bankside, notoriously a district of ill fame, and there is no doubt that the galleries of the Globe and the Fortune afforded excellent occasions for light-fingered rogues and for gallant importunities not always resisted. Much of this outcry against the theatre as encouraging immorality and crime was, nevertheless, unfair. The licence of the times came thereby into the open, but the theatre cannot be held responsible for social habits which it merely reflects, and it should not be forgotten that the Bishop of Winchester was a proprietor of stews for generations before these unwholesome sites were acquired for the comparatively decent business of housing the plays of Shakespeare and such-like corrupters of youth. In any case the outcry against the theatre as a focus of ill-doing was essentially irrelevant to the main issue. The real motive of the controversy must be sought elsewhere.

The new morality was in essentials based on the assumption that men might be improved by consistently pretending to be better than they were. Possibly there is something to be said for the assumption that only by a resolute hypocrisy can men or nations ever hope to improve their hearts and minds. Unfortunately the theory is seldom honestly defended. The inhibitionists prefer to claim for their negations that they represent a positive state of grace.

This, in fact, was the real issue between the humanists and the Puritans. On one side were the claims of intellect and sensibility working towards a free development of human faculty—in effect that discovery of man which was an even more important feature of humanism than the discovery of the physical world. On the other side was a moral discipline which ultimately diverted the spiritual energy of the Renaissance towards a moral regeneration of mankind based on an elaborate and essentially primitive system of repression and denial.

These issues, however, were successfully concealed. The Puritans attacked stage plays for what they contained and the conditions under which they were given. They found in the tragedies of the period nothing but examples to honest citizens of murders, treacheries and rebellions, and in the comedies nothing but intrigues and wantonness. Such compositions corrupted the imagination of youth and the chastity of matrons. The theatre was a school of abuse and bawdry, the nest of the devil, a consistory of Satan. In the playhouse was focused all the sin of the City. Men came there to waste their substance and to meet women. All this rhetorical abuse was in the last resort inspired by a deep sense of incompatibility between the classic and Christian dispensation. The Church, then as always, desired to use the imagination of man for its own peculiar purpose, and the theatre has always been its most effective and dangerous rival. In the theatre a man may vicariously enjoy and possess the faculties whose exercise is denied him in common life. There he may find his emotions intensified, his sense of the beauty and variety of experience enlarged. He may lord it with Caesar, come into the dominion of his five senses with the great lovers and exquisites, reach out in speculation beyond the Index of Rome or the Institutes of Geneva, realise for a moment the full splendour of his inheritance. In Elizabethan London men were squarely confronted with this secular issue as never before in the course of English history. Sunday was the usual day for plays. The trumpets blew for the performances at the Curtain or the Globe as the bells were tolling him to prayer. He must choose between these invitations, and in choosing the theatre he was not merely exciting the hatred of ministers defrauded of custom, not merely violating a conventional sense of decency and virtue ; he was definitely challenging the whole Pauline conception of man as a creature that must die to this world before he can inherit the next.

The pamphlets and dissertations of the Puritan authors are much alike. They spoke a language which hardly varied in matter or manner for a century. Anthony Munday, to whom Jonson frequently alludes, may be taken as their typical author. Common plays, jesting and rhyming he declares to be public enemies of virtue and religion, allurements unto sin, corrupters of good manners, the cause of security and carelessness, mere brothel houses of bawdry. They bring the Gospel into slander, the Sabbath into contempt and men's souls into danger. Munday frequently alludes, in the Salvationist tradition, to his own backsliding : " I confess ", he wrote in 1580, " that ere this I have been a great affecter of that vain art of playmaking, insomuch that I have thought no time so well bestowed as when my wits were exercised in the invention of these follies." With a sad relish he describes the abuses from which he has been weaned :

> Mine own ears have heard honest women allured with abominable speeches. Sometimes I have seen two knaves at once importunate upon one light huswife ; whereby much quarrel hath grown to the disquieting of many. . . . There is the practising with married wives to train them from their husbands and places appointed for meeting and conference. When I had taken note of all these abuses and saw that the theatre was become a consultory of Satan, I concluded with myself never to employ my pen to so vile a purpose nor to be an instrument of bringing the wicked together.

Or again :

> Whosoever shall visit the chapel of Satan, I mean the theatre, shall find there no want of young harlots, utterly

Ben Jonson

past shame; who press to the forefront of the scaffolds
to the end to show their impudency and be as an object
of all men's eyes. Yea, such is their open shameless behaviour as every man may perceive by their wanton gestures whereunto they are given. For often without respect
of the place and company which behold them they commit
that filthiness openly which is horrible to be done in secret.
For neither reverence, justice, nor anything beside can
govern them.

Stephen Gosson, writing in 1582, with a host of
others, further colours the picture :

In the playhouses at London it is the fashion of youths
to go first into the yard and to carry their eye through
every gallery ; then, like unto ravens, where they spy the
carrion thither they fly and press as near to the fairest as
they can. They gave them pipins, dally with their garments to pass the time ; they muster talk upon all occasions and either bring them home to their houses on small
acquaintance or slip into taverns when the plays are done.
He thinketh best of his painted sheath and taketh himself
for a jolly fellow that is noted of most to be busiest with
women in all such places.

All these writers abound in the recital of such
enormities. The good Philip Stubbs, in his *Anatomy
of Abuses* (1583), invited his readers to mark the
wanton gestures and bawdy speeches, " such laughing
and fleering, such kissing and bussing, such clipping
and culling, such winking and glancing of wanton
eyes " as was wonderful to behold. Nor must we
lose sight of what followed when the play was done.
For the good man followed the spectators home, where
" in their secret conclaves " unmentionable consequences ensued. The theatre was the cause of all
the wickedness in life :

If you will learn falsehood ; if you will learn cosenage ;
if you will learn to deceive ; if you will learn to play the
hypocrite, to cog, lie and falsify ; if you will learn to jest,
laugh and fleer, to grin, to nod and mow ; if you will

learn to play the vice, to swear, tear and blaspheme both
heaven and earth ; if you will learn to become a bawd,
unclean, and to devirginate maids, to deflower honest wives ;
if you will learn to murder, slay, kill, pick, steal, rob and
rove ; if you will learn to rebel against princes, to commit
treasons, to consume treasures, to practise idleness, to sing
and talk of bawdy love or venery ; if you will learn to
deride, scoff, mock and flout, to flatter and smooth ; if you
will learn to play the whoremaster, the glutton, drunkard
or incestuous person ; if you will learn to become proud,
haughty and arrogant ; and, finally, if you will learn to con-
temn God and all his laws, to care neither for heaven nor
hell, and to commit all kind of sin and mischief, you need
to go to no other school, for all these good examples may
you see before your eyes in interludes and plays.

Sir Edmund Chambers, in his work on the Elizabethan stage, has collected and analysed some striking
specimens of Puritan indictment. Except for superficial differences of language and deportment, the
controversy has not varied in its essentials for over
three hundred years. Jeremy Collier a century later
repeated the whole performance with special reference
to Congreve and his contemporaries. Anthony Munday and Philip Stubbs still write to *The Times* and sit
on Vigilance Committees in England to-day. Their
main line of attack has never varied. The theatre
is made responsible for all the evils which the Church
has failed to remove, and the imagination of man,
being prone to evil, must be suitably discouraged.
In this perpetual quarrel Jonson clearly defined his
personal attitude and faith in one of the later masks.
We shall find him in *Pleasure Reconciled to Virtue*,
performed on Twelfth Night in 1619, venturing to
assert that there is no essential incompatibility between
a reasonable cultivation of the five senses and the
conduct of a good Christian. Meanwhile, at the Hope
Theatre on Bankside in October, 1616, he gave to
the public, in the most popular of all his plays, the

liveliest and best portrait of a Puritan in the English language. The circumstances under which the comedy was written have already been noted ; but the play itself calls for special attention both for its quality and as a significant expression of its author's general attitude to the life of the time and the world in general.

In parentheses it must be noted that Jonson, even in holiday mood, cannot forgo an induction wherein he glances at his critics and directs his admirers. But the references are happier than usual. There is nothing bitter or sour to mar the fun of the fair :

> He that will swear *Jeronymo* or *Andronicus* are the best plays yet shall pass unexcepted at here as a man whose judgment shows it is constant, and hath stood still these five-and-twenty or thirty years. Though it be an ignorance, it is a virtuous and staid ignorance ; and, next to truth, a confirmed error does as well ; such a one the author knows where to find him.

Even the offence of hunting for libels and false allusions is condemned in a spirit of good humour. The spectators are asked to guarantee :

> That they neither in themselves conceal, nor suffer to be concealed, any state-decipherer, or politic picklock of the scene, so solemnly ridiculous as to search out who was meant by the gingerbread woman, who by the hobby-horse man, who by the costardmonger, nay, who by their wares ; or that they will pretend to affirm on their own inspired ignorance what mirror of magistrates is meant by the justice, what great lady by the pig-woman, what concealed statesman by the seller of mouse-traps, and so of the rest.

The author, moreover, in declaring his intentions, is less truculent here than in his fighting comedies. He insists upon his fidelity to nature without offence to those who would improve upon reality. No person is to expect more than he knows or better ware than a fair will afford ; he is not to look for a nest of antiques, for the author is loth to make nature afraid in his plays like those who beget tales, tempests or drolleries. Nevertheless, he concludes, " let the concupiscence of jigs and dances reign as strong as it will amongst you, yet, if the puppets will please anybody, they shall be entreated to come in ".

Jonson is nowhere more tolerant, open of mind and sense than in this play. It is a fit expression of the merry England which was passing. It is the play of a faithful and fearless lover of life and it is throughout a true bill. There is no false gilt on the gingerbread. Never did such a gallery of rogues prey so happily upon so complete a company of fools. In character, incident and phrase the comedy is gross, vital and abundant. The author looks upon the common life of the time without daintiness or scruple. We are not invited to condone its iniquities ; yet we must feel it more wholesome to frequent the booths of St. Bartholomew than to sit at home with the zealots.

It is not possible to follow the author in his detailed presentation of over thirty characters, of the incidents in which they figure and of the systematic surprises and complications of his plot. The principal action is set on foot by Win-the-Fight Littlewit, the young wife of John Littlewit, the proctor. Littlewit is eager to visit the Fair, but Mrs. Littlewit fears that her mother, Dame Purecraft, being a Puritan, will never consent to their going. Littlewit, however, has a device. His wife, being pregnant, must fall sick of a longing for roast pig. Dame Purecraft will not dare to deny her daughter's craving—especially as she is secretly partial to pig herself. Dame Purecraft first tries to dissuade her daughter : " O resist it, Win-the-Fight. It is the tempter, the wicked tempter. You may know it by the fleshly motion of pig." But the longing persists and Dame Purecraft calls upon

her spiritual adviser, " Zeal-of-the-LandBusy ", as
a faithful fortification against this charge of the
adversary. Busy will find a way. He is called from
the pantry, where he is discovered with his teeth in a
cold turkey-pie, a great white loaf on his left hand
and a glass of malmsey on his right. He enters wip-
ing his beard and the case is put.

First he rules that pig may be eaten :

> Verily for the disease of longing it is a carnal disease,
> or appetite, incident to women ; and, as it is carnal and
> incident, it is natural, very natural ; now pig, it is a meat,
> and a meat that is nourishing and may be longed for, and
> so consequently eaten ; it may be eaten ; very exceeding
> well eaten ; but in the Fair, and as a Bartholomew pig,
> it cannot be eaten ; for the very calling it a Bartholomew
> pig, and to eat it so, is a spice of idolatry, and you make
> the Fair no better than one of the high places. This, I
> take it, is the state of the question : a high place.

This, however, will not do. Win-the-Fight Littlewit desires to eat her pig in the Fair and Busy is
begged to consider whether this, too, might not, under
necessity, be lawful. Needless to say he proves equal
to the occasion :

> It may be eaten and in the Fair, I take it, in a booth,
> the tents of the wicked. The place is not much, not very
> much. We may be religious in the midst of the profane,
> so it be eaten with a reformed mouth, with sobriety and
> humbleness, not gorged in with gluttony or greediness :
> there's the fear. For should she go there as taking pride
> in the place, or delight in the unclean dressing, to feed
> the vanity of the eye or lust of the palate, it were not well,
> it were not fit, it were abominable and not good.

So promising an argument may be taken further
yet. Why, for example, should Busy himself stay
behind ?

> I will go and eat. I will eat exceedingly and prophesy.
> There may be a good use made of it, too, now I think

on't. By the public eating of swine's flesh, to profess our hate and loathing of Judaism, whereof the brethren stand taxed. I will therefore eat, yea, I will eat exceedingly.

The pilgrimage of Mr. and Mrs. Littlewit and Dame Purecraft, conducted by Busy through the Fair, is recounted along with the adventures of another set of characters : Winwife and Quarlous, gentlemen in search of fun and fortune ; Bartholomew Cokes, esquire of Harrow, an ingenious fool, admired of King Charles II, who presumably had a fellow feeling for a man unable to say " no " ; Justice Overdo, playing providence in a series of strange disguises ; Grace Wellborn, ward of the Justice and one of the few charming and sensible women to be found in Jonson's comedies. The incidents in which they participate are appropriately designed to reveal their several characters against the full and vivid background of the Fair. Jonson has concentrated here all the resources of his peculiar realism. Nowhere is his odd blend of fancy, deliberate and systematic, with a naturalism, accurate and observed, more strikingly displayed. Lanthorn Leatherhead the toyman, Ezechial Edgworth the cutpurse, Nightingale the ballad-singer, Mooncalf the tapster, Val Cutting the bully, Captain Whit the bawd, Joan Trash with her gingerbread, Ursula the pigwoman, with their helpers and servers, are authentic figures of their class and time, but presented with a meditated extravagance. Ursula queens it here, her language greasier than her pigs, all fire and fat and bottle-ale, dropping two stone of suet a day, the very womb and bed of enormity, a walking sow of fallow and inspired vessel of kitchen stuff, in whom a man might sink and be drowned a week ere any friend could find him ; 'twere like falling into a whole shire of butter and they had need be a team of Dutchmen should draw him out. Her exchange of courtesies with friends and rivals is not for a squeamish reader ; nor can the pious object that Jonson has in any way tried to sweeten or embellish her enticements.

The author devotes all his second act to this picture of the Fair, leaving his audience in joyous expectation of Busy and his friends. In due course they arrive, Busy in control and full of exhortation :

> Walk in the middle way, foreright ; turn neither to the right hand nor to the left ; let not your eyes be drawn aside with vanity nor your ears with noises.

The pilgrims are set upon instantly by the vendors and showmen :

> What do you lack, what do you buy, Mistress ? A fine hobby-horse to make your son a tilter ? a drum to make him a soldier ? a fiddle to make him a reveller ? what is't you lack ? little dogs for your daughters ? or babies, male or female ?

Busy is prompt in counsel :

> Look not towards them, hearken not ; the place is Smith-field or the field of Smiths, the grove of hobby-horses and trinkets ; the wares are the wares of devils and the whole Fair is the shop of Satan ; they are hooks and baits, very baits, that are hung out on every side, to catch you and to hold you, as it were by the gills and by the nostrils as the fisher doth. Therefore you must not look nor turn toward them. The heathen man could stop his ears with wax against the harlot of the sea ; do you the like with your fingers against the bells of the beast.

Mrs. Littlewit pertinently asks her mother how they shall find a pig unless they look for a pig. Will it run off the spit into their mouths ? Busy, however, has an answer :

> No, but your mother, religiously wise, conceiveth it may offer itself by other means to the sense, as by way of steam,

Bartholomew Fair

which I think it doth here in this place—huh, huh—yes
it doth. (*He scents after it like a hound*.) And it were a
sin of obstinacy, great obstinacy, high and horrible obstinacy, to decline or resist the good titillation of the famelic
sense, which is the smell. Therefore be bold—huh, huh, huh
—follow the scent; enter the tents of the unclean for
once, and satisfy your wife's frailty. Let your frail wife
be satisfied; your zealous mother and my suffering self
will also be satisfied.

He adds a further edifying consideration to the effect
that, in finding a pig quickly, they will the sooner
escape other vanities of the Fair. Promptly, therefore,
they enter the booth of Ursula, for " here be the best
pigs and she does roast them as well as ever she did ".
The voice of Busy is heard uplifted within : a pig
prepare presently, let a pig be prepared. Eating his
fill, he nevertheless finds time to preach against long
hair, bottle ale and tobacco. Sated with good meat
he comes again upon the scene in full tide :

For long hair, it is an ensign of pride, a banner; and
the world is full of those banners. And bottle-ale is a drink
of Satan's, a diet drink of Satan's, devised to puff us up and
make us swell in this latter age of vanity, as the smoke
of tobacco to keep us in mist and error; but the fleshly
woman which you call Ursula is above all to be avoided,
having the marks upon her of the three enemies of man;
the world, as being in the Fair; the devil, as being in
the fire; and the flesh, as being herself.

Win-the-fight Littlewit has come not only to eat
pig but to see the Fair. But Busy has small sympathy
with such trivial pleasures. For him the hobby-horse
has no attraction. The " hobby-horse is an idol, a
very idol, a fierce and rank idol; the drum is the
broken belly of the beast; the gingerbread stall is a
basket of popery and a nest of images ". The vendors
of the Fair entreat him to be silent, but, " having

eaten two-and-a-half pigs to his share and drunk a pailful," there is no holding him :

> Hinder me not woman. I was moved in spirit to be here this day, in this Fair, this wicked and foul Fair ; and fitter may it be called a Foul than a Fair ; to protest against the abuses of it, the foul abuses of it, in regard of the afflicted saints, that are troubled, very much troubled, exceedingly troubled, with the opening of the merchandise of Babylon again and the peeping of popery upon the stalls, here, in the high places. See you not Goldylocks, the purple strumpet there, in her yellow gown and green sleeves ? the profane pipes, the tinkling timbrels ?

He begins to overthrow the stall, to pull down this "idolatrous grove of images, this flasket of idols", till at last, refusing to stop his noise, he is carried off to punishment :

> 'Tis a sanctified noise. I will make a loud and strong noise, till I have daunted the profane enemy. And for this cause I will thrust myself into the stocks, upon the pikes of the land.

Busy in the stocks reveals himself the complete Puritan—stubborn in adversity, glorying in the conceit of his martyrdom, foretelling the destruction of fairs, May-games, wakes, Whitsun ales, sighing and groaning for the reformation of these abuses, triumphing in his extraordinary calling " done for his better standing, his surer standing, hereafter ". Escaping subsequently from the stocks, he takes up the good cause with undiminished zeal and, raging through the Fair, happens upon a puppet show. The tragical story of Hero and Leander is being enacted in a booth :

> Down with Dagon ! down with Dagon ! 'tis I, I will no longer endure your profanations. . . . I will remove Dagon there, I say, that idol : that heathenish idol, that remains, as I may say, a beam, a very beam—not a beam of the

sun, nor a beam of the moon, nor a beam of a balance, neither a housebeam, nor a weaver's beam, but a beam in the eye, in the eye of the brethren, a very great beam, an exceeding great beam; such as are your stage-players, rimers and morris-dancers, who have walked hand in hand, in contempt of the brethren and the cause, and been borne out by instruments of no mean countenance.

The showman protests that he presents nothing but what is licensed by authority; he has the hand of the master of the Revels for his play. Busy falls upon him headlong:

> The master of the rebels' hand thou hast, Satan's! Hold thy peace, thou scurrility, shut up thy mouth; thy profession is damnable and in pleading for it thou dost plead for Baal. I have long opened my mouth wide and gaped. I have gaped as the oyster for the tide after thy destruction; but cannot compass it by suit or dispute; so that I look for a bickering ere long and then a battle.

There follows a controversy between Busy and the showman, in which Jonson brings forward some of the more common arguments used by the Puritans against the players. In conclusion Busy confesses himself confuted—Jonson's sole lapse from the veracity of his portrait. But Busy had perforce to be beaten. The audience wished his discomfiture and had to be satisfied.

Zeal-of-the-Land Busy is a true picture. His style of speech, with its meaningless repetitions and tiresome playing with worn tags and phrases, was as characteristic of the nonconformist orators of the sixteenth century as of their present heirs. In cases where one might reasonably suspect a malicious exaggeration of their style, a short reading of any tract of the times shows that Jonson was remarkably sober in his transcriptions. " I have gaped as the oyster for the tide, for thy destruction," exclaims

Busy in his wrath. Here, if anywhere, parody would seem to be indicated. Nothing of the kind. We find, as a specimen of Puritan oratory, this actual simile in Eachard's contempt of the clergy : " Our souls are constantly gaping after thee, O Lord, yea, verily, our souls do gape, even as an oyster gapeth." Not only is Jonson's Puritan a true portrait ; he is a timely warning of what was coming to Jonson's England. Busy might be confuted in a play, but he, nevertheless, prophesied a bickering and a battle, and in the bickering and the battle, when it came, the cause of mirth and sanity was lost. Jonson in 1614, taking the measure of the Puritan movement, foretold its ultimate triumph some thirty years before the event.

We have reviewed *Bartholomew Fair* as the progress of a Puritan. The other aspects of the play must, therefore, be neglected. We might as profitably have followed the adventures of Justice Overdo ; the vicissitudes of the gentlemen adventurers, Quarlous and Winwife ; the plucking of Cokes, most engaging of comic simpletons ; or the ingenious operations of Ezechial Edgworth, the cutpurse, and his confederates. To even better purpose, with sufficiently a love of life to accept without misgiving the grosser works of nature, might we choose to linger beside the booth of Ursula, the pig-woman, with her carnal vocabulary and ready violence of image and epithet :

Ay, ay gamesters, knock a plain, plump wench of the suburbs, do, because she's juicy and wholesome ; you must have your thin, pinched ware, pent up in the compass of a dog-collar (or 'twill not do), that looks like a long-laced conger set upright, and a green feather, like fennel in the joll on't. . . . Hang 'em, rotten, roguey cheaters, I hope to see them plagued one day with lean playhouse poultry, that has the bony rump sticking out like the ace of spades or the point of a partizan, that every rib of them is like the tooth of a saw ; and will so grate them with their hips and shoulders as (take 'em altogether) they were as good lie with a hurdle.

Or, for a contrast, there is sweeter company in Grace Wellborn, wooed by her gentlemen adventurers. She has the clear wit and sense of the humanist generation which was passing :

> How can I judge of you, so far as to a choice, without knowing you more ? You are both alike to me yet, and so indifferently affected by me, as each of you might be the man, if the other were away ; for you are reasonable creatures, you have understanding and discourse ; and if fate send me an understanding husband, I have no fear at all but mine own manners shall make him a good one.

Here is candour, dignity and a steady appreciation of what is due to herself and her importunate suitors.

But we cannot stay longer among the booths of St. Bartholomew. Nor, perhaps, is it necessary ; for this is a play which may still be read and not abandoned, like so much of Jonson's work, to the antiquarians and savoured only in the synopses and citations of the critics. It is, indeed, almost essential to read it. For this is England's carnival or farewell to flesh.

CHAPTER XI

The Happy Laureate

JONSON in 1617 was forty-three years of age. He had written his best plays. He had published his works in a first collected edition. On February 3rd of that year he was granted by the King a pension of one hundred marks which, though the title had not yet been invented or the position created, made him in effect the first poet laureate of England. He presented now a very different figure from the lank and haggard youth, back from the wars, who had killed Gabriel Spencer some sixteen years previously. The "raw-boned anatomy" of *Every Man out of His Humour*, "who walks up and down like a charged musket", had begun to put on flesh and soon, since he could no longer hope to redeem his figure, he would be driven to jest upon it. "Twenty stones less two pounds" was shortly to be his confession. In 1619 he walked from London to Edinburgh and back again. Was it a last despairing effort to keep hard in body as in mind? It was an heroic remedy, but unsuccessful. For another eight or ten years he remained outwardly at the height of his powers, but the dissolution was begun.

The visit to Scotland is the first important event of this middle period. Winding up the old year with a *Mask for Christmas*, presented at Court in 1616, he started the New Year with *The Mask of Lethe*, written for Lord Hay, who was entertaining the French Ambassador at his house on February 22nd, 1617.

Then came *A Vision of Delight*, *Lovers Made Men*, *Pleasure Reconciled to Virtue*, and *For the Honour of Wales*, all presented at Court previous to his departure. In 1619 he set forth on his valiant pilgrimage.

There seems to have been some friendly chaff at his expense and some, perhaps, which was not so friendly. It happened that in this very year John Taylor, the water-poet, also decided to walk to Scotland. The King had preceded them both in 1618 and all London was buzzing with reports of a lean but pleasant land, not at all so barbarous as had been commonly believed. Jonson was hearing everywhere of Scotland, and something of what he heard was doubtless from the King himself. All this talk of persons and places beyond the Tweed may have pricked the lowland blood in his veins. Taylor's pilgrimage was for self-advertisement, but Jonson thought it was in mockery. It was in any case unfortunate that a laureate of England and missioner of the muses should have been thus forestalled by the " King's water-poet and Queen's waterman ", as Taylor was in the habit of styling himself.

This Taylor was one of the quaint figures of the time. He had worked hard all his life at being what is commonly known as a character. He had been with Essex to the Flores. Then, after a brief spell as a Thames waterman, he had taken a public-house at Oxford where his illiterate jingles brought him good custom. When the loyalists were driven from Oxford he opened a public-house under the sign of the Crown in Phoenix Alley. His principal advertisement was to take strange journeys, as from London to Queenborough in a boat made of brown paper or his very merry, wherry, ferry voyage to York. The best of him was loyalty to the King whom he so familiarly carried in his pocket ; for, when Charles lost his head, the Crown in Phoenix Alley became the Mourning Crown to the displeasure of all good republicans.

That John Taylor should announce from his tavern that he intended to take the low road to Scotland, when Jonson was taking the high road, was a coincidence to be received with loud approval by the Mermaid wits. It was far, however, from the honest waterman's thoughts to make a mock of his rival. He devoutly followed his King, hoping to get by the way excellent matter for the bar parlour and stuff for a new sheet to be spread among his customers: "The Penniless Pilgrimage or the Moneyless Perambulation of John Taylor—how he travailed on foot from London to Edinburgh in Scotland."

"Taylor was sent along here to scorn him"—such was Jonson's angry comment to Drummond. Jonson suspected a conspiracy to make him ridiculous. Not only had Taylor come to Scotland in his despite; he had been *sent*. The sequel is characteristic of the man whom Drummond himself was shortly to describe as "passionately kind and angry". Jonson, arriving in Scotland, was waited upon by the very merry, wherry, ferry poet at Leith. It is Taylor who tells the story. Jonson apparently went straight to the point and accused the waterman roundly of mockery and malice, his fingers itching upon the ever-ready cudgel. John Taylor, however, indignantly denied the charge. He writes quite honestly on his pilgrimage:

Reader, these travails of mine into Scotland were not undertaken, neither in imitation nor emulation of any man, but only devised by myself, on purpose to make trial of my friends, both in this kingdom of England and that of Scotland, and because I would be an eye witness of divers things which I had heard of that country; and whereas

many shallow brained critics do lay an aspersion on me
—that I was set on by others, or did undergo this project,
either in malice or mockage of Master Benjamin Jonson,
I vow by the faith of a Christian that their imaginations
are all wide, for he is a gentleman to whom I am so much
obliged for many undeserved courtesies that I have received
from him, and from others by his favour, that I durst
never be so imprudent or ungrateful as to suffer any man's
persuasions or mine own instigation to incite me to make
so bad a requital for so much goodness.

Jonson, to whom all this must have been said after
his declaration to Drummond, found the sculler a true
man and gave him a gold piece of the value of two
and twenty shillings to drink his health in England.
" So ", concludes the waterman, " with a friendly
farewell I left him as well as I hope never to see him
in a worse estate ; for he is amongst noblemen and
gentlemen that know his true worth and their own
honours, where with much respective love he is
worthily entertained."

Jonson stayed with Drummond some three weeks,
but now and then made visits to other gentlemen.
Taylor at Leith found him at the house of one Robert
Stuart. The names of his hosts, recovered from stray
letters and records, mean nothing to us now. Only
Drummond matters. Did Jonson go to Hawthornden
by invitation ? Drummond had visited London some
years previously and, being interested in poets and
learning, could hardly have overlooked the author of
Volpone and the greatest scholar of his time. More
probably Jonson went with letters of introduction,
possibly with recommendations from the King. All
we know of the journey is that he travelled by the
great north road through Yorkshire and Northumber-
land, and bought a new pair of shoes at Darlington.
At Edinburgh the fog lifts a moment. We find him
publicly welcomed and entertained by the Town

Ben Jonson

Council at a cost of £221 6s. 4d. Scots, and admitted as a burgess and guild brother. That was in September. Almost certainly he saw Drummond then—perhaps under the legendary sycamore in Drummond's garden. That Drummond started to his feet with a " Welcome, welcome royal Ben ", is unlikely. Drummond was not that sort of man—a slight, frail, sickly fellow, with a baby mouth and a natural shrinking from the rudeness of life, a man of gentle and limited enthusiasms. Genius that went beyond his range of feeling and intelligence subdued him, but he resented it. There had been nothing yet in his life but his books, a devoted mother and sisters, and a romantic passion nipped untimely by the death of his first and only love.

That Jonson went to Hawthornden was a kindly act to posterity. Drummond was waiting for him with a notebook and at every turn of his career these notes must be called in evidence. Without them Jonson's character would have remained but a shadow of the figure we have come to know. Admittedly the Conversations are a distorting mirror. Drummond was not large enough to reflect him truly. His notes, moreover, were random jottings, intended rather to fix impressions than to be of any real service to others —scrawls hastily entered without regard to their relevance and in contempt of syntax.

Drummond has been heartily scolded for not better appreciating his opportunities. He should, it is urged, have realised that here was his chance of being Boswell to a mighty time. He should at any rate have been careful to convey a just idea of his famous guest. Some even accuse him of downright malice. Gifford blames him for the whole deep-rooted legend of Jonson as a cantankerous, envious and malignant creature, which he so vehemently challenged and destroyed.

WILLIAM DRUMMOND OF HAWTHORNDEN
Engraved by E. Smith

[face p. 212

Gifford, face to face with Drummond, can hardly contain himself. " Cankered hypocrite " is one of the mildest of his references, and he mourns repeatedly that his hero should have fallen into such unworthy hands—a man who spied upon his guest, lay in wait for him, recorded his unguarded sayings without context or explanation, betrayed him over the winecups into indiscretions to be noted down without mitigation or remorse. Even Cibber hazarded the view that " it was not altogether fair of Mr. Drummond to commit to writing things that passed over a bottle, and which perhaps were heedlessly advanced. As few people are so wise as not to speak imprudently sometimes, it is not the part of a man who invites another to his table to expose what may drop inadvertently." To which it may be answered that Jonson said and wrote many worse things than are recorded in the Conversations and would have stood publicly by anything he may have uttered for a private ear ; that Drummond did not intend his notes for posterity but for himself ; that there is no wilful malice in his jottings ; that the Conversations, though Drummond knew it not, are more damaging to himself than to his guest ; that no fair charge of hypocrisy can be brought against a man who, in spite of the respect which he feels for a great figure of the time, reserves his right of private judgment.

Posterity cannot honestly accuse Drummond of treachery, but it can cordially regret that he was too limited and complacent a man to come within easy speaking distance of his visitor. Drummond was overwhelmed by Jonson's staggering vitality, his violent enthusiasms and superlative dislikes, his loud and sweeping opinions, his blunt disregard of established prejudices and reputations, his contempt of authority and compromise. A bull had broken into his china shop and Drummond was ultimately left to assess the damage and to compose his shattered peace. A very natural, almost an engaging, resentment looks through the pauses of his inventory.

Drummond, completing his notes—apparently dictated and never revised, for no man of letters could have set down even in his private diary anything so crabbedly in his proper hand—attempted a brief summing-up of his impressions in a character sketch which shall be quoted in full :

> He (Jonson) is a great lover and praiser of himself ; a contemner and scorner of others ; given rather to lose a friend than a jest ; jealous of every word and action of those about him (especially after drink, which is one of the elements in which he liveth) ; a dissembler of ill parts which reign in him, a bragger of some good that he wanteth ; thinketh nothing well but what either he himself or some of his friends and countrymen have said or done ; he is passionately kind and angry ; careless either to gain or keep ; vindictive, but if he be well answered, at himself.
>
> For any religion, as being versed in both. Interpreteth best sayings and deeds often to the worst. Oppressed with fantasy, which hath ever mastered his reason, a general disease in many poets. His inventions are smooth and easy ; but above all he excelleth in a translation.

Admittedly this is not a kind or generous portrait of a man who, sitting at table with his host, unpacked his heart in words. But Drummond, having suffered assault and battery, was feeling his bruises. Jonson never had much regard for his audience, and Mermaid manners in the house of a prim Scottish laird, of a sickly constitution and reclusive disposition, were not likely to be well received. There is no active spite in the delineation. Drummond merely notes, for his private satisfaction, characteristics of the poet which at one time or another had made him intermittent enemies even among the hard-bitten poets of London

accustomed to give and receive as good as they got.
Drummond is sore, but honest appreciation looks
through his censure. His criticisms are more than
balanced by gleams of cordial perception. " Passionately kind and angry " is a high-light that atones for
many shadows. " Careless either to gain or keep "
is also good. Most admirable of all is the precious
phrase : " vindictive, but, if he be well answered, at
himself ".

This portrait, moreover, was written on a bad day
when Drummond, abandoned by his guest, was left
to count the empty bottles and recover from the strain
of living under a Lord of Misrule. The Conversations
reveal an intimacy and a range of topics which show
that the two men liked and respected one another.
Delicate subjects were safely handled, more particularly the subject of Drummond's own performances
as a poet : " His censure of my verses was that they
were all good, especially my epitaph of the Prince,
save that they smelled too much of the Schools and
were not after the fashion of the time. For a child
(says he) can write, after the fashion of the Greeks
and Latins, verses running : yet that he wished, to
please the King, that piece of Forth Feasting had been
his own." This is not too easy of digestion for a
sensitive minor poet ; but it is recorded with modest
calm. Jonson was kind to Drummond as to a man
who did not sufficiently stand up for himself. Had
Drummond made extravagant claims for his verses,
Jonson, who clearly thought but little of their
quality (for a child can write after the fashion of the
Greeks and Latins), would have taken him down a
peg.

Drummond listened in horror and respect to Jonson's
opinions—respect for their substance and horror at
the enthusiastic violence of their expression. He

never questions or comments on the sayings he records
—except in one place to suggest that Jonson, not being
able to read French, had no right to judge of the
merits of Cardinal du Perron's translation of Vergil.
Of his scholarship Drummond stood quite candidly
in awe : " He was better versed and knew more in
Greek and Latin than all the poets of England."
Perhaps he protested now and then against the energy
with which Jonson laid about him, for he records a
saying of Jonson that sounds like a retort to some
such objections : " He told me I was too good and
simple and that oft a man's modesty made a fool of
his wit."

Jonson met his host without reserve. Their talk
was by turns general and particular, lively and serious. The personal touches in the Conversations are
many and various. We read that Jonson, in his merry
humour, was wont to name himself the poet ; that
of all styles he loved most to be called honest ; that
he disliked music with his meals ; that he despised
Owen as a pedantic schoolmaster who swept his living
from the posteriors of little children ; that he could
set horoscopes but trusted not in them ; that sundry
times he had devoured his books, in other words sold
them all for necessity, but that every new year he
received twenty pounds from the Earl of Pembroke
to buy more ; that he was much chaffed for his efforts,
largely unsuccessful, to grow a beard. We learn that
he liked a simple riddle : what is it that the more you
cut it, groweth still the longer ?—a ditch. He delighted
in odd stories, such as the tale of a packet of letters
which fell overboard and was devoured of a fish, the
fish being taken at Flushing and the letters safely
delivered in London to him, to whom they were
addressed.

He was pleased with the simplest jest, telling of

one who, being asked of another who was bald why he suffered his hair to grow so long, answered : it was to see if his hair would grow to seed that he might sow it on naked pates. He liked to tell of things that discredited those who affected to be better than their fellows, as of a gentlewoman who fell in such a fantasy or frenzy with one Mr. Dod, a Puritan preacher, that she requested her husband that, for the procreation of an angel or saint, he might lye with her—which, having obtained, it was but an ordinary birth.

Meanwhile, famous names dropped from his lips with trenchant and sometimes surprising judgments. Spenser's stanzas pleased him not, nor his matter ; Daniel was a good honest man, but no poet ; Donne's *Anniversary* was profane and full of blasphemy, but he was the first poet in the world for some things ; Shakespeare wanted art ; only Fletcher and Chapman, next himself, could make a mask ; Francis Beaumont loved too much himself and his own verses ; there were no books like Hooker's *Ecclesiastical Polity* for church matters or Selden's *Titles of Honour* for antiquities ; if he might have written Southwell's *Burning Babe* he would have been content to destroy many of his own pieces ; there was no such good ground for an heroic poem as King Arthur's fiction ; Sir Philip Sidney was no pleasant man in countenance, his face being spoiled with pimples ; Salisbury never cared for any man longer than he could make use of him ; my Lord Chamberlain of England (Bacon) wringeth his speeches from the strings of his band; Selden was the " bravest man in all languages ".

Suddenly, however, the talk would become more intimate, so that Drummond's notes, recording the gist of Jonson's confessions, anecdotes and reminiscences, must be called in evidence at every turn of his life. He spoke of his wife, of curious incidents in his affairs with women, of the death of his son, of his mother, of the money he made by his plays, of his poverty, of his religion. Would he have talked so much at his ease with a cankered hypocrite?

Drummond's final portrait of Jonson must be read in the light of the Conversations themselves. It then appears as the inevitable reaction of a weak man from the fascination of a stronger spirit. The Conversations, moreover, must themselves be read with circumspection. Judgments and opinions, noted out of their context, with nothing to guide us as to the spirit in which they were uttered, should not be taken too precisely. Drummond recorded Jonson as saying that Shakespeare wanted art, and that Shakespeare was careless, having wrecked a ship on the shores of Bohemia. This would seem to indicate that Drummond was defending Shakespeare from disparagement. Jonson, however, put Shakespeare with the greatest poets of all time, whereas Drummond had no idea that Shakespeare was effectively greater than Daniel or Alexander and describes him in one of his prefaces as " one among several authors who have written of love ". The only play of Shakespeare's in Drummond's library—described by Gifford as a " collection of rubbish not worth the hire of the cart that took it away "—was *Love's Labour's Lost*. Drummond loved all books, but he had neither taste nor judgment. His shrill enthusiasms and indiscriminate amateur reactions could hardly fail to provoke his guest and to raise in him the spirit of mischief. It is clear that many of his " notes " are a solemn record of things thrown off in jest or uttered to stagger and confuse. Drummond, praising Shakespeare in the same breath with Sir William Alexander, was more than enough to raise in Jonson the demon of perversity. One could hardly discuss the author of " Hamlet " with such a man. So Jonson stopped him carelessly in full career : Shakespeare wanted art and he wrecked a ship on the coasts of Bohemia. So, too, with Spenser. Jonson is noted as declaring that " Spenser's stanzas pleased him not, nor his matter ". So might any competent critic, provoked by falsetto ardours of the amateur, deliver himself in the heat of the moment. But we know that Jonson truly admired Spenser and had by heart the *Shepherd's Calender* :

> For Bacchus' fruit is friend to Phoebus wise,
> And when with wine the brain begins to sweat,
> The numbers flow as fast as spring doth rise.

Or again :

> O ! if my temples were distained with wine,
> And girt in girlands of wild Yvie twine,
> How I could rear the Muse on stately stage,
> And teach her tread aloft in buskin fine,
> With quaint Bellona in her equipage !

The judgment on Spenser was not so hard a saying as it seemed. Jonson disliked a complicated system of rhyme and condemned all sonnets as a bed of Procrustes for the muse. He disliked, equally, complicated, allegorical romances and he had chastised the euphuists—of which Spenser was the finest flower—in his plays. Drummond, on the other hand, was in his element with Spenser. He doted on the Faerie Queene and even maintained that its author, like Shakespeare, was fully equal to Daniel. How was it possible to corroborate so promiscuous an arbiter, even though one agreed with him in substance ? Jonson, as in his observations on Shakespeare, was exasperated into heresies and contradictions. Spenser's stanzas pleased him not, nor his matter. Yet later, when the subject recurred, for Drummond could not keep off his favourite poet, Jonson talked of Spenser with real emotion, relating with a feeling that shines through the crabbed record of his words, " that the Irish having robbed Spenser of his goods and burnt his house and a little child newborn, he and his wife escaped ; and after, he died for lack of bread in King Street, and refused twenty pieces sent to him by my Lord of Essex and said he was sorry he had no time to spend them ".

It was Jonson's impulse to contradict even those who agreed with him. Passionately kind, he often found the kindness of other men inadequate. Then he would grow splenetic, snubbing the praises which to him fell so far short of his own enthusiasm. Contradictions that abound in the conversations with Drummond cannot be otherwise explained. When Drummond commended Francis Beaumont, Jonson, mourning his young contemporary who had died untimely at thirty years of age, declared that the fellow " loved too much himself and his own verses ". This was no considered disparagement, but an irritable gesture pricked out of him by commendations that were indiscriminate and distasteful. The remark was one of many noted by Drummond for its singularity. What Jonson really thought of Beaumont and of many others whom he is recorded in the Conversations as scolding over the wine for this or that blemish must be sought elsewhere. Thus in a famous epigram Jonson begins :

How I do love thee Beaumont and thy muse

and he concludes :

What art is thine that so thy friend deceives !
When even there, where most thou praisest me,
For writing better, I must envy thee.

There are glimpses here and there in these Con-

versations of a nature deeply sensitive. There is, in
particular, that sudden gust which prompted him to
say of the unhappy Southwell, ten times tortured
and executed at Tyburn : that Southwell was hanged ;
yet had he written that piece of his the Burning Babe,
he would have been content to destroy many of his.
It was Jonson's habit to declaim the verses which he
brought in evidence:

> As I in hoary Winter's night
>   Stood shivering in the snow,
> Surprised I was with sudden heat,
>   Which made my heart to glow ;
> And lifting up a fearful eye
>   To view what fire was near,
> A pretty Babe, all burning bright,
>   Did in the air appear ;
>
> Who scorchèd with excessive heat,
>   Such floods of tears did shed,
> As though his floods should quench his flames,
>   Which with his tears were bred.
> Alas ! (quoth he), but newly born
>   In fiery heats I fry,
> Yet none approach to warm their hearts
>   Or feel my fire but I ;
>
> My faultless breast the furnace is,
>   The fuel wounding thorns ;
> Love is the fire, and sighs the smoke,
>   The ashes shames and scorns ;
> The fuel justice layeth on,
>   And mercy blows the coals,
> The metal in this furnace wrought
>   Are men's defiled souls ;
>
> For which as now on fire I am
>   To work them to their good ;
> So will I melt into a bath,
>   To wash them in my blood.
> With this he vanished out of sight,
>   And swiftly shrunk away,
> And straight I called unto mind
>   That this was Christmas Day.

The voice of the best reader of his day fades away.
Drummond shifts uneasily in his chair. Such feeling
was too deep and tender for him. He shrank from
these intensities. But the moment left its mark and
he made a note of it.

There is another point to be remembered in reading
the Conversations. Drummond noted down only what
to him was most striking and unexpected. Jonson
may have praised Shakespeare for an hour before
being driven to that bold assertion that he wanted
art. He may have witnessed to all the qualities that
made Beaumont his friend and pupil before hinting
that the young man thought too well of himself.
There is, in fact, only one serious and consistent
estimate of a living writer embodied in Drummond's
notes—namely, the appreciations scattered up and
down the record of the works of Donne. They help
us to understand why Jonson, as a critic, was a power
in the land. He had an immense admiration for
Donne, but admiration never troubled his discretion
or blinded him to what he regarded as blemishes in
any man. "He esteemeth John Donne the first poet
in the world for some things," Drummond records.
This was a good beginning and left no room for
subsequent misunderstanding, especially as Jonson not
only praised Donne but quoted him: "His verses of
the Lost Chain he hath by heart and that passage
of the Calm":

> In one place lay
> Feathers and dust to-day and yesterday.

But Jonson admired always with judgment. He found
that Donne's obscurity was a fault to be regretted,
not the token of a profundity to be admired. "That
Donne, himself, for not being understood, would
perish" was one of his riders. "That Donne, for

not keeping of accent, deserved hanging " was another, and he further declared the *Anniversaries* which Donne had written to commemorate the death of Elizabeth Drury to be " profane and full of blasphemy ". To compare a lady with a church, declare that Satan could not arrest the thoughts within her breast because she was a Sovereign State, and to affirm that men should strive after heaven merely because she was there and better worth a visit than the Virgin Mary struck Jonson as being not merely quaint but wicked. Coleridge, of a later generation, overlooked the wickedness ; but he, too, declared Donne's accent to be deplorable, described his convolutions as fantastic and stiff, and classed him with the metaphysical poets who delighted to " wreathe iron pokers into true love knots ". Donne's fanciful treatment of divine mysteries struck his more normal friend as lacking in the reverence and simplicity of mind with which men should approach such high matters. He had no natural sympathy with the more intricate and familiar intensities of religious experience.

Jonson admired in Donne the young man who had written all his best poems at twenty-five. Of the marvellous Dr. Donne, who preached from the pulpit at St. Paul's to my lords and ladies in the vein of Hamlet addressing the skull of poor Yorick, he was driven sadly to add : " and now, since he was made doctor repenteth highly and seeketh to destroy his poems ". This was treason to the muse ; but Jonson, though he regrets it, still remembers with gratitude the early faith and promise of the renegade :

> Whose every work, of thy most early wit
> Came forth example and remains so yet.

Jonson, moreover, paid to Donne a higher tribute

than praise in submitting to his friend work of his own for judgment :

> Read all I send ; and if I find but one
> Marked by thy hand, and with the better stone,
> My title's sealed.

It is difficult to resist the temptation to reconstruct from Drummond's memoranda the mood and occasion that elicited or led to the opinions recorded. Such excursions, however, are perilous. Suffice it that Jonson's reputation, which suffers under a hasty reading of those random jottings, is enriched and fortified by a more careful approach. By the exercise of a little common understanding, we catch inevitable and precious glimpses of a great English worthy traversing at his ease the whole scale of human experience. Passionately kind and angry, he ranges up and down, qualifying or destroying reputations, sitting in proud or enthusiastic judgment on great and small, confessing to his own human accidents and frailties, a man with nothing to conceal of himself or his opinions, incorruptible in his love of life and respect for his vocation. Most precious of all are the sudden preferences he shows for simple things—for slight, ribald jests, sallies of a mind which, being old with learning in boyhood, had remained for ever young in its sensibilities, with all the gawkiness, assurance and enthusiastic bitterness of youth. It should be noted, moreover, that, when he feels himself free to quote from poets by the hour and comes by way of Horace, Spenser and the rest to his own measures, it is not the railings of Asper or the splendid corruption of Volpone which he brings to this feast of Apollo, but such small perfections as :

> Drink to me only with thine eyes,
> And I'll not ask for wine ;

or trifles such as this :

> For love's sake kiss me once again ;
> I long and should not beg in vain ;
>   Here's none to spy or see.
>   Why do you doubt or stay ?
>   I'll taste as lightly as the bee,
> That doth but touch his flower and flies away.

Jonson's visit remained the most important event in the life of Drummond. It would be long before he could fill the silence or mend the gap left by the departure of his prodigious friend. Evidently at parting there was much reciprocal vowing of perpetual amity. Drummond was to send Jonson local particulars for a fisher or pastoral play on Loch Lomond, an arrangement of which Jonson reminded him on his return to London in May, 1619. Drummond kept his promise in July. " If there be any other thing in this country ", he writes, " which my power can reach, command it. There is nothing I wish more than to be in the catalogue of them that love you." He signed the letter : " your loving friend ". Jonson, meanwhile, sent to Drummond some pleasant epigrams. One of them, *On a Lover's Dust, Made Sand for an Hour Glass* was thus inscribed :

> To the Honouring Respect
>   Born
> To the Friendship contracted with
>   The Right Virtuous and Learned
>   Master William Drummond,
> And the Perpetuating the same by all offices of
>   Love Hereafter,
>   I, Benjamin Jonson,
> Whom he hath honoured with the leave to be called his,
>   Have with my own hand, to satisfy his Request,
>   Written this Imperfect Song,
>   On a Lover's Dust, made sand for an
>   Hour-glass.

Another poem, entitled *My Picture left in Scotland,*

concluded with some familiar touches—Jonson's muse visiting his friend in slippers :

> I now think Love is rather deaf than blind ;
>   For else it could not be
>   That she,
>   Whom I adore so much, should so slight me
> And cast my suit behind.
> I'm sure my language to her was as sweet,
>   And every close did meet
>   In sentence of as subtle feet,
>   As hath the youngest he
>   That sits in shadow of Apollo's tree.
>
>   Oh ! but my conscious fears,
>   That fly my thoughts between,
>   Tell me that she hath seen
>   My hundreds of gray hairs,
>   Told six and forty years,
> Read so much waste as she cannot embrace
> My mountain belly and my rocky face ;
> And all these, through her eyes, have stopt her ears.

How much of Britain north of the Tweed was seen by Jonson can only be conjectured. We may assume that he was at least as handsomely received as the water-poet who, shortly before, had been entertained by the Earl of Mar at Kindrochit Castle, put into a kilt and invited to witness such sporting and feasting as he had never thought to see in these islands and such feudal houses as had not been found in England for two hundred years. Jonson was at any rate impressed, and went back the richer in memory and experience. He meant to write an account of his journey to be entitled a *Discovery* as well as a pastoral play on Loch Lomond. But alas ! the *Discovery*, or what was written of it, perished in a fire that destroyed his library in 1623, and the play was never written at all. One line only survives of his tribute to Scotland. It is addressed to Edinburgh,

> The heart of Scotland, England's other eye.

The Happy Laureate

King James' reception of the valiant pilgrim has already been noted. " He professed (thank God) some joy to see me," Jonson wrote to Drummond, " and is pleased to hear of the purpose of my book . . . a most catholic welcome and my reports not unacceptable to his Majesty."

So ended the famous journey to Scotland.

There is another visit to be recorded at this time. In the summer of 1619 Jonson went to Oxford. Master of Arts in both Universities, by their favour and not his study—such is the brief summary noted by Drummond of his academic position. When the honour was conferred by Cambridge is unknown, but clearly he had in effect received both his degrees prior to the Scottish visit. The journey to Oxford in 1619, however, gave the University an opportunity of confirming the distinction, and on July 19th he was formally inducted in full convocation. Jonson's correspondence with Oxford and Cambridge was of long standing, as shown by his dedication of *Volpone* to the sister universities and by their performance of the play in 1606.

Jonson was drawn to Oxford in 1619 by his friend Richard Corbet, Senior Student at Christ Church, afterwards Bishop of Norwich. Jonson had known Corbet in London as a friendly scholar and a mighty drinker of sack. No one in those early days had expected that he would ever be a bishop. Corbet was a man of fancy who believed in fairies, a genial mystic who passed untimely into the shadow of reform. Jonson reached Oxford to find that his friend had just lost his father. The elder Corbet was nearly eighty when he died. Jonson had known him at Twickenham, a gardener among his flowers and trees, and he wrote at Oxford an epitaph touched with envy that any man could be so peaceful and so good.

Ben Jonson

A life that knew nor noise nor strife;
But was, by sweetening so his will,
All order and disposure still.
His mind as pure and neatly kept,
As were his nurseries, and swept
So of uncleanness or offence
That never came ill odour thence.

.   .   .   .   .   .

Much from him I profess I won,
And more and more I should have done,
But that I understood him scant.

Jonson could love this wise stillness of an old man
in his garden, but it was at the same time a thing
that awed him with its strangeness. Meditation, surrender and the open mind—these were things remote
from his disposition. The contemplative life, though
he felt its charm, was something which Jonson was
never brought to comprehend.

CHAPTER XII

Discoveries

JONSON is rarely to be found in slippers, and the nearest thing to catching him in the confessional mood is to read the commonplace book quaintly published among his collected works as the *Discoveries*. You will not take him by surprise. These notes are set down, with deliberation, to be read. But they ramble through a multitude of subjects, and the care used in their writing does not detract from the sincerity of the views expressed.

The reader will look first for things personal and he will find that they are few. There are, however, some precious lines upon memory in which the secret of Jonson's great learning is revealed. He laments that memory is the first of our faculties to be invaded by age: " I myself could, in my youth, have repeated all that I had ever read and so continued till I was past forty: since, it is much decayed in me. Yet I can repeat whole books that I have read and poems of some selected friends." Later he explains that memory is a natural gift in men of a slow habit of writing, thus confessing that he himself is neither swift nor ready: " Such as torture their writings and go into council for every word must needs fix somewhat and make it their own at last, though but through their vexation."

There is another passage in which, writing generally of good and bad men, Jonson looks suddenly at himself. " An innocent man ", he writes, " needs no

Ben Jonson

eloquence; his innocence is instead of it, else I had
never come off so many times from those precipices
whither men's malice pursued me." He then briefly
reviews the hazards of his career:

> It is true I have been accused to the Lords, to the King,
> and by great ones. But it happened my accusers . . . were
> driven, for want of crimes, to use invention . . . nor were
> they content to feign things against me, but to urge things
> feigned by the ignorant against my profession. . . . Nay,
> they would offer to urge my own writings against me;
> but by pieces (which was an excellent way of malice), as
> if any man's context might not seem dangerous and offen-
> sive if that which was knit to what went before were de-
> frauded of his beginning; or that things by themselves
> uttered might not seem subject to calumny which, read
> entire, would appear most free.

There follows a passage which brings him nearer
yet. For his enemies, he says, had also upbraided
his poverty:

> I confess she is my domestic; sober of diet, simple of
> habit, frugal, painful, a good counsellor to me, that keeps
> me from cruelty, pride, or other more delicate impertinences
> which are the nurse children of riches. But let them look
> over all the great and monstrous wickednesses, they shall
> never find those in poor families. They are the issues of
> the wealthy giants and the mighty hunters: whereas no
> great work, worthy of praise, but came out of poor cradles.
> It was the ancient poverty that founded commonweals,
> built cities, invented arts, made wholesome laws, armed
> men against vices, rewarded them with their own virtues
> and preserved the honour and state of nations till they
> betrayed themselves to riches.

There is more than a hint in these *Discoveries* that
Jonson might have followed his friends, Donne,
Corbet, Herrick and the rest, into the pulpit with
credit and conviction. For, on the vanities of this
world, he stands squarely with the prophets and

divines.　There are pages here and there that recall
the best of Latimer :

> What need hath nature of silver dishes, multitude of
> waiters, delicate pages, perfumed napkins ?　She requires
> meat only and hunger is not ambitious.　Can we think
> no wealth enough but such a state for which a man may
> be brought into a premunire, begged, proscribed, or
> poisoned ?　Oh, if a man could restrain the fancy of his
> gullet and groin, and think how many fires, how many
> kitchens, cooks, pastures and ploughed lands ; what orchards,
> stews, ponds and parks ; what velvets, tissues, embroideries,
> laces, he could lack ; and then, how short life is. . . .
> Have I not seen the pomp of a whole kingdom and what
> a foreign king could bring hither ?　All to make himself
> gazed and wondered at, laid forth as it were to the shew,
> and to vanish all away in a day ?　And shall that which
> could not fill the expectation of a few hours entertain and
> take up our whole lives ? . . .　While it boasted itself, it
> perished.　It is vile and a poor thing, to place our happiness
> on these desires.

Or again :

> There is nothing valiant or solid to be hoped for from
> such as are always kempt and perfumed, and every day
> smell of the tailor ; the exceedingly curious, that are wholly
> in mending such an imperfection in the face, in taking
> away the morphew in the neck, or bleaching their hands
> at midnight, gumming and bridling their beards, or making
> the waist small ; binding it with hoops while the mind
> runs to waste.　Too much pickedness is not manly. . . .
> Yet this is that wherewith the world is taken and runs
> mad to gaze on ; clothes and titles, the birdlime of Fools.

Here again is the preacher :

> I am glad when I see any man avoid the infamy of a
> vice ; but to shun the vice itself were better.　Till he do
> that he is but like the prentice, who, being loth to be
> spied by his master coming forth of Black Lucy's, went
> in again.　To whom his master cried : The more thou
> runnest that way to hide thyself the more than art in the
> place . . . I have known lawyers, divines, yea, great ones,
> of this heresy.

Ben Jonson

This is Jonson of Annandale, ready to bear witness. Sometimes the vein is short and we remember that this was, after all, no more than a commonplace book, such as any honest man might keep in all humility. " Ill fortune never crushed that man whom good fortune deceived not." Our idea of Jonson would not be complete if we did not know that he could be sententious and prepared to hold forth on occasion, and England was never too merry to listen to such Sabbatical exercises. Even Shakespeare capitulated to her love of an apothegm :

> There is a soul of goodness in things evil
> Would men observingly distil it out.

There are many sayings scattered through the *Discoveries* very proper to the man who of all titles liked best to be called honest. " I will have no man addict himself to me," he declares. " But if I have any thing right, defend it as Truth's, not mine, save as it conduceth to a common good. It profits not me to have any man fence or fight for me, to flourish or take a side. Stand for truth and 'tis enough."

Or again :

> Truth is man's proper good ; and the only unmortal thing was given to our mortality to use . . . Homer says he hates him worse than hell-mouth that utters one thing with his tongue and keeps another in his breast. Which high expression was founded on divine reason ; for a lying mouth is a stinking pit.

Elsewhere he writes :

> I have seen that poverty makes men do unfit things ; but honest men should not do them ; they should gain otherwise. Though a man be hungry, he should not play the parasite. That hour wherein I would repent me to be honest there were ways enow open to me to be rich. Flattery is a fine picklock of tender ears.

Much of this is common form, but, every now and

then, the poet comes breaking through. Note the unexpected conclusion of the following passage, in which a single warm phrase lifts it from the level of mere prophesying :

> What a deal of cold business, doth a man mis-spend the better part of life in ! in scattering compliments, tendering visits, gathering and venting views, following feasts and plays, making a little winter love in a dark corner.

Next to the passages in which Jonson takes himself for a theme or reveals a temperament are those in which he discusses questions directly concerning his own vocation. He writes in many places of style, of his debt to the ancients, of the poet's small reward, of his training and special qualities. All that we have been told or might suspect of Jonson's habit of composition is abundantly confirmed in the *Discoveries*. Jonson informed Drummond that he always wrote down his poetry first as prose. First he must know what exactly it was that he wished to say. So here he writes :

> In style, to consider first what ought to be written and after what manner, the writer must first think and excogitate his matter, then choose his words and examine the weight of either. Only then should he rank matter and words, so that the composition may be comely. He must beware of the froward conceits and first words that offer themselves ; often repeat what he has formerly written. The sum of all is that ready writing makes not good writing, but good writing brings on ready writing. Even, however, when we think we have got the faculty it is good to resist it. Though the practised author should work with his own faculties, it is good for the young writer to study others. Those who are familiar with the best authors will ultimately find in their own work something of their predecessors, and it will be all to their advantage to do so. For a man to write well there are three necessities : to read the best authors, observe the best speakers and much exercise of his own style.

Ben Jonson

Many striking passages witness to Jonson's unsleeping sense of language as the true measure of mind. *Oratio imago animi* he writes :

> Language most shows a man. Speak, that I may see thee. It springs out of the most retired and inmost parts of us and is the image of the parent of it, the mind. No glass renders a man's form or likeness so true as his speech.

Of all qualities in style Jonson insisted most upon the classical excellence. A man in his writing and in his speech must above all things be clear and accessible. Elegance should be the result of good order, restraint and concentration upon the matter in hand :

> A man should so deliver himself to the nature of the subject whereof he speaks that his reader may take knowledge of his discipline with some delight ; and so apparel fair and good matter that the studious of elegancy be not defrauded, redeem arts from their thorny and brakey seats, where they lie hid and overgrown with thorns, to a pure, open and flowery light ; where they may take the eye and be taken by the hand.

Jonson deprecated any deliberate singularity in style, but at the same time insisted that it should be individual and definite. He comments with equal asperity on both extremes—the writer who goes out of his way to be harsh and original and the writer who allows his pen to run with a spineless facility. Of the former he writes :

> There are others that in composition are nothing but what is rough and broken, and if it would come gently they trouble it of purpose. They would not have it run without rubs, as if that style were more manly that strokes the ear with a kind of unevenness. These men err not by chance but knowingly and willingly. They are like men that affect a fashion by themselves, have some singularity in a ruff, cloak or hatband ; or their beards specially cut to provoke beholders and set a mark upon themselves.

But on the smooth writers he is even more severe :

> Others there are that have no composition at all. . . .
> It runs and slides and only makes a sound. . . . You
> may measure these wits and find the depth of them with
> your middle finger. They are cream bowl or but puddle
> deep.

The termagant style of tragedy, which he frequently
mocks in his comedies, he subjects to a sober and
reasoned criticism. The language of poets should
differ from common speech, but their art should
give always the allusion of reality and their devices be
appropriate and, therefore, unobtrusive.

> The true artificer will not run away from nature as he
> were afraid of her, or depart from the life and the like-
> ness of truth, but speak to the capacity of his hearers.
> And though his language differ from the vulgar somewhat,
> it shall not fly from all humanity with the Tamerlanes
> and Tamer-Chams of the late age, which had nothing in
> them but scenical strutting and furious vociferation to
> warrant them to the ignorant gapers. He knows it is his
> only art so to carry it as none but artificers perceive it.

Jonson's debt to the ancients has been critically
considered elsewhere. His own declarations on the
subject are especially significant in view of the charges
brought against him so frequently that he was little
more than a " translating scholar ". There was
nothing pedantic or slavish in his allegiance. To
every age its wisdom. Each succeeding generation
must bring to the test of experience the observations
and conclusions of the authors of antiquity. Nothing,
he writes, can conduce more to letters than to examine
their writings, but no one should rest in their sole
authority or take anything upon trust from them.
They opened the gates and made the way that went
before us, but as guides not commanders. We
should admire and respect their wisdom, but we may

dissent from them without ingratitude, for they would be the last to envy their posterity for what it might add to the sum of human knowledge. Jonson emphatically repudiates the assumption that men should look back rather than forward :

> I cannot think Nature is so spent and decayed that she can bring forth nothing worth her former years. She is always the same, like herself ; and, when she collects her strength, is abler still.

All that Jonson writes of his vocation is candid, modest and sincere. His sense of dedication never failed him in misfortune. Others who had started with him turned aside, seeking other employment or confessing other loyalties. Jonson looked askance at them without envy. Only now and then, comparing the rewards of these fickle ones with his own hardship and poverty, did he venture a reproach to the Muse he had served so faithfully through the years :

> Poetry, in this latter age, hath proved but a mean mistress to such as have wholly addicted themselves to her or given their names up to her family. For those who have but saluted her on the by, and then tendered their visits elsewhere, she hath done much and advanced in the way of their own professions (with the law and the gospel) beyond all they could have hoped or done for themselves without her favour. Wherein she doth emulate the judicious but preposterous bounty of the times grandees, who accumulate all they can upon the parasite or freshman in their friendship ; but think an old client or honest servant bound by his place to write and starve.

Of politics and religion Jonson writes as a man who has not thought long or deeply. In such matters he was of the Renaissance not of the Reformation. His politics went no further than commendation of a good prince and his religion no further than an indifferent conformity and a plentiful lack of sympathy with the Puritans who mistrusted his calling.

Of the wise prince he wrote like a good subject born under the Tudors :

> After God nothing is to be loved of man like the prince ; he violates nature that doth it not with his whole heart. For when he hath put on the care of the public good and common safety, I am a wretch and put off man, if I do not reverence and honour him in whose charge all things divine and human are placed.

With the wisdom of the good prince he continually contrasts the folly and perversity of the vulgar :

> A prince has more business and trouble with them than ever Hercules had with the bull or any other beast, by how much they have more heads than will be reined with one bridle. There was not that variety of beasts in the ark as is of beastly natures in the multitude, especially when they come to that iniquity to censure their sovereign's actions.

The prince, however, must think and rule, not for himself, but for his people. His divine right rests on wisdom, service and clemency. The poet's eulogy and respect of good princes is only equalled by his stern censure of sceptred fools. " A prince without letters is a pilot without eyes," he declares ; and in another place he affirms : " A good King is a public servant." The prince must have a care, moreover, that the respect with which he is surrounded shall not give him an illusion of wisdom and skill which in reality he lacks :

> They say Princes learn no art truly but the art of horse-manship. The reason is, the brave beast is no flatterer. He will throw a prince as soon as his groom.

There is nothing slavish or mystical in Jonson's devotion to the throne and he glances severely at the vices of absolute rule : the good prince needs no spies, intelligencers to entrap true subjects ; he fears no libels, no treasons ; his people speak what they think ; he is guarded with his own benefits. There was here an implicit criticism of the King sitting in Star Chamber, which discounted much of the admiration given to a perfect sovereign. " Many punishments ", says the poet, " as much discredit a Prince as many funerals a physician, and those who counsel him to suppress opposition with severity are but the hangman's factors. The only way for a King to sit secure is so to govern his people that they shall have need of his administration."

> He ought to shear not to flay his sheep ; to take their fleeces not their fells. . . . He is the soul of the commonwealth and ought to cherish it as his own body. . . . He is an ill prince that so pulls his subjects feathers as he would not have them grow again, that makes his Exchequer a receipt for the spoils of those he governs.

There is much in this vein which would make uneasy reading for his royal masters. The royal breviary is arduous and complete :

> Study piety towards the subject ; show care to defend him. Be slow to punish in divers cases ; but be a sharp and severe revenger of open crimes. Break no decrees or dissolve no orders to slacken the strength of laws. Choose neither magistrates, civil or ecclesiastic, by favour or price, but with long disquisition and report of their worth by all suffrages. Sell no honours, nor give them hastily ; but bestow them with counsel and for reward . . . But above all the prince is to remember that, when the great day of account comes, which neither magistrate nor prince can shun, there will be required of him a reckoning for those whom he hath trusted as for himself, which he must provide. And if piety be wanting in the priests, equity in the judges, or the magistrate be found rated at a price, what justice or religion is to be expected ? Which are the only two attributes make Kings akin to gods.

Discoveries

What then of the King who is neither wise nor merciful ? Is it to be an axiom that the King can do no wrong ? It must be confessed that, for all his shrewd criticism of bad princes, Jonson came very near to the doctrine of non-resistance. The condition of the times may be such that innocence falls under suspicion and is punished :

> Let no man therefore murmur at the actions of the prince, who is placed so far above him. If he offend, he hath his discoverer. God hath a height beyond him. But where the Prince is good Euripides saith : God is a guest in a human body.

It is striking evidence of the tenacity of the Tudor system of government that a man like Jonson, by temperament rebellious, impatient and incapable of compromise or submission in the things that mattered, should still be faithful to ideas which a younger generation would soon be in arms to destroy or mitigate. His submission was instinctive and involuntary, but it was already hedged about with reservations. When Jonson praised a good prince, as when he paid his addresses to James or Charles, there was often more exhortation than compliment in his tributes.

Jonson on religion looks equally back to the Renaissance. " The strength of Empire is in religion "— that was as far as he would go. He writes a great deal of morality, but he writes like a pagan philosopher. Virtue is its own reward. There is never a hint in Jonson's writings of another world in which earthly wrongs and inequalities will be set right or any appeal to mystical sanctions and powers. There is never a suggestion that he has more respect for the Hebrew than for the classic poets and philosophers. His indifferent conversion to the Roman sect was natural enough in this essentially pagan husband of a Catholic wife. The kind gods of Olympus survive in the calendar of saints, and, though the yoke of Peter be heavy and his burden far from light, it involves less essential frustration and a negation of human values less entire than the tyrannies of Calvin or Knox. That Jonson was for many years a Catholic without prejudice is as comprehensible as his return to the protestant faith in a spirit of genial conformity. His religion was elsewhere. He can rise to no eloquence in matters of faith, and there is nowhere in his life or works any suggestion of mystical experience. For him there is no God but knowledge, and God hath no enemy but ignorance. You will look vainly in him for any deep sense or conviction of sin, and he expressly dismissed the whole Christian doctrine of evil.

> I know no disease of the soul but ignorance. . . . Great understandings are most racked and troubled with it : nay, sometimes they will choose to die than not to know the thing they study for. Think then what an evil it is, and what good the contrary.

The ignorance of which he writes, however, is not a mere lack of knowledge or training in the arts and sciences. It is rather a state of mind or condition of being—a wilful shutting of the reason and the faculties in blind submission to prejudice or authority. Of the " contrary " he declares :

> Knowledge is the action of the Soul, and is perfect without the senses, as having the seeds of all science and virtue in itself ; but not without the service of the senses ; by these organs the Soul works ; she is a perpetual agent, prompt and subtle ; but often flexible and erring, entangling herself like a silkworm ; but her reason is a weapon with two edges, and cuts through. In her indagations, ofttimes she takes in errors into her by the same conduits she doth truths.

Jonson, who knew no disease of the soul but ignorance, looked on at the theological controversies under

THE COUNTESS OF BEDFORD AS PENTHESILEA
Design by Inigo Jones for the Mask of Queens
Copyright of the Duke of Devonshire

which the Renaissance was stifled with indifference or disgust. But only once does he express himself with any heat on the subject :

> Some controverters in divinity are like swaggerers in a tavern, that catch that which stands next to them, the candlestick or pots ; turn everything into a weapon : oft-times they fight blindfold and both beat the air. The one milks a he-goat ; the other holds under a sieve. Their arguments are as fluxive as liquor spilt upon a table, which with your finger you may drain as you will. Such controversies or disputations (carried with more labour than profit) are odious ; where most times the truth is lost in the midst or left untouched. And the fruit of their fight is that they spit upon one another and are both defiled.

It is a fitting conclusion. Within a few years Milton was at war with Salmasius. Salmasius described his antagonist in doctrine as a blind puppy with guttering eyelids. Milton retorted in kind and in Whitehall the saints were ruling.

CHAPTER XIII

The Later Masks

THE masks have so far been taken as incidents in Jonson's career as a poet and dramatist with a livelihood to secure. They have also served to show that the " supposèdly rugged old bard " could be light, ingenious and merry, when his mood and company permitted, or stagger the world with his learning and logic when he so desired. The later masks reveal more completely the depth and variety of his genius and the environment in which he worked as the first laureate of England.

This later series began with *Christmas His Mask* presented at Court in December, 1616. Christmas, Christmas of London, Captain Christmas, has not yet assumed his long white beard and his scarlet gown. He wears round hose and long stockings, a close doublet, a high-crowned hat, little ruffs and white shoes. His gaiters and scarves are tied across and his drum is beaten before him. His beard is long and thin. He is no dangerous person, but old Gregory Christmas still, and, though he comes out of Pope's Head Alley, professes to be as good a Protestant as any in his parish. He travels with his sons and daughters—Misrule, like a reveller; Carol, with his song book; Minced Pie, like a fine cook's wife; Gambol, like a tumbler; Post and Pair, with a pair-royal of aces in his cap; New Year's Gift, with his hat full of broaches and a collar of ginger-bread; Mumming, in a masking pied suit; Wassel, with a brown bowl. Offering and Baby-Cake bring up the

rear. It is an innocent, familiar gambol, in which
Cupid appears as a London apprentice and Venus as
a deaf but loquacious tirewoman.

The Mask of Lethe, presented in February of the
following year in the house of Lord Hay by divers
of noble quality, his friends, for the entertainment of
the French Ambassador, was elegant rather than
familiar. Imaginary ghosts conveyed by Charon over
Styx are found to be but wan lovers who come to
drink of the waters of Lethe and be cured:

> Come do not call it Cupid's crime
> You were thought dead before your time;
>   Go, take the ladies forth, and talk,
>   And touch and taste too; ghosts can walk.
> 'Twixt eyes, tongues, hands, the mutual strife
> Is bred that tries the truth of life.

Jonson was in this year a happy man. *The Mask
of Lethe* was followed at Christmas by *A Vision of
Delight*. Delight brings with her to Whitehall Grace,
Love, Harmony, Revel, Sport, Laughter and Wonder.
Fancy also bears a part; and, if she be ingenious
rather than free-footed, Wonder atones by celebrating
the pleasures of Spring in numbers, rare in our poet,
showing that he can walk with pleasure under open skies:

> How comes it winter is so quite forced hence
> And locked up underground? that every sense
> Hath several objects? trees have got their heads,
> The fields their coats? that now the shining meads
> Do boast the paunce, the lily, and the rose?

There is a fluid grace in these pastoral exercises:

> How is't each bough a several music yields?
> The lusty throstle, early nightingale,
> Accord in tune, though vary in their tale?
> The chirping swallow, called forth by the sun,
> And crested lark doth his division run?
> The yellow bees the air with murmur fill?
> The finches carol, and the turtles bill?
> Whose power is this? what god?

Ben Jonson

The poet's questions receive a royal answer :

> Behold a King
> Whose presence maketh this perpetual spring.

Even in the royal presence Jonson, however, keeps his head. The herds, the flocks, the grass, the trees do all confess King James, but Chorus points quickly away to where the courtiers are waiting to enter for the dance. These were growths that confessed the King with a more obvious propriety.

Pleasure Reconciled to Virtue, presented before King James on Twelfth Night in January, 1618–19, was the first mask in which Prince Charles was allowed to take part. It opens with a mighty hymn, sung in full chorus :

> Room! room! make room for the Bouncing Belly.

Jonson, introducing Comus and his crew, was here presenting England's carnival, and King James liked it so well that he had it repeated, with additions, most appropriately, on Shrove Tuesday of the same year. Comus was not yet the enemy of souls. Fifteen years later Milton was to write the last and greatest of English masks—a hymn to chastity and meditation. Comus would then be shown as a damned magician, lord of the Sensual Stye. Milton's Comus was a hymn to the saints triumphant. Jonson's Comus, borne in triumph as the god of cheer, his head crowned with roses and his hair curled, entering to the wild music of cymbals, flutes and tabors, was a tribute to man secular and unredeemed. He breaks all his girdles, but breaks forth a god. He is prime master of arts and the giver of wit. His good cheer is of the flesh, but honest men may drink of the bowl of Hercules if it be remembered that such draughts were the reward of thirsty heroes. Jonson censures his Comus in excess but not in kind, and nowhere does his author more plainly declare himself to be of the school of Epicurus :

> There should be a cessation of all jars
> 'Twixt Virtue and her noted opposite.

The real enemy is immoderation. The secret of life is to take your pleasures wisely, and Hercules, chiding the followers of Comus, rebukes, not their enjoyment of good things, but their folly in destroying a wise appetite by overfeeding :

> Can this be pleasure to extinguish man
> Or so quite change him in his figure ? Can
> The Belly love his pain, and be content
> With no delight but what's a punishment ?
> These monsters plague themselves.

In the end pleasure is reconciled to virtue. What though Comus, god of cheer, be beaten from his grove ?

> Though pleasure lead,
> Fear not to follow.
> They who are bred
>   Within the hill
>   Of skill
> May safely tread
> What path they will ;
> No ground of good is hollow.

King James showed excellent taste in commending this small morality which agreeably combines a sound ethic with a merriment as robust and free as its author. Jonson, repeating it on Shrove Tuesday—the day was an omen—added appropriately, since Prince Charles was the first performer, an anti-mask in Honour of Wales. The poet is scolded by visitors from that country for having gone to Africa for the mountain which served his maskers for a background. Why Atlas ? Has not Wales as good mountains to show ? " There is a great huge deal of anger upon you from all Wales and the nation ", protests one of these offended gentlemen to the King himself, " that your worship should suffer our young Master Charles, your worship's son and heir and Prince of Wales, the first time he ever dance, to be put up in a mountain (God knows where) by a palterly poet . . . when it is known his Highness has as goodly mountains and as tall hills of his own (look you, do you see now) and of as good standing and as good descent as the proudest Atlas christened." His Majesty is familiarly urged to come to Wales and judge of the matter for himself. This Welshman has little regard for the poet's maskers, dancing about Comus in the form of bottles and tuns ; the very beasts of Wales can do better. The goatherd's wife makes music to the goats as they come from the hills, and the Welsh goat is an excellent dancer. The country itself is a very garden and seed-plot of honest minds and men, never mutinous, but stout, valiant, courteous, hospitable, temperate, ingenious, capable of all good arts, most lovingly constant, charitable, great antiquaries, religious preservers of their gentry and genealogy, as they are zealous and knowing in religion.

The masks of this period are happy work. Jonson has thrown off the load of learning carried by *The Mask of Queens*, and there is none but the gentlest satire even by the way.

News from the New World Discovered in the Moon, presented in 1620 before the King on Twelfth Night and again on Shrove Tuesday, was perhaps the happiest of them all. Jonson had just returned from his journey to Scotland. The King had missed him and confessed as much. To a chorus of friendly compliment and persuasion Jonson had been put to work again.

The new mask was written for the most part in prose and it prompts a regret that the author did not use prose more often. The fun is all in the best of humour. Jonson has become a public institution and is, therefore, good enough matter for a public jest. His poet has been to the moon and there is one who would know : " Did he undertake this journey, I pray you, to the moon on foot. . . . Because one of our greatest poets went to Edinburgh on foot, and came back. Marry, he has been restive ever since." But this poet did not go to the moon on foot. Nor in Endymion's way, by rapture in sleep or a dream. Nor in Menippus' way, by wing. Nor in the way of Empedocles who, " when he leaped into Etna, having a dry sear body and light, the smoke took him and whift him up into the moon, where he lives yet moving up and down like a feather, all soot and embers, coming out of that coal pit ". He went, seemingly, " by the neat and clean power of poetry, the mistress of all discovery ".

There is this, too, of taverns, between a factor and a herald :

Factor. What inns or alehouses are there in the moon. Does he tell you ?
Herald. Truly I have not asked him that.
Factor. Nor were you best, I believe.
Herald. Why in travel a man knows these things without offence. I am sure, if he be a good poet, he has discovered a good tavern in his time.
Factor. That he has. I should think the worse of his verse else.

The poet was glancing, in all security, at his own foibles. One was taverns. The other was antiquity. To one who shows small respect for the stale ensigns of the man in the moon—his dog and his bush of thorns—the wanderer exclaims : " Sir, nothing against antiquity, I pray you. I must not hear ill of antiquity." It is pleasant to find Jonson so completely disarmed.

Ben Jonson

He has a smile for everyone in this holiday mood : for the anabaptists who in the moon, having no controversies, live dumb as fishes and have leave only to hum and ha, not daring to prophesy or start up upon stools to raise doctrines; for the lovers, as fantastic in the moon as on the earth, but happier in that they have a covert when they please more private than any Hyde Park in christendom for " they do all in clouds there ; they walk in the clouds, they sit in the clouds, they lie in the clouds, they ride and tumble in the clouds ". Their coaches are clouds, and the coachman, with cheeks like a trumpeter and a wind in his mouth, to blow them along. Best of all, there are mists in the moon and a man that owes money needs no other protection.

There followed a dance of curious fowl and of maskers who came down from the region of the moon covered with icicles which melt in the warmth and splendour of the King's Majesty to broken verses such as James, author of " Reulis and Cautelis of Scottis Poesie ", was likely to approve.

The Gipsies Metamorphosed, thrice presented to King James, first at Burleigh on the Hill, next at Belvoir and lastly at Windsor in August, 1621, is a notable example of the thoroughness with which Jonson mastered any subject with which he chose to concern himself. He writes of gypsies as though he had been born and bred in a caravan, and finds for them, conscientiously, a vocabulary as coarse as their condition. But the erudite veracity of the piece—there was no sea-coast in this Bohemia—was less remarkable than the familiarity with which the author approached his distinguished audience. Since this was a mask of gypsies, those present must have their fortunes read and the poet was not afraid to be saucy to King, Prince or ladies. He reads in the royal hand that his

The Later Masks

Majesty loves horse and hound; that he hunts the stag for the weal of his body; that he is no great wencher, although by no means incapable; that he is an honest, good man who has a care to his bairns; that he has some bookcraft. In the Prince's hand he looks for evidence of what his bride may expect from her marriage. What should it be:

> Save the promise before day
> Of a little James to play,
>   Hereafter,
> 'Twixt his grandsire's knees, and move
>   All the pretty ways of love
>   And laughter.

There were some charming lines for my lady of Rutland:

> To be loved where most you love
> Is the worst that you shall prove;
> And by him to be embraced,
> Who so long hath known you chaste,
> Wise and fair; whilst you renew
> Joys to him, and he to you;
>   And, when both your years are told,
>   Neither think the other old.

The hand of my lady of Buckingham proclaims, however, the greatest felon in the land. She has a face too slippery to be looked upon by any man with safety. My Lord Keeper has an innocent hand—luckily, for he carries the King's conscience in his breast. The Lord Treasurer has a clean palm, which again is lucky, because he has charge of the King's purse.

On Twelfth Night of the following years, 1622-3-4, were presented at Court in succession *The Mask of Augurs, Time Vindicated to Himself and his Honours* and *Neptune's Triumph.*

The Mask of Augurs contained several anti-masks, in which the author brought in characters from the buttery-hatch—a brewer's man, a lighterman, an ale-

Ben Jonson

wife and a bearman with three dancing bears. Apollo
was commanded by Jove to visit King James and to
rear in Britain a college of tuneful augurs to assist
his Majesty with their divining skill. The signs were
relevant. The birds that flew were a dove bringing
peace and an owl bringing wisdom and content.
Finally, Jove throned in heaven was disclosed presiding
over a senate of the gods and promising the Earth
that King James shall long be spared :

> Your wish is blest,
> Jove knocks his chin against his breast
> And firms it with the rest.

Time Vindicated was presented as a defence of the
age against its satirists. Prince Charles, who had led
the tuneful Augurs, again played the principal part,
treading his measures with the wife of the French
Ambassador. The anti-maskers were of mutes ador-
ing Chronomastix, armed with a whip to lash the
age, and of tumblers and jugglers, brought on by a
cat and fiddle. It is a token of Jonson's happy mood
that Chronomastix, claiming to scourge the vices of
men, is put to shame. Some critics identify him as
George Wither, author of *Abuses Stript and Whipt*.
Wither drove a lively pen on behalf of the Puritans
and was fair game for a poet who found his inspiration
in a tavern. The mask concluded with a cunning
chorus in praise of hunting :

> Hunting, it is the noblest exercise,
> Makes men laborious, active, wise ;

Let all men look to the King :

> Turn hunters then,
> But not of men ;
> Follow his ample
> And just example,
> That hates all chase of malice and of blood,
> And studies only ways of good,

250

To keep soft peace in breath.
Man should not do mankind to death,
  But strike the enemies of man.
  Kill vices, if you can:
  They are your wildest beasts,
And, when they thickest fall, you make the
  Gods true feasts.

In October, 1623, Prince Charles returned from his visit to Spain in search of a royal wife. With Buckingham for a master of the ceremonies, he had successfully scandalised the Spanish nation, and his failure to secure a Spanish princess had made him for the moment almost a popular hero. Here, in any case, was a relevant subject for a mask, and Jonson, on Twelfth Night of the year following, celebrated, with unusual magnificence, *Neptune's Triumph for the Return of Albion*.

  The mighty Neptune, mighty in his styles,
  And large command of waters and of isles

had sent forth his son Albion to Celtiberia. For his conveyance home he had since dispatched a floating island. This was a triumph of uncommon magnificence. The heavens opened above the island to disclose Apollo, Mercury and the goddess Harmony, the palace or house of Oceanus being discovered later with loud music. The anti-masks were of savoury dishes, issuing from a pot and a service of pickled sailors. The mask contains a protest on the part of the poet-presenter against the introduction of anti-masks as being " things heterogeneous to all device, mere by-works and at best outlandish nothings "—an odd fling from an author who made the anti-mask an important and effective feature of his compositions in this kind.

Pan's Anniversary or *The Shepherds*, produced in 1625, was the last of the masks witnessed by King James. It reveals a side of Jonson, lover of nature, which appeared but seldom in his plays till he wrote his last dramatic elegy of *The Sad Shepherd*. It is startling to discover that Jonson knew his wild flowers as well as any countryman :

> Well done, my pretty ones, rain roses still,
> Until the last be dropt : then hence and fill
> Your fragrant prickles for a second shower.
> Bring corn-flag, tulips, and Adonis' flower,
> Fair ox-eye, goldylocks and columbine,
> Pinks, goulands, king-cups, and sweet sops-in-wine,
> Blue harebells, pagles, pansies, calaminth,
> Flower-gentle and the fair-haired hyacinth.
> Bring rich carnations, flower-de-luces, lilies,
> The checked and purple-ringèd daffodillies,
> Bright crown-imperial, kingspear, holyhocks,
> Sweet Venus-navel and soft lady-smocks.
> Bring too——

But the list is already long enough to show that this poet of the tavern could walk in the fields and lanes with an open eye and a mind at ease.

The mask concludes with a series of hymns to Pan, disclosing a feeling for nature which is commonly reserved, against all evidence, for the romantic poets of the nineteenth century :

> Pan is our all, by him we breathe, we live,
> We move, we are ; 'tis he our lambs doth rear,
> Our flocks doth bless, and from the store doth give
> The warm and finer fleeces that we wear.
> He keeps away all heats and colds,
> Drives all diseases from our folds ;
> Makes everywhere the spring to dwell,
> The ewes to feed, their udders swell ;
> But, if he frown, the sheep, alas !
> The shepherds wither and the grass.

Prince Charles had now for several years taken the lead in the yearly masks at Twelfth Night. He was praised for his elegance and Jonson wisely provided that he should be ever grave and magnificent, screening him from the familiarities of presenters and the rude entries of the anti-mask. King James had always liked to be approached as a good fellow. But how would the new King receive such liberties? Jonson prudently refrained from experiment. The masks which he wrote for King Charles show a careful respect for the throne.

The first of them, presented under the name of *The Fortunate Islands*, was mainly repetition. Charles, remembering with pleasure how in 1624 he had played Albion in *Neptune's Triumph*, asked that the mask should be revised and presented in 1626. In a new introduction the presenter, Johphil, an airy spirit, appears in a lightly satirical sketch of the Rosicrucian mysteries. The subject was topical, for it was then the fashion to be burying white wands in the ground to catch fairies and to be muttering prayers in the woods to raise a salamander. The anti-mask culminated in a dance of famous characters raised by a magic ointment, of whom the chief was Master Skelton, whom Jonson admired as a poet who had contrived to utter much sound sense and effective criticism under a cloak of ragged rhymes and boisterous conceits. The foolery was kept within decent bounds; but, even so, the royal indulgence was craved: great King, your pardon if desire to please have trespassed. Jonson himself could not, alas! be present. With the death of James his happy period had passed and already he had been struck with the palsy from which he never wholly recovered. His muse, as he phrases it later, was "fixed to the bed and boards."

It was four years before Jonson, working with Inigo Jones, presented *Loves Triumph through Callipolis*. The characters of the mask were foolish lovers "whose distracted comedy and confused affections were contrasted with the right, noble way of loving" illustrated in the mask itself. The royal orders were exacting and precise. The inventors had been commanded "to think on something worthy of his Majesty's putting into act, with a selected company of his lords and gentlemen, for the honour of his court and the dignity of that heroic love and regal respect borne by him to his unmatchable lady and spouse the Queen's majesty". The King appeared in person as the Heroical Lover. Supporting him were lovers severally described as Provident, Judicious, Secret, Valiant, Witty, Jovial, Secure, Substantial, Modest, Candid, Courteous, Elegant, Rational and Magnificent.

This was a King's Mask, presented to the Queen. On the following Shrove Tuesday the compliment was returned and *Chloridia*, a Queen's Mask, was presented to the King. It was agreed, after consultation, that the composition should celebrate "some rites done to the goddess Chloris", who, in a general council of the gods, was to be proclaimed goddess of the flowers. Inigo Jones provided a pleasant landscape, with fountains and young trees and adorned with flowers "which did imitate the pleasant spring". The principal part in the anti-mask was borne by Jeffrey Hudson, the Queen's dwarf, richly apparelled as a prince of Hell, whither Cupid, smarting from neglect by the gods, had gone to make a party against them. Hudson was a very proper man, only eighteen inches high when, at nine years old, he had first been presented at Court. At Burleigh in 1626 he had been served up to the King and Queen in a pie, and the Queen, taking a fancy to him, had put him among her pages at Whitehall. Jonson wrote for him a pretty speech telling how Cupid had put Hades to sixes and sevens : Tantalus is fallen to his fruit and has a river before him running excellent wine : Ixion, loosed from his wheel, has turned dancer and is cutting capers ; Sisyphus is grown a master bowler, challenging all the parsons to a game ; the Furies are playing at nine-pins. The anti-mask was a dance of Tempest, Winds, Lightnings, Thunder, Rain and Snow. The scene was then " changed into a delicious place "— the bower of Chloris where the Queen sat as Chloris herself with fourteen nymphs.

This was the last mask written by Jonson in collaboration with Inigo Jones. A fierce and famous quarrel had broken out between them, and King Charles, preferring Inigo to Ben, called no more upon his father's faithful servant. There remain two small " Entertainments " to record—both written for the Earl of Newcastle, who in 1633 and 1634 entertained the King first at Bolsover and afterwards at Welbeck. Charles in 1633 was going north to his coronation in Scotland. In 1634 he was returning to London. Many great families feasted him, but none so splendidly as Newcastle. Clarendon wrote in his history :

> Both the King and court were received and entertained by the Earl of Newcastle, and at his own proper expense, in such a wonderful manner and an excess of feasting as had scarce ever before been known in England, and would be still thought very prodigious if the same noble person had not within a year . . . made the King and Queen a more stupendous entertainment, which, God be thanked, though possibly it might too much whet the appetite of others to excess, no man ever after imitated.

Jonson's share in these splendours was to contribute, in *Love's Welcome to Welbeck* and *Love's Welcome to Bolsover*, a short introduction to a course at quintain performed by the local gentry. The first Welcome cost the Earl five thousand pounds and the second from fourteen to fifteen thousand pounds.

The quarrel between Ben Jonson and Inigo Jones, which was one of the principal reasons of Jonson's neglect and poverty in his last years, was of long standing. There was no serious breach until 1630 ; but Jonson in 1619 was already intimating that the partnership was enforced rather than friendly. Drummond records him as saying to Prince Charles that " when he wanted words to express the greatest villain in the world he would call him an Inigo ", and Drummond notes in another place : " Jones having accused him (Jonson) for naming him, behind his back, a fool, he denied it ; but, says he, I said he was an arrant knave and I avouch it." The collaboration, however, was too profitable to be broken and it continued for another fourteen years. Jones was vain, greedy of honours, a bad friend and a mean antagonist. But he was good company. He could set the table on a roar and, if his wit failed, he would jump over the chairs to amuse his royal master. The relations between Jones and Jonson at Whitehall were curiously similar, even in detail, to those which existed later between Molière and Lulli at Versailles. Jones, like Lulli, clowned his way into the royal favour, and finally engrossed it. Jones jumped over chairs to the royal delight. Lulli on one occasion jumped from the stage crash into the middle of a harpsichord, splitting it to fragments.

To Jonson, priest of Apollo, poetry was the soul of the mask ; spectacle was no more than the outward form. To Jones the mask lived or died by its investiture. It was the show folk came to see, and the poetry was merely his opportunity. *Chloridia* brought the question of precedence to a head. Jonson, publishing his mask, recorded on the title-page that the " inventors " were Ben Jonson and Inigo Jones. Jones thought the names should be reversed. Jonson, on the contrary, thought it was hardly necessary for the name of Jones to be mentioned at all. Jonson never stood a chance with Charles against such a courtier and Inigo prevailed. A year later, on January 12th, 1631, Mr. Pory, writing to Sir Thomas Packering, informed him that a new mask, then under preparation, was by one, Aurelian Townshend, " Ben Jonson being for this time discarded by reason of the predominant power of his antagonist, Inigo Jones, who this time twelvemonth was angry with him for putting his own name first in the title page ".

Jonson, though sick, was not easily put down. Nor might he be persuaded to a peace. From his bed he issued a famous *Expostulation with Inigo Jones*, glancing bitterly—for this was what really mattered— at those who in a mechanic age were more taken with properties and engines than with the poet's art. In conclusion, he left his enemy in possession of the field. Inigo, claiming everything for himself, had grown too strong : he could now swim without cork. Thus far the *Expostulation*. It was supplemented by two epigrams, the first concluding with the only good line that came out of the quarrel :

Thy forehead is too narrow for my brand.

The matter, however, was not yet concluded. In 1633 Jonson submitted to the Master of the Revels a new comedy entitled *A Tale of a Tub*. Therein was found a ferocious satire upon Inigo Jones, appearing under the name of Vitruvius Hoop. The office book of the Master of Revels contains the following entry : " Vitruvius Hoop's part wholly struck out, and the motion of a tub, by command from my Lord Chamberlain ; exceptions being taken against it by Inigo Jones, surveyor of the King's Works, as a personal injury unto him." Posterity was thus spared or cheated of seeing Jonson, increasingly a derelict of the great world, attacking with savage impotence the man on whom for the moment success was shining. Only a mutilated passage here and there remains of the original satire. Vitruvius Hoop in the permitted version was replaced by one Medley, son of a weaver and a professor among the architects, learned in the social dimensions (rumour had it that Jones was then hoping to become a marquis):

> I have upon my rule here
> The just proportions of a knight, a squire,
> With a tame justice, or an officer rampant,
> Upon the bench, from the high constable
> Down to the headborough or tithing man,
> Or meanest minister of the place.

It is the poet's fortune, wrote Jonson in his Epilogue to this play, to be up early but never to be near the prizes. It is your Medlays who win the house. Jonson glances here and there at the effective blend of self-conceit and servility which made Jones so dangerous an antagonist, but his enemy hides safely enough from posterity in pages that few will read.

It was characteristic of Jonson that, though his quarrel with Inigo was clearly putting him out of favour with the Court, he did not shrink from pursuing it even in the royal presence. When the King came to Bolsover in July, 1634, Vitruvius, driven from his tub, appeared in the course of *Love's Welcome* as a surveyor conducting a dance of mechanics. Therein Inigo was mocked, along with his musical, arithmetical and geometrical gamesters, his true mathematical boys. Faithful friends looked with misgiving upon these exercises. Jones was too strong to be dislodged and the King made no secret of his displeasure. Howell, one of the younger sons of Ben, wrote in May, 1635, to his honoured friend and father, Mr. Ben Jonson, referring to the *Expostulation* and warning him to let sleeping surveyors lie : " I heard you censured lately at Court that you have lighted too foul on Sir Inigo, and that you write with a porcupine's quill, dipt in too much gall." On July 5th Howell was moved to send his friend a more specific warning : " If your spirit will not let you retract, yet you shall do well to repress any more copies of the satire ; for, to deal plainly with you, you have lost some ground at Court by it ; and, as I hear from a good hand, the King, who hath so great a judgment in poetry (as in all things else) is not well pleased therewith."

Jonson listened at last to honest reason so frankly conveyed. He recalled the *Expostulation*. It was too late, however, to recover all the copies, and Jonson, though he never recovered the King's ear, still has the ear of posterity.

CHAPTER XIV

Decline and Fall

MISFORTUNES came not single spies but in battalions. In 1623 Jonson lost his library. In 1625 he lost King James. In 1626 he was struck with the palsy. In 1628 he became somehow involved with the authorities in connection with the assassination of the Duke of Buckingham. From 1626 to 1631, for four years, there was no mask at Court. He returned to the stage in 1628 with *The New Inn*, but the play was so ill-received that he swore never to write another. In 1629 he was in such straits for money that he was driven to petition his Majesty for a hundred pounds. In 1630 came the final breach with Inigo Jones. In 1631 the City, which in 1628 had appointed him chronologer, an office which brought him in a " chanderly pension " of £33 6s. 8d. per annum, withdrew the grant " until he should have presented to the Court some fruits of his labours in that place ". The Aldermen evidently regarded the appointment as involving certain obligations towards the City clocks. Jonson had regarded it as a sinecure.

Jonson told Drummond in 1618 that often he had been obliged by necessity to devour his books. But as often as he sold them he replenished his store and we know that every year Pembroke gave him twenty pounds to buy such as he fancied or required. The books burned in 1623 were, therefore, less regretted than certain unpublished works of his own which also perished. Jonson commemorated the event in an *Execration upon Vulcan* in which he gave a list of the MSS. destroyed. There was a complete translation of Horace's *Art of Poetry*, illustrated with notes from Aristotle, an English grammar, an account of his journey into Scotland, an unfinished drama on Persephone, a history nearly finished of the reign of Henry V of England and the results of his reading for twenty-four years of divine and pagan authors. The grammar, he says, was to teach children the purity of language, an office neglected by their nurses, while the account of the journey into Scotland contained " all the adventures ". To the history of Henry V Carew, Selden and Cotton had contributed. All this work was irreplaceably lost except the text of the translation from Horace, published after Jonson's death, and a few fragments of the English grammar.

The *Execration*, in view of these losses, is in excellent humour. The poet can think of no reason why Vulcan should have singled him out as a victim, to destroy in an hour so many years of labour. There was nothing on his shelves to call down fire—no heresy, imposture, witchcraft, lewdness or folly. And what a waste of good fuel !

> Thou might'st have yet enjoyed thy cruelty
> With some more thrift and more variety ;
> Thou might'st have had me perish piece by piece,
> To light tobacco or save roasted geese,
> Singe capons or crisp pigs, dropping their eyes ;
> Condemned me to the ovens with the pies.

Vulcan, moreover, should have given warning of his intention. The poet would then have crammed his shelves in happy haste with things fit for burning—heathen abominations like the Talmud and the Alcoran ; the whole sum of errant knighthood, with its dames and dwarfs, its mad Rolands and sweet Olivers ; the works of alchemists ; pamphlets and papers from the Pope's Head Alley and the mad preachings of Ball.

Other famous fires are remembered. Jonson had seen the fire that burned down the Globe on Bankside in 1613. That was a crime for which Vulcan doubtless had reasons of his own, for Burbage's theatre was built on a site dedicated from time immemorial to the service of Venus. There she had " maintained the mystery," and still it smouldered. Jonson might have added that on Bankside her rites were wont to be performed in so disorderly a fashion that the King had ordered all her houses to be pulled down, despite the fact that they paid good rent to the Bishop of Winchester. The poet, in conclusion, urges the lame god to confine his activities henceforth to foreign lands. There is scope for him enough in the Low Countries, where he may do his mischiefs to the satisfaction of all concerned : blow up, mine, countermine, produce his engines of murder, and be praised for all his devices :

> We ask your absence here ; we all love peace,
> And pray the fruits thereof and the increase ;
> So doth the King, and most of the King's men
> That have good places.

Little is known of the obscure interrogation to which Jonson was submitted as a sequel to the assassination of the Duke of Buckingham in 1628. Apparently the whole affair was due to a misunderstanding. There were many people in the country who felt that the life of Buckingham who, in 1626, had avoided impeachment only by the dissolution of Parliament, was in justice forfeit to the nation. So long as he had been idle or employed upon ludicrous foreign missions he had been no more than a public nuisance. As an active leader of the English forces, naval or military, he was a public calamity. Felton, who slew him in

August, 1628, was very properly hanged, but was secretly regarded as a general benefactor. Verses to that effect, committed to paper by a person unknown and addressed to Felton, the man of Suffolk, fell into the hand of Sir Robert Cotton, one of the oldest and best friends of Jonson :

> Farewell ! for thy brave sake we shall not send
> Henceforth commanders enemies to defend ;
> Nor will it ever our just monarch please
> To keep an Admiral to lose our seas.

Cotton showed Jonson the verses and asked whether he knew the author. Perhaps he suspected Jonson himself. Jonson not only denied all knowledge of the author but condemned the sentiment. At this stage the authorities intervened, and Jonson was asked in October to call upon the Attorney-General. Jonson swore upon his hope of heaven that the only copy of the verses he had ever seen or handled was the one which Cotton had shown him. Suspicion fell upon a certain Townley, student of Christ Church and a popular preacher. Townley was Jonson's friend and had fled to Holland. Jonson must, therefore, explain his friendship. Had he not once given a dagger to Townley ? The drift of the question is not clear. The gift of a dagger to a man who was alleged to have written a poem in praise of an assassin was presumably regarded as a highly suspicious circumstance. Jonson did not deny the dagger. He was even circumstantial about it. It had a white handle and he had worn it at his belt. One day, after a sermon at St. Margaret's, Townley had admired it, and a few days later, after supper, Jonson had given it to his friend. All this doubtless seemed uncommonly sinister to the authorities, but no connection could be proved between the present to Townley and the assassination of Buckingham. There was a dagger in both, and there it ended. Jonson was released, but there had been enough to alarm and disturb an ageing poet, not in the best of health. There seemed to be no trouble in the State which did not sooner or later come his way.

The death of King James was a more serious disaster. King Charles remembered with kindness that Jonson had helped him frequently to appear with distinction in a series of entertainments which the poet's learning and high position had redeemed from frivolity. He remembered also that Jonson had not inelegantly amused and distracted his father. But Charles, in his tastes and pleasures, was negative and fastidious. It was not in his nature to love the presence of a man who weighed twenty stone, spoke his mind with force and freedom, and brought with him into Whitehall airs from the tavern. There were to be no more quips and quiddities or telling of royal hands. Charles would be kind, when reminded that kindness was necessary, but he would never be familiar.

Three of the King's interventions in Jonson's favour are historic. There is a fourth, better known than all the rest, invented by Colley Cibber and inserted by Smollett in his *History of England*. Cibber relates, not in malice but because the fiction pleased him, that Jonson in 1629 was sick, poor, and lodged in an obscure alley. The King, supplicated in his favour, sent him ten guineas. When the messenger delivered the sum Jonson took it in his hand and said : " His Majesty has sent me ten guineas because I am poor and live in an alley ; go and tell him that his soul lives in an alley." This is a grotesque inversion. Jonson, poor and sick, as the fiction truthfully records, personally applied to the King for assistance. Charles sent him not ten guineas, but a hundred pounds, and

Decline and Fall

the poet, sincerely grateful, replied in an epigram. He referred to the holy gifts of grace annexed to the person of his Majesty which enabled him to cure the King's evil in his subjects, and added with a grim, respectful wit :

> But thou wilt yet a kinglier mastery try,
> To cure the *poet's evil*, poverty.

In the same year Jonson addressed a second epigram to the great and good King Charles upon his birthday. It was inscribed as by his Majesty's most humble and *thankful* servant, Ben Jonson. He was still drawing the hundred marks a year, accorded to him as the laureate of King James, and in March, 1630, he petitioned King Charles to convert them into pounds. Charles consented, issuing a warrant which smiled in its conclusion upon the poet's known addiction to good wine, adding to the pension a tierce of canary to be continued to his successors for three hundred years. The hundred pounds is to be paid quarterly " in consideration of the good and acceptable service done unto us and our said father by the said Ben Jonson, and especially to encourage him to proceed in those exercises of his wit and pen which we have enjoined unto him and which we expect from him ". The King also gives and grants to the said poet " one terse of canary wine yearly to have, hold, perceive, receive and take . . . out of our store of wines yearly and from time to time remaining at or in our cellars within or belonging to our palace of Whitehall ".

Such was the original charter of our English laureates. Jonson regarded it as conveying an office not a pleasantry. In the first year of his appointment he celebrated in epigrams the King's birthday, the birth of a prince and the lying-in of the Queen. For the Queen's birthday an epigram, however, would

Ben Jonson

not suffice. All the nine muses in nine graceful
stanzas commemorated her Majesty in an ode. Jonson's performances as a laureate were not remarkable.
Their chief merit was to be punctual.

Jonson, performing the duties of his office, claimed
also the rewards. The King's household in 1630
was dilatory. Jonson, wishing to have, hold, perceive, receive and take his quarterly allowance of sack,
addressed to them an expostulation :

> What can the cause be, when the King hath given
> His poet sack, the Household will not pay ?
>
> . . . . . .
>
> Twere better spare a butt than spill his muse;
> For in the genius of a poet's verse
> The King's fame lives. Go now, deny his terse !

Of the noble friends who stood by Jonson in adversity the most notably generous was the Earl of Newcastle. It was to Newcastle that Jonson complained
when the Aldermen withdrew his annuity as Chronologer to the City. On another occasion Jonson
declares that he has neither fortune to repay nor
security to engage ; yet ventures to ask succour for
his present necessities at this good time of Easter.
More welcome than charity, however prompt and
gracious, was honest employment. It was at the
darkest moment of the poet's career, on the morrow
of his quarrel with Inigo Jones, when even the King
had intimated displeasure, that Newcastle sent for
Jonson and asked him to write the *Welcome to Welbeck*.
On this occasion Jonson wrote : " God sends you
these chargeable and magnificent honours of making
feasts to mix with your charitable succours dropt
upon me, your servant ; who have nothing to claim
of merit, but a cheerful undertaking whatsoever your
lordship's judgment thinks me able to perform."
There is only one epigram to Newcastle, and it is

wistful reading. Jonson, visiting his lordship's stables, could almost wish himself a horse :

> For never saw I yet the Muses dwell,
> Nor any of their household, half so well.

Jonson, mendicant, is a sad theme. He was of necessity a beggar, but nothing he wrote for alms diminishes our respect for his essential independence of spirit. It is his vocation rather than himself that pleads. An epistle mendicant, addressed in 1631 to the Lord High Treasurer of England, may be taken as a model of its kind. It is impersonal ; it states the facts ; it offers the recipient an opportunity to render a service if he so desires :

> My lord,
> Poor wretched states, prest by extremities,
> Are fain to seek, for succours and supplies,
> Of princes aids, or good men's charities.
>
> Disease the enemy, and his ingineers,
> Want, with the rest of his concealed compeers,
> Have cast a trench about me, now five years ;
>
> And made those strong approaches by faussebrayes,
> Redouts, half-moons, horn-works, and such close ways,
> The Muse not peeps out, one of hundred days ;
>
> But lies blocked up and straitened, narrowed in,
> Fixed to the bed and boards, unlike to win
> Health, or scarce breath, as she had never been ;
>
> Unless some saving honour of the crown
> Dare think it, to relieve, no less renown,
> A bed-rid wit, than a besiegéd town.

Weston, High Treasurer of England, answered this petition with forty pounds.

Jonson's private reflections upon the benefits he received from his patrons were candidly set forth in an undated epistle to the Earl of Dorset, written probably during his first illness in 1626. Dorset had come to Jonson's assistance spontaneously. There would be fewer proud, hard and ungrateful men in the world, says the poet, if all those who were able to do good turns could time them so well and knew so well how a service should be rendered. Gifts that are long in coming or come reluctantly, after delays and excuses, or are negligently made, corrupt the thanks and make the suppliant sorry for what he has obtained. There is a noble way both of giving and receiving. Both parties should be of a cheerful countenance and the man is unworthy who is ashamed of his obligations, begs in a whisper, will receive nothing but in corners, is loth to leave any print, record or token of his benefit and runs from its memory. His own gratitude shall be plainly rendered for all to read and his final prayer shall be that his patron may ever remain such a man as he may continue to love, even though the gift had never been.

To poverty and sickness was added a loss of dramatic power which, on his return to the stage in 1626, even his friends were driven to admit. The series of plays which began with *The Staple of News* in 1626 and concluded with *The Magnetic Lady* in 1632 detracted inevitably from the reputation of the author of *Volpone* and *The Alchemist*. Dryden unkindly, but not unfairly, referred to these later works as the dotages.

The Staple of News was produced by the King's Men either at the end of 1625 or the beginning of 1626. It was nine years since Jonson had written for the stage and he had lost touch. The best of the play is a literary satire directed in a sub-plot against contemporary journalism. The main action is too much in the style of a mask. There is a tendency to allegory which is dangerous in a comedy, where hidden meanings are often worse than no meaning at all. Jonson, however, is not yet sick, and professes himself to be in excellent spirits. Sitting on the stage is a company of gossips : Mirth, Tattle, Expectation and Censure. One of them has been to see the actors in the tiring house where he has had a glimpse of the poet :

> Yonder he is within, rolling himself up and down like a tun in the midst of them. . . . His sweating put me in mind of a good Shroving dish. . . . He hath torn the book in a poetical fury and put himself to silence in dead sack.

The fun is hearty rather than brilliant, but it shows the author in good spirits and facing an audience in which he hoped to find friends to laugh with him rather than against him.

The prologue strikes a more serious and a too familiar note. Jonson appeals once again from the foolish to the wise spectators. He hopes, too, that they have come to hear rather than to see his play, for he has little to offer in the way of a show. He would have his audience listen attentively and not start talking of the coaches in Hyde Park or the bill of fare at Medley's. The old arrogance flashes out in conclusion, for, if the play, says he, should fail to please you, it can only be that you are unable to judge of its merits.

The Staple of News is topical and, therefore, dangerous. Fleet Street was not yet a highway of the fourth estate. Press headquarters were then in Pope's Head Alley where Nathaniel Butter and Captain Gainsford brought forth a hebdomadal newsheet, known as the *Weekly Courant*. The third act of the play shows us the office of *The Staple*—a travesty of Butter and his myrmidons at work. There is a foreign department : the King of Spain has been elected pope ; the grand Turk has turned Christian and means to visit the church at Amsterdam ; a burning glass has been found in Galileo's study which is to be used for burning up fleets at sea ; the Dutch have invented a submarine—an automatic invisible eel which is to be sent into Dunkirk and sink all the ships in the harbour.

Jonson's satire upon contemporary journalism was not too well received. The audience was not quite sure how to take it, and the author even found it necessary to explain, on publication, that the news given out at the Staple Office was not authentic. There were too many honest folk in those days who believed things far less extraordinary than anything Jonson could invent. The wonder is that he was not called to account by the authorities. Spreading false rumours was a Star Chamber matter in those days.

The reception of *The Staple of News* was merely disconcerting. The production of *The New Inn* by the King's Men in January, 1629, was an unqualified disaster. The play has its apologists—even its champions. Charles Lamb found in it some beautiful passages. Hazlitt commended one of the characters. But the actors could make nothing of their parts, and the audience could make nothing of the plot. It would not hear the play to an end. Jonson published it in 1631 with an angry title-page : *The New Inn* or *The Light Heart*, a comedy, as it was never acted, but most negligently played, by the King's servants and more squeamishly beheld by others, the King's subjects. He appealed in a preface from the crowd that had hooted his comedy from the stage to the reader who might, he hoped, be induced to receive it with understanding " There is more hope of thee ", he writes, " than of a hundred fastidious impertinents who were there present the first day." These people had merely come " to see and to be seen ; to make a general muster of themselves in their clothes of credit and possess the stage against the play; to dislike all, but mark nothing; and, by the confidence of their rising between the Acts in oblique lines, make affidavit to the house of their not understanding one scene. Armed with this prejudice, as the stage furniture or arras-clothes, they were there, as spectators, away, for the faces in the hangings and they beheld alike." Therefore, he says, " I do trust myself and my book rather to thy rustic candour than all the pomp of their pride and solemn ignorance to boot. Fare thee well and fall to. Read."

Jonson, writing this play, was already " fixed to the bed and boards ". He is plaintive in respect of his physical condition, and the epilogue—which, alas ! was never reached on the first night—begins with what for a moment looks like a plea for indulgence :

> If you expect more than you had to-night,
> The maker is sick and sad. But do him right;
> He meant to please you; for he sent things fit
> In all the numbers, both of sense and wit,
> If they have not miscarried. If they have,
> All that his faint and faltering tongue doth crave
> Is that you not impute it to his brain;
> That's still unhurt; although, set round with pain,
> It cannot long hold out. All strength must yield;
> Yet judgment would the last be in the field,
> With a true poet.

Like a hurt child, he hardly knows whether to be rebellious or pitiful. In one breath he declares that, though " the carcase die, this art shall live ", but in the next he allows us to see how deeply he felt the neglect of his royal master. As Bardolph said of Falstaff, the King hath killed his heart. The lines fall from his pen as from a dying man :

> And had he lived the care of King and Queen,
> His art in something more yet had been seen.

The audience at Blackfriars, had the epilogue been reached, might have allowed its wrath to be turned aside ; but the prologue had unfortunately invited retribution rather than mercy :

> If any thing be set to a wrong taste,
> 'Tis not the meat there, but the mouth's displaced.

This was not the way to introduce a play which called for deep attention and some indulgence, if its merits were to be appreciated at a first hearing. The public was soon out of hand. Jonson had given to a chambermaid at the New Inn the name of Cis. Someone found it amusing, and the jest was taken up. Those who have seen an audience at a popular theatre who, failing to find entertainment in the play before them, seize on the smallest opportunities for their diversion will easily conjecture the sequel. Each time the unlucky name was mentioned, the uproar increased. Jonson, on being told of it, altered the name and wrote a special epilogue in protest and amazement, so that, in the second volume of his collected works, we read : Another epilogue there was made for the play, in the poet's defence, but the play lived not, in opinion, to have it spoken :

> We think it would have served our scene as true,
> If, as it is, at first we had called her Prue,
> For any mystery we there have found,
> Or magic in the letters or the sound.

The reception accorded to *The New Inn* was a shrewd test for the sons of Ben, and not all of them, alas ! survived it. Jonson, disdaining to call for a champion, went first into the lists. " The just indignation the author took at the vulgar censure of his play by some malicious spectators begat the following "— thus Jonson introduced a famous ode to himself which called forth a whole series of parodies and rejoinders. It was a spirited performance, in which for the second, but not the last, time Jonson took his farewell of the theatre :

Come leave the loathèd stage,
And the more loathsome age ;
Where pride and impudence, in faction knit,
Usurp the chair of wit !
Indicting and arraigning every day
Something they call a play.
Let their fastidious, vain
Commission of the brain
Run on and rage, sweat, censure and condemn ;
They were not made for thee, less thou for them.

Say that thou pour'st them wheat,
And they will acorns eat ;
'Twere simple fury still thyself to waste
On such as have no taste !
To offer them a surfeit of pure bread,
Whose appetites are dead !
No, give them grains their fill,
Husks, draff to drink and swill ;
If they love lees, and leave the lusty wine,
Envy them not, their palate's with the swine.

   .   .   .   .   .   .

Leave things so prostitute,
And take the Alcaic lute ;
Or thine own Horace, or Anacreon's lyre ;
Warm thee by Pindar's fire :
And though thy nerves be shrunk, and blood be cold
Ere years have made thee old,
Strike that disdainful heat
Throughout, to their defeat,
As curious fools, and envious of thy strain,
May, blushing, swear no palsy's in thy brain.

There is a final stanza in which the poet dedicates himself to the glories of his King and to tuning forth the acts of his sweet reign. This is gratitude rather than policy. It was immediately after the failure of *The New Inn* that Charles came to the relief of the author with a hundred pounds.

Ben Jonson

The ode was a trumpet call and the tribe came flocking. Young Randolph was first in the field :

> Ben, do not leave the stage,
> Though 'tis a loathsome age ;
> For pride and impudence will grow too bold,
> When they shall hear it told
> They frightèd thee. Stand high as is thy cause ;
> Their hiss is thy applause ;
> More just were thy disdain,
> Had they approved thy vein ;
> So thou for them, and they for thee were born,
> They to incense, and thou as much to scorn.

The poet's best revenge, he urges, is to give them of the best of his muse. Let them die of hunger amid her dainties and thirst though her wine be at their lips. Others, like Cleveland, set no bounds to their advocacy :

> Proceed in thy brave rage,
> Which hath raised up our stage
> Unto that height as Rome in all her state,
> Or Greece might emulate.

There were some, however, sealed of the tribe, who were not prepared to lose their heads in such a cause. Thomas Carew was such a one. It was true that Ben had branded the times with a just satire. Still *The New Inn* was not *Volpone* or *The Alchemist* :

> Thy comic Muse from the exalted line,
> Touch'd by the Alchemist, doth since decline
> From that her zenith, and foretells a red
> And blushing evening, when she goes to bed.

This was painful reading. Carew might at such a moment have spared the suggestion that his old master had done finer things in his time. Otherwise, the verses were kind enough. For the red and blushing evening of so great a poet, Carew continues, will outshine the following stars. It matters not greatly whether this or that of Ben's eaglets has the stronger

BEN JONSON

Engraved by R. Vaughan

Portrait from the 1616 Edition of Ben Jonson's Works

[face p. 274

wing, since all are his own and there is none of the
flock of cackling geese to compare with his choir of
swans. The poet's friends, however, must be permitted to discriminate between the children of his
muse :

> Though one hand form them, and though one brain strike
> Souls into all, they are not all alike.

The poet should forbear to blast his immortal bays
by seeming to resent a lack of appreciation in an
unworthy public. Let them mock his deliberation,
accuse him of robbing the authors of antiquity. He
shall wear these spoils as trophies :

> Thy labour'd works shall live, when time devours
> The abortive offspring of their hasty hours.
> Thou art not of their rank ; the quarrel lies
> Within thine own verge. Then let this suffice,
> The wiser world doth greater thee confess
> Than all men else, than thyself only less.

That Carew should thus address his master shows
how shrewd a wind was blowing. There was harder
proof to come. To his shame Owen Feltham, author
of *The Resolve*, expressed the feeling of the town in
a parody which in the circumstances was ungenerous :

> Come leave this saucy way
> Of baiting those that pay
> Dear for the sight of your declining wit.

Feltham was running before the storm. Too late,
when Ben was lying in Westminster, he made amends
with an ode, putting the dead poet whom he had
skinned alive with Shakespeare and Beaumont—one
of the three brightest gems in the crown of the stage.
The height of Pindar, the wit of Plautus, the weight
of Seneca, the sensibility of Horace—all met in him.
Each line from his strong quill distilled like a diamond
drop. He stripped Thalia, before like a Maytime

girl, of her mimic jigs. Old authors would find themselves so admirably rendered in his verse that their ghosts would be vexed that the renderings were not their own. What though his muse were slow ? The larger planets move more deliberately than light Venus and the giddy moon :

> The boy may make a squib ; but every line
> Must be considered where men spring a mine.

Such praises, after the event, only make it more difficult for us to forgive Feltham for deserting his master at this unhappy moment.

Feltham's parody was painful proof that only those who loved him could bear with the sick poet in his adversity. It was also a further indication that Jonson, who made during his whole life only two hundred pounds out of the theatre, paid for his meagre earnings with abundant vexation. The plays are few that do not increase his troubles. *The New Inn* was misliked by the public. *The Magnetic Lady* or *The Humours Reconciled*, presented at the Blackfriars Theatre in 1632, was misliked by the authorities. The actors, finding the dialogue tame, larded it freely with oaths. Hard swearing was falling out of fashion, and the King's Reader was spending much of his time in expunging or attenuating such expletives as the more hard-mouthed writers still permitted themselves. The actors were brought before the High Commission to answer the offence and, Jonson being confined to his bed, they did not at once make it clear that the swearing was their own. Luckily Jonson himself notoriously disliked oaths and profanity, and his interpreters were finally driven to confess themselves.

The Magnetic Lady was not ill-received, but there was no call for enthusiasm and Jonson had now to reckon with a host of critics. He had estranged the new journalists under Nathaniel Butter. He had a yet more dangerous enemy in Wither and his Puritan following, while Inigo Jones was now supreme at Court. A certain master Gill, whose father Jonson had chastened for praising Wither overmuch, came forward to remind the public that Ben, in his youth, had been a bricklayer.

> Thou better know'st a groundsel how to lay
> Than lay the plot or groundwork of a play.
> Fall then to work in thy old age agen,
> Take up your trug and trowel, gentle Ben ;
> Let plays alone.

But the comedy excited little comment one way or the other. The public was tired of baiting the old bear.

The year following the production of *The Magnetic Lady* was again disastrous. In the heat of his quarrel with Inigo Jones Jonson had written and sent to the King's Reader *A Tale of a Tub.* How passages offensive to Inigo were detected and by order excised from the MS. has been related. The comedy, thus emasculated, was played before the King and Queen on January 14th, 1634, and coldly received. It excited such little interest in the public that there remains no record of its manner of production.

More serious was the sudden death in 1633 of a dear friend and benefactor. Of his male companions none was more to his heart and fashion than Sir Kenelm Digby—poet, man of fashion, adventurer by land and sea :

> In him all virtue is beheld in state ;
> And he is built like some imperial room
> For that to dwell in, and be still at home.
> His breast is a brave palace, a broad street,
> Where all heroic ample thoughts do meet.

Dearer and more admired than Digby was Digby's wife Venetia. She was as lovely and kind as she was clever. Ben adored her with something of that romantic love with which he turned his mind at the last into green pastures. Listening, he found her voice—

> so sweet, the words so fair,
> As some soft chime had stroked the air ;
> And though the sound had parted thence,
> Still left an echo in the sense.

She died suddenly and two men were desolate. Jonson's lament was in feeling the deepest he ever penned :

> 'Twere time that I died, too, now she is dead,
> Who was my muse and life of all I did.

Here for the moment, so near the end, we leave him. The mood of these last years, when, fixed to the bed and boards, he saw the world go by, will be explored in a final chapter.

CHAPTER XV

The Dotages

SUCH biography, as can be gleaned from the later plays of Jonson, beginning in 1616 with *The Devil is an Ass* and ending in 1633 with *A Tale of a Tub*, has already been presented. Indulgence might be extended to a critic who shrank from the task of assessing these productions and retrieving from them such pages as are necessary to a complete appreciation of the author's work. The task cannot, however, be honestly avoided. The fact that none of these plays is ever likely to be performed again upon the stage and that few are likely to be read with attention, even by those who are familiar with the best of Jonson's work, makes it all the more necessary to examine them. They contribute to an understanding of his mind and method. They contain, moreover, a great deal that is worth recovery and add to our appreciation of the author's versatility and range.

Dryden's epithet is misleading. These are not dotages in the common sense of the word. They are dotages in the sense that Browning's *Prince Hohenstiel-Schwangau, Saviour of Society* or Wagner's *Parsifal* is a dotage : the products of a mind, increasingly secluded, ever more firmly set in its methods, applying a process from habit rather than inspiration. The last works of an author of genius often tend to read like an able parody of the works of his prime. They show us gleams of his finer quality, but equally they

Ben Jonson

exhibit, for our instruction, faults which were inherent but hardly visible when he worked under a stronger impulse. They indicate a hardening rather than a softening of the poet's brain. Jonson, elaborate in his realism when he wrote *The Alchemist*, was yet more elaborate in *The Staple of News* ; complicated in the construction of his plots when he wrote *Volpone*, he devised the most intricate situation ever presented to an audience in *The New Inn* ; liable to run his fancies to death in *The Silent Woman*, he killed them twice over in *The Magnetic Lady*. These are not dotages in the sense that they exhibit impotence or decay. They are marked, on the contrary, by a deliberate and determined development of character-istics which always distinguished the work of Jonson from that of other men.

The process is not yet apparent in the first of the plays which has still to be considered. *The Devil is an Ass*, produced in 1616, stands chronologically nearer to the works of Jonson's maturity, which ended in 1614 with *Bartholomew Fair*, than to the later group which began with *The Staple of News* in 1625. It is not, however, one of the major plays. Jonson started with an ingenious theme, but failed to develop its satirical implications. The induction promised more than the author actually performed. Therein Satan is importuned by Pug, one of the lesser fiends, for leave to visit the Earth in the service of his master. Satan doubts whether Pug would be equal to such a mission. Is there any form of evil in which any devil may now hope to compete successfully with mankind :

> Stay in your place, know your own strength and put not
> Beyond the sphere of your activity.
> You are too dull a devil to be trusted
> Forth in those parts, Pug, on any affair

The Dotages

That may concern our name on earth. It is not
Everyone's work. The state of hell must care
Whom it employs, in point of reputation,
Here about London.

Hell can no longer breed vices strange or fast enough
for Earth, which now has studs of her own. It is
useless to send down the old iniquities ; subtle and
extraordinary sins are now the fashion. It is even
difficult for an honest devil to tell the vices of earth
from the virtues :

They wear the same clothes, eat the same meat,
Sleep in the self-same beds, ride in those coaches,
Or very like, four horses in a coach,
As the best men and women.

The fears of Satan are justified. Pug finds himself
unable to cope with the complicated knaveries of
earth. He is outwitted at every turn. The devil is
an ass.

Jonson, however, allows his principal subject to
fall into the second place. For once he does not seem
to have made up his mind what exactly he intended
to do. His theme is indicated rather than explored.
The best scenes of the play are incidental rather than
necessary. The character of Meercraft, for example,
in which Jonson satirises the manners and methods
of company promoters, essentially the same in his
day as our own, is among his best creations. He has
all the tricks of the trade. He is magnificently general
or minutely technical ; talks in enormous figures or
produces his accounts to a farthing ; uses with equal
address the lie by implication and the lie by statistics,
adapting himself cleverly to the moods and abilities
of his customers. It is a contemporary satire of
permanent application, to be admired apart from the
play in which it is embedded.

The strangely original scene in which the wife of Fitzdottrel, a foolish squire, is exposed by her husband to the ingenious addresses of Witipol, a city gallant, is equally remote from the main purpose of the play. Fitzdottrel, for the price of a fine cloak, undertakes to allow Witipol to address his wife for ten minutes without interruption in his presence. Contact with the lady is barred, and he commands her, moreover, to answer nothing in return. Fitzdottrel is the type of man who insists on the accidents of loyalty, and entirely misses its essentials. He feels secure because he has attached to the interview so many restrictions that no visible and immediate harm can possibly ensue. The lady is solicited under her husband's nose. Witipol speaks without regard to the presence of her lord, allowing her to perceive that he pities her condition, married to a simpleton, and that he fully understands her predicament. He assumes that her husband has forfeited all right to her consideration, and that she cannot but be grateful to a lover who has paid so dearly for the bare privilege of speaking his mind. There is an attractive blend of frankness and delicacy in these addresses, which, taken with the pleasant artifice of the situation, anticipates the comedies of Marivaux. The lady in their subsequent encounters is the equal of her ingenious suitor in frankness, quickness of apprehension and sensibility to the finer shades of conduct. She appreciates his sympathy and even suggests, in riddling terms, ways and means of communication.

Witipol, reading her riddles, presses his suit in a passage wherein Jonson loses himself, as he will do ever more readily as the years advance, in his own conceits. Love, reviewing the charms which now he has the honour to approach :

could make
More wanton salts from this brave promontory,
Down to this valley, than the nimble roe ;
Could play the hopping sparrow 'bout these nets,
And sporting squirrel in these crispèd groves ;
Bury himself in every silkworm's kell
Is here unravelled ; run into the snare
Which every hair is, cast into a curl
To catch a cupid flying ! bathe himself
In milk and roses here and dry him there,
Warm his cold hands to play with this smooth, round
And well-torned chin, as with the billiard ball ;
Roll on these lips, the banks of love, and there
At once both plant and gather kisses.

Jonson for once was presenting a woman of sense.
She was moved and flattered, but she hoped to find that
a man of such brain and spirit would employ his parts
to better purpose than in provoking her to a step
which she had no wish to take :

'Tis counsel that I want and honest aids,
And in this name I need you for a friend ;
Never in any other ; for his ill
Must not make me, Sir, worse.

This, in 1616, was a surprising end to a suit that
promised a more worldly conclusion. Incidentally, it
should be noted as a not unworthy tribute to this
virtuous lady, that Witipol was permitted to indite
for her the exquisite verses :

Have you seen but a bright lily grow,
Before rude hands have touched it ?

Pug has meanwhile entreated his master to recall
him from a world which has passed beyond the
simpler forms of temptation. To bring a vice from
hell to earth was like bringing coals to Newcastle
or oranges to Spain. Among other indignities he
has become servant to a lady of fashion. It is too

much. He would return to his more familiar
penances :

> Catching the winds together in a net,
> Mustering of ants and numbering atoms ; all
> That hell and you thought exquisite torments, rather
> Than stay me here a thought more. I would sooner
> Keep fleas within a circle, and be accomptant
> A thousand year which of them, and how far,
> Outleaped the other, than endure a minute
> Such as I have within. There is no hell
> To a lady of fashion ; all your tortures there
> Are pastimes to it.

It was nine years before Jonson came again to the
stage. *The Staple of News*, as we have seen, was a
play rich in biography and dangerously topical. It
was definitely the first of the dotages. The satire
upon contemporary journalism has already been noted.
The main plot of the play, though it elicited from
the author passages that rank with some of his best
work, exhibited characters more fitted to a mask or
allegory. Queen Pecunia, Mortgage, Statute, Band
and Wax are pure abstractions. Other characters
are wholly lost in their calling or profession. Such
are Picklock, the man of law, Lickfinger, the master-
cook, Fashioner, the tailor, Leatherleg, the shoemaker.
Often we are in doubt whether to read the play as a
comedy of persons or a formal morality. Too often
we must read it as an exercise. Except in the lighter
diversions of the underplot, and in occasional speeches
wherein the poet runs off with his fancy like some
happy dog with a promising bone, the play is difficult
reading for any but a disciplined admirer. Gifford
declared : There are few of Jonson's dramatic works
which exhibit stronger marks of his peculiar talents.
For that reason he loved it, and for the same reason
Swinburne followed him ; equally for the same reason
many who read with admiration the greater comedies

find it impossible to reach the end. The " peculiarity " of the talents here exhibited makes them too difficult of approach.

The main subject is an allegory upon the use and abuse of wealth, in which Queen Pecunia is served and worshipped by three Pennyboys and a suite of admirers. Pennyboy the first is young and spend-thrift ; Pennyboy the third is covetous and a usurer ; Pennyboy the second is in effect a moder-ator between them and pronounces the moral of the play :

> Believe it, brother,
> The use of things is all and not the store ;
> Surfeit and fullness have killed more than famine ;
> The sparrow with his little plumage flies,
> While the proud peacock, overcharged with pens,
> Is fain to sweep the ground with his grown train
> And load of feathers.

Queen Pecunia at the close recommends the golden mean and a safe frugality. She would be neither a slave unto men's pleasures nor a tyrant over their fair desires. Up and down the play are scattered wise sayings and eloquent speeches on the right employ-ment of money. It is a sin against Pecunia to smother her in chests or to strangle her in bags, but the prodigal who spends his riches on externals is equally rebuked :

> Why that's the end of wealth : thrust riches outward,
> And remain beggars within ; contemplate nothing
> But the vile sordid things of time, place, money,
> And let the noble and the precious go.
> Virtue and honesty—hang them, poor thin membranes
> Of honour ! Who respects them ?

Pennyboy the third has a notable outburst in praise of thrift :

What fires, what cooks, what kitchens might be spared ?
What stews, ponds, parks, coops, garners, magazines ?
What velvets, tissues, scarfs, embroideries,
And laces they might lack ?   They covet things
Superfluous still, when it were much more honour
They could want necessary.   What need hath nature
Of silver dishes or gold chamber-pots ?
Of perfumed napkins, or a numerous family
To see her eat ?   Poor, and wise, she requires
Meat only ;   hunger is not ambitious.

There is good preaching from all sides, and in each
of the characters a firm conviction that he has found
the ultimate secret of things.   Lickfinger, the cook,
for example, finds in the kitchen, with its boiler,
range and dresser, the fountain of all wisdom :

A master cook !   why he's the man of men,
For a professor !   he designs, he draws,
He paints, he carves, he builds, he fortifies,
Makes citadels of curious fowl and fish ;
Some he dry-dishes, some moats round with broths,
Mounts marrow bones, cuts fifty-angled custards,
Rears bulwark pies and, for his outer works,
He raiseth ramparts of immortal crust,
And teacheth all the tactics, at one dinner ;
What ranks, what files, to put his dishes in,
The whole art military.   Then he knows
The influence of the stars upon his meats,
And all their seasons, tempers, qualities,
And so to fit his relishes and sauces.
He has nature in a pot, 'bove all the chymists,
Or airy brethren of the Rosie-cross.
He is an architect, an engineer,
A soldier, a physician, a philosopher,
A general mathematician.

All pay court in their several styles to Queen Pecunia,
and the celebration of her charms culminates in a
litany of admiration.   She has the foot of Venus, the
neck of Hebe, the arms of Juno, the face of Leda,
the breasts of Hermione, the cheeks of Flora, the
mouth of Helen.   She has a front too slippery to be
looked upon—*vultus nimium lubricus aspici*.   She kisses

her suitors to sweet music, while Pennyboy the second, chorus to the play, moralises the spectacle :

> Look, look, how all their eyes
> Dance in their heads, observe, scattered with lust,
> At sight of their brave idol ! how they are tickled
> With a light air, the bawdy saraband !
> They are a kind of dancing engines all,
> And set by nature thus to run alone
> To every sound ! all things within, without them,
> Move but their brain, and that stands still ! mere monsters,
> Here in a chamber of most subtle feet.
> These are the gallant spirits of the age,
> The miracles of the time ; that can cry up
> And down men's wits, and set what rate on things
> Their half-brained fancies please.

All this bright worship of Pecunia is the prelude to a bitter denunciation of her congregation. The false doctor, poet, courtier, miser, spendthrift, are all rebuked, humbled or rated, the worst fate being reserved for Pennyboy the third, who runs stark mad and solemnly tries his two dogs for conspiracy. Only those are forgiven at the last who confess their errors and, Pecunia being restored to them, undertake to serve her with discretion.

* *

The New Inn, in its management and construction, falls unhappily among the dotages. In substance, however, it will be more appropriately considered later as a product of the elegiac mood in which Jonson, nearing the end of his life, indited *The Sad Shepherd*. The biographical importance of the play has already been emphasised, and it will be necessary to review it again as an indication of the mood in which its author met the neglect and misfortune of his later years.

Jonson was always apt to be too ingenious in his plots. His incidents do not start one from another ;

the action seldom flows. All is constructed and arranged. His situations are devised to fulfil a definite purpose, and the artificer exhibits a virtuosity which is sometimes disconcerting. He takes pleasure in complicating plot and counter-plot. He keeps his characters continually on the move, exhausting all their possible relations, or bringing them to cross purposes till the reader finds it difficult to hold the threads. *The New Inn* starts from a situation so preposterous that it is difficult to present it at all clearly. Inveterate habit has assumed control with the result that we seem to be dealing with a travesty.

Lord Frampul, an eccentric nobleman, has two daughters, Frances and Letitia. His wife, to whom he was sincerely attached, left him after the birth of Letitia under the impression that she was misliked for failing to produce him an heir. With her infant child she roams the world as an Irish gipsy. Lord Frampul, stricken with remorse, has meanwhile abandoned his estates to his elder daughter Frances, and wandered off in search of his wife, assuming the character and habits of a tinker. Finally he settles down as the eccentric proprietor of the New Inn or the Light Heart. To the New Inn comes his wife, still an Irish gipsy, bringing Letitia, whom she has disguised as a boy. Lord Frampul, over a period of years, recognises neither his wife nor the sex of the " boy ", of whom he assumes the care, and who passes under the name of Frank. Nor does Lady Frampul recognise her lord. Later there comes also to the New Inn Frances, the elder daughter of Lord Frampul, who, on the disappearance of her parents, inherited the family estates. None of the members of this strange family knows or recognises another.

Frances has come to the Inn for her pleasure. She

brings with her two suitors, Lords Beaufort and Latimer.
Already at the Inn, moreover, is one Lovel, a melancholy lover who has long sighed for her in vain.
Gallant sports are devised, in which Lovel is required
to discourse of true love and of true valour.   Frances,
wishing to enliven these proceedings, and having taken
a fancy to the " boy " Frank, dresses him up in woman's
clothes, in which guise he is wooed with enterprise by
Lord Beaufort.   Thus we have a girl, disguised as a boy,
passing now for a girl in sooth—in other words she
is pretending to be herself.   Incidentally, she is
entertaining a party of strangers which includes her
sister, with the permission of mine host, who, unknown
to them all, is her father.   There was in Jonson's
time the further complication that the part of Letitia
was played by a male actor.

On this situation, here set forth as a supreme
example of a " dotage " in construction, Jonson constructed a series of light variations.   On it are built
the court of Love and Valour in which Lovel wins
the heart of the lady ; a series of mystifications in
which Prue, a chambermaid, tragically misnamed Cis
in the first version, queens it over a noble company ;
irruptions of sub-plots fashioned by a tailor's wife,
a militia man and Sir Glorious Tipto, penultimate hero
of the long line of which Bobadil was now a remote
ancestor.   Such is the mechanism from which the
essential play astonishingly emerges as the tranquil
expression of a poet's autumn.

* *
*

The Magnetic Lady or *The Humours Reconciled,* produced in 1632, presents another form of dotage.   It
illustrates a formal method taken to extremes.   It is
difficult to discover what, in nature, the author was
trying to do.   No one has come anywhere near a

satisfactory explanation of his process, which must, therefore, be taken or left by the reader as the author himself announced it in the induction. Master Damplay inquires : Why *Humours Reconciled* ? He is answered by a boy of the house : " The author beginning his studies of this kind with *Every Man in His Humour*, and, after, *Every Man out of His Humour*, and since continuing in all his plays, especially those of the comic thread, whereof *The New Inn* was the last, some recent humours still, or manners of men, that went along with the times ; finding himself now near the close, or shutting up of his circle, hath fancied to himself in idea this magnetic mistress, a lady, a bountiful brave housekeeper and a virtuous widow, who, having a young niece ripe for a man and marriageable, he makes that his centre attractive, to draw thither a variety of guests, all persons of different humours, to make up his perimeter."

But still we ask : Why *Humours Reconciled* ? And we continue to ask that question through the play, though Jonson is at pains to comment on the progress of his scheme in further inductions which increase rather than alleviate our bewilderment.

The characters of the play are repetitions : Captain Ironside, the soldier ; Sir Diaphanous Silkworm, the courtier, Sir Moth Interest, the usurer ; Practice, the lawyer ; Bias, the politician—we have met them all before. The style has grown equally stiff with the characterisation. For a taste of the old habit of elaboration carried to excess, a scene in which Rut, the physician, prescribes for the moral health of Sir Moth Interest is typical. First the diagnosis :

> Give me your hand, Sir Moth. Let's feel your pulse ;
> It is a pursiness, a kind of stoppage,
> Or tumour of the purse, for want of exercise,
> That you are troubled with. Some ligatures

The Dotages

In the neck of your vesica, or marsupium,
Are so close knit that you cannot evaporate ;
And, therefore, you must use relaxatives.
Beside, they say you are so restive grown,
You cannot but with trouble put your hand
Into your pocket to discharge a reckoning ;
And this we sons of physic do call *chiragra*,
A kind of cramp or hand gout.

Prescription follows :

I'll first prescribe him
To give his purse a purge, once, twice a week,
At dice or cards ; and, when the weather is open,
Sweat at a bowling alley ; or be let blood
In the lending vein, and bleed a matter of fifty
Or thousand ounces at a time : then put your thumbs
Under your girdle and have somebody else
Pull out your purse for you, till with more ease
And a good habit you can do't yourself.

An epitaph to *The Magnetic Lady* was written with point and mischief by Howell in a letter which he addressed to Jonson upon its production :

FATHER BEN,—
Nullum fit magnum ingenium sine mixtura dementiae : there 's no great wit without some mixture of madness, so saith the philosopher ; nor was he a fool who answered : nec parvum sine mixtura stultitiae : nor small wit without some alloy of foolishness. Touching the first, it is verified in you, for I find that you have been oftentimes mad. You were mad when you writ your *Fox*, and madder when you writ your *Alchemist* ; you were mad when you writ *Catiline*, and stark mad when you writ *Sejanus*. But when you writ your *Epigrams* and *Magnetic Lady*, you were not so mad. Insomuch that I perceive that there are degrees of madness in you. Excuse me that I am so free with you. The madness I mean is that divine fury, that heating and heightening of the spirit, which Ovid speaks of.

This is but a tactful paraphrase from Macbeth : Time was that, when the brains were out, the man would

Ben Jonson

die. These late characters of Jonson are ghosts at a
banquet.

* *

It is a sad comment on the uncertainties of literary
appreciation that critics should have raised the question
whether *A Tale of a Tub*, produced in 1633, was not
perhaps an early work of Jonson reserved for publication until the years of his decline. The suggestion
rests on references here and there in the play to
Queen Elizabeth. There is no record of an early
text—nothing in fact on which to base so unlikely a
theory. Jonson alluded to Queen Elizabeth because
he meant his play to be deliberately archaic. He
wrote it, as Gifford suggests, " to relieve the tedium
and misery of long disease ". In plot, character,
style and incident it is the last of the dotages.

Jonson introduces it in a prologue in which he
declares his play to be stuffed with " acts of constables
and clowns ". It is derived—

> from old records
> Of antique proverbs, drawn from Whitsun-lords,
> And their authorities, at Wakes and Ales,
> With country precedents and old wives' tales ;

his design being—

> to show what different things
> The cotes of clowns are from the courts of kings.

The play may be read as an effort to achieve bucolic
realism or as an obscure satire upon contemporary
figures disguised in smock and kirtle. The heart of
the satire, being the presentation of Inigo Jones as
In-and-In Medlay of Islington, cooper and head-
borough, was removed by order of the King's Reader
and it would be tedious to follow up the few slender
clues that remain to other identities. The antique

292

village setting is hardly more than a literary device, uncertainly maintained. These rustic pleasantries invoke the protection of St. Valentine, under whose simple auspices they are conducted to a dubiously merry conclusion. For modern readers the most striking of the jests was not intended. This is a rustic piece in which we are invited to appreciate the pastoral attractions of Maribone, Pancras and Kentish Town.

Why *Humours Reconciled*? The answer was not as clear as it might have been. Why *Tale of a Tub*? It were better not to inquire too closely. There is a reference to Diogenes in the fourth act, and the first gentleman of the piece is one Squire Tub of Totten Court. There may be more in this than meets the eye, but it is hardly surprising that no critic has yet ventured to retrieve it.

CHAPTER XVI

Anthology

DRUMMOND wrote of Jonson that in his merry humour he was wont to name himself the Poet. That he constructed stage plays or invented masks was accidental. The heart of his mystery lay in the wider term. Of Jonson, the poet, much has been incidentally quoted, but the examples given of his quality, the best and worst of him, have so far been cited only so far as they revealed his character, witnessed to events in his life or illustrated his dramatic progress. A small anthology of his poetry submitted for its own sake is, therefore, necessary. A presentation of Jonson's work which neglected *A Celebration to Charis*, with his epigrams, odes and elegies would clearly be incomplete.

Jonson's work is all of a piece. His qualities as a poet are those which we have found in him as the author of *Sejanus* and of *Volpone*. He wrote his lyrics with the same intentness, decision, habit of elaboration and deliberate intelligence. He achieved excellence by a calculated aptness of expression. They are work of the hammer and the file. Sometimes he achieved perfection and the effort is concealed, but more often the stubborn lines show only too clearly that they are the wrought speech of the scholar and not a free singing of the spirit. Jonson could neither write easily himself nor believe that any other poet could do so. " Who casts to write a living line must sweat," he declared in his last tribute to Shakespeare,

294

and in the *Apologetical Dialogue* he wrote of himself :

> I that spend half my nights and all my days
> Here in a cell, to get a dark pale face,
> To come forth worth the ivy or the bays.

We do not need, however, either his own confession
or the persistent gibing of his critics to know that
Jonson wrote never upon an impulse, but always with
a mind firm fixed and a pen that must be driven to fit
his terms to a clear thought or an image kept steadily
in view. Effort can be detected in all that he did—
whether it be triumphant or defeated.

Jonson left for publication over one hundred and
thirty epigrams. They are of all lengths from a solitary
couplet to a substantial poem of over two hundred
lines. Jonson claimed for his epigrams that they
represented the " old way and the true " of composing
such occasional pieces. His only rule was that they
should be short, rather than long, and limited to the
exposition of a single idea or event. He denounces
the notion that an epigram is necessarily satirical,
declaring that those who look in his book for something
bold and licentious, full of gall, a petulant thing, in
which the author hurls ink and wit as a madman stones,
will be disappointed. Satire there may be, but a book
of epigrams may contain almost anything, short of
a narration.

The peculiar quality of an epigram—something
concise, considered, classical in style, chiselled and
clear-cut, free of atmosphere or passion—is one which
belongs to most of the collected poems of Jonson and
the description would fit almost equally well the
collections which were put together under the odd
titles of *Underwoods* and *The Forest*. These headings
look strange to a modern eye. Let the author himself

explain : "the ancients called that kind of body *sylva* or *"Υλη*, in which there were works of divers nature and matter congested ; as the multitude call timber-trees promiscuously growing, a Wood or Forest : so am I bold to entitle these poems of later growth by this of Underwood, out of the analogy they hold to the Forest in my former book." It is an introduction which might stand equally well before any one of the three main collections or anthologies into which Jonson's poems are divided and it sufficiently warns the reader that in this Forest his ear is unlikely to be caught with native wood-notes.

The best of the epigrams are those which most nearly correspond to the popular idea of what an epigram should be. They are compact and pointed. They drive home an idea or impression. Examples in this kind may be taken almost at random :

On Something, that Walks Somewhere

At court I met it, in clothes brave enough,
To be a courtier ; and looks grave enough,
To seem a statesman : as I near it came
It made me a great face ; I asked the name.
A Lord, it cried, buried in flesh and blood,
And such from whom let no man hope least good,
For I will do none ; and as little ill,
For I will dare none. Good Lord, walk dead still.

Detachment is the necessary spirit of such work as this, and here Jonson is safe. Feeling, which may touch a poem here and there to beauty, but which more often betrays this poet into oddity or extravagance, is entirely absent. In all these hundred and thirty-three epigrams there are only a few lines here and there in which emotion is successfully conveyed and only one, among them all, in which the mood of the poet is aptly expressed from the first line to the

last, namely, the beautiful epitaph on Salathiel Pavy,
a child of Queen Elizabeth's chapel :

> Weep with me, all you that read
>   This little story :
> And know, for whom a tear you shed
>   Death's self is sorry.
> 'Twas a child that so did thrive
>   In grace and feature,
> As Heaven and Nature seemed to strive
>   Which owned the creature.
> Years he numbered scarce thirteen
>   When Fates turned cruel,
> Yet three filled zodiacs had he been
>   The stage's jewel ;
> And did act, what now we moan,
>   Old men so duly,
> As, sooth, the Parcae thought him one,
>   He played so truly.
> So, by error to his fate
>   They all consented ;
> But viewing him since, alas, too late !
>   They have repented ;
> And have sought to give new birth,
>   In baths to steep him ;
> But being so much too good for earth,
>   Heaven vows to keep him.

Jonson is here kept true to his mood by running true
to his initial fancy. The feeling is carried by a series
of conceits logically connected. It is an intellectual
performance, but the effort is concealed, and the whole
composition, despite its secret elaboration, reads like
a simple expression of affection and regret.

The poems published by Jonson himself in 1616
under the title of *The Forest* consist of fifteen pieces.
Apart from addresses to friends or patrons, which
have already been noted, the collection contains the
songs to Celia. The best of these is the most famous
of all Jonson's lines, sung and quoted by thousands
who could not tell us the name of the author :

Drink to me only with thine eyes,
   And I will pledge with mine ;
Or leave a kiss but in the cup,
   And I'll not look for wine.
The thirst that from the soul doth rise
   Doth ask a drink divine ;
But might I of Jove's nectar sup,
   I would not change for thine.

I sent thee late a rosie wreath,
   Not so much honouring thee,
As giving it a hope, that there
   It could not withered be.
But thou thereon didst only breathe,
   And sent'st it back to me ;
Since when it grows, and smells, I swear,
   Not of itself, but thee.

It is a lyric without lapse or flaw. The initial fancy is just sufficiently exploited. The author has not time or room to complicate or expand it beyond measure. It is, in fact, a perfect exception that proves all we have generally learned about Jonson's habit of composition. Its simplicity and easiness suggest a strong impulse that keeps the poet true. But they are found on inspection to be the result of a deliberate and successful application of a single idea, and the spontaneity is wholly fallacious, for the poem, couplet for couplet, is carefully based on a collection of love letters written by the sophist, Philostratus : " Drink to me with thine eyes only. Or, if thou will't, putting the cup to thy lips, fill it with kisses and so bestow it upon me." Here is crowning proof that Jonson was never more natural than when he uttered himself in quotations.

Two other songs to Celia in this collection may be quoted as examples of Jonson's light but studied excursions in gallantry. The first of them was sung by Volpone, wooing the wife of Corvino in *The Fox* :

Come, my Celia, let us prove,
While we may, the sports of love ;
Time will not be ours for ever ;
He at length our good will sever.
Spend not then his gifts in vain.
Suns that set may rise again ;
But if once we lose this light,
'Tis with us perpetual night.

Why should we defer our joys ?
Fame and rumour are but toys.
Cannot we delude the eyes
Of a few poor household spies ;
Or his easier ears beguile,
So removèd by our wile ?
'Tis no sin love's fruit to steal,
But the sweet theft to reveal ;
To be taken, to be seen,
These have crimes accounted been.

The second is upon the same theme of stolen love.
It runs featly but only just escapes the monotonous
elaboration to which Jonson was always liable :

Kiss me sweet : the wary lover
Can your favours keep and cover,
When the common courting jay
All your bounties will betray.
Kiss again ; no creature comes.
Kiss, and score up wealthy sums
On my lips thus hardly sundred,
While you breathe. First give a hundred,
Then a thousand, then another
Hundred, then unto the other
Add a thousand, and so more ;
Till you equal with the store,
All the grass that Rumney yields,
Or the sands in Chelsea fields,
Or the drops in silver Thames,
Or the stars that gild his streams,
In the silent summer-nights,
When youths ply their stolen delights ;
That the curious may not know
How to tell 'em as they flow,
And the envious, when they find
What their number is, be pined.

Ben Jonson

The Forest was a collection selected and published by the author himself. *Underwoods*, published in 1641, was a collection put together by his literary executors. It consists of pieces found among his papers after his death, or taken from works already published. The duties of the editor were carelessly performed, and the collection includes a good deal that Jonson would probably have destroyed. It opens with *Poems of Devotion*, passes to *A Celebration of Charis* in ten lyric pieces, presents one hundred and one poems under the heading of Miscellaneous, and concludes with a tribute to the Lady Venetia Digby.

The *Poems of Devotion* need not long detain us. Jonson in his religion accepted without much searching of heart or mind what lay humanly nearest. That he professed the Catholic or Anglican conventions was neither here nor there. There is no deep sense of spiritual issues anywhere in his plays. These poems of devotion are a pious exercise, of interest only as showing how even the most powerful and independent minds can honestly subscribe to doctrines without allowing them seriously to affect their conduct or vital concerns. We have seen him deeply moved by *The Burning Babe* of Southwell, and we find him declaring in a hymn on the Nativity:

> To see this Babe, all innocence,
> A martyr born in our defence;
> Can man forget his story?

This, however, merely means that Jonson's imagination was touched by the Christian legend. More characteristic is a Hymn to God the Father, for here the stoic speaks:

> Hear me, O God!
> A broken heart
> Is my best part;
> Use still thy rod,
> That I may prove
> Therein Thy love.

The only religious utterances of Jonson, except for these *Poems of Devotion*, are a prayer published as a conclusion to *The Forest*, and certain passages in the tribute to Venetia Digby. The prayer is that of a pagan stoic uttered in Christian phrase:

> I feel my griefs too, and there scarce is ground
> Upon my flesh t' inflict another wound.
> Yet dare I not complain, or wish for death,
> With holy Paul, lest it be thought the breath
> Of discontent; or that these prayers be
> For weariness of life, not love of Thee.

The tribute to Venetia Digby dwells at length on her certainty of heaven as the reward of piety:

> Dare I, profane, so irreligious be,
> To greet or grieve her soft euthanasy
> So sweetly taken to the court of bliss.

Or again:

> He knows what work He hath done, to call this guest
> Out of her noble body to this feast;
> And give her place according to her blood
> Amongst her peers, those princes of all good!
> Saints, martyrs, prophets, with those Hierarchies,
> Angels, Archangels, Principalities,
> The Dominations, Virtues and the Powers.

It is the expression of an orthodoxy to which imagination has remained indifferent, and the lack of imaginative reaction is the more significant in that the poet, who in this tribute writes conventionally of heaven as a place of angels and rewards, was deeply and sincerely moved by the loss he had sustained.

Not even a cruel bereavement could provoke him to a really individual religious utterance.

In *A Celebration of Charis* Jonson presents his most serious effort as a lyrical poet. Significantly he has waited to sing of love till he is fifty, and begins with *His Excuse for Loving* :

> Let it not your wonder move,
> Less your laughter, that I love.
> Though I now write fifty years,
> I have had, and have my peers ;
> Poets, though divine, are men ;
> Some have loved as old again.
> And it is not always face,
> Clothes or fortune, gives the grace ;
> Or the feature, or the youth ;
> But the language, and the truth,
> With the ardour and the passion,
> Gives the lover weight and fashion.

It is a fair taste of the author's quality. Later he declares :

> This is she
> Of whose beauty it was sung :
> She shall make the old man young,
> Keep the middle age at stay,
> And let nothing high decay ;
> Till she be the reason why
> All the world for love may die.

Is there another poet of love who alludes to middle age as a prelude to ecstasy ? Note also that Charis is a universal mistress. There is nothing personal or private here. This is to be a classical tribute and the celebration rises to its highest and most clearly sustained note in a number entitled *Her Triumph*, wherein the poet's lady rides in a chariot, for all the world to see, to a general and public proclamation of her beauties :

See the chariot at hand here of Love,
  Wherein my Lady rideth !
Each that draws is a swan or a dove,
  And well the car Love guideth.
As she goes, all hearts do duty
    Unto her beauty ;
And enamoured do wish, so they might
    But enjoy such a sight,
That they still were to run by her side,
Through swords, through seas, whither she would ride.

Do but look on her eyes, they do light
  All that Love's world compriseth !
Do but look on her hair, it is bright
  As Love's star when it riseth !
Do but mark, her forehead's smoother
    Than words that soothe her ;
And from her arched brows, such a grace
    Sheds itself through the face,
As alone there triumphs to the life
All the gain, all the good of the elements' strife.

Have you seen but a bright lily grow,
  Before rude hands have touched it ?
Have you marked but the fall o' the snow
  Before the soil hath smutched it ?
Have you felt the wool of bever ?
    Or swan's down ever ?
Or have smelt o' the bud o' the brier ?
    Or the nard in the fire ?
Or have tasted the bag of the bee ?
O so white ! O so soft ! O so sweet is she !

Jonson never wrote a better poem of equal length, and those who admire his work most and know it best can only feel surprised that he should have succeeded in penning thirty lyric lines, without a single serious lapse into obscurity or violence. The faults to which his muse, intellectually driven, with no immediate impulse to keep it vital and true, is so often liable are here avoided. Even so, who would not be tempted to curtail the poem by two-thirds, leaving only the last stanza, in which fancy and feeling, meditated and refined, meet for one perfect moment on companionable terms ?

Jonson, in conversation with Drummond, quoted from this sequence the seventh number, and Drummond mentions it as " the most commonplace of his repetitions," i.e. a special favourite of the author and frequently delivered. Here again is a poem which could hardly be omitted from a judicious anthology of seventeenth-century verse. It is entitled : *Begging Another*, *On Colour of Mending the Former* :

> For Love's sake, kiss me once again,
> I long, and should not beg in vain.
>   Here's none to spy or see ;
>   Why do you doubt or stay ?
>   I'll taste as lightly as the bee,
> That doth but touch his flower, and flies away.
>
> Once more, and, faith, I will be gone,
> Can he that loves ask less than one ?
>   Nay, you may err in this,
>   And all your bounty wrong ;
>   This could be called but half a kiss ;
> What we're but once to do, we should do long.
>
> I will but mend the last, and tell
> Where, how, it would have relished well ;
>   Join lip to lip, and try ;
>   Each suck the other's breath,
>   And whilst our tongues perplexed lie,
> Let who will think us dead, or wish our death.

The last stanza begins to fall into that habit of elaboration and insistence of which we have already seen so many examples. Its extreme particularity is disconcerting. The lyric lift is not strong enough to carry the physical details. Join lip to lip and the result is not necessarily, for poetic purposes, a kiss.

These ten lyric pieces are in divers moods : From *Her Man described by Her Own Dictamen*, some stanzas may be quoted as an example of the running style

which Jonson frequently used in his masks. It is
a portrait by Charis of the perfect lover, and it is
written in the vein of Catullus, which Jonson often
followed with success :

> Young I'd have him too, and fair,
> Yet a man ; with crispèd hair,
> Cast in thousand snares and rings,
> For Love's fingers and his wings ;
> Chestnut colour, or more slack,
> Gold, upon a ground of black ;
> Venus and Minerva's eyes,
> For he must look wanton-wise.
>
> Eyebrows bent like Cupid's bow,
> Front, an ample field of snow ;
> Even nose, and cheek withal,
> Smooth as is the billiard-ball ;
> Chin as woolly as the peach ;
> And his lip should kissing teach,
> Till he cherished too much beard,
> And made Love or me afeard.
>
> He should have a hand as soft
> As the down, and shew it oft ;
> Skin as smooth as any rush
> And so thin to see a blush
> Rising through it ere it came ;
> All his blood should be a flame,
> Quickly fired, as in beginners
> In Love's school, and yet no sinners.
>
> .   .   .   .   .   .
>
> All his actions to be such,
> As to do no thing too much ;
> Nor o'er praise, nor yet condemn,
> Nor out-value, nor contemn ;
> Nor do wrongs, nor wrongs receive,
> Nor tie knots, nor knots unweave ;
> And from baseness to be free,
> As he durst love Truth and me.

From *A Celebration of Charis* we pass in these
Underwoods to a collection of over a hundred poems
of all lengths, types and qualities. Many lines from
this collection have been quoted in reference to inci-

dents in the poet's life. Our anthology would not be complete, however, if we did not quote again, this time in full, *My Picture Left in Scotland* :

I now think Love is rather deaf than blind,
    For else it could not be,
        That she,
    Whom I adore so much, should so slight me,
And cast my suit behind.
I'm sure my language to her was as sweet,
    And every close did meet
    In sentence of as subtle feet,
    As hath the youngest he
    That sits in shadow of Apollo's tree.

Oh ! but my conscious fears,
    That fly my thoughts between,
Tell me that she hath seen
    My hundreds of gray hairs,
        Told six and forty years,
Read so much waste as she cannot embrace
    My mountain belly and my rocky face ;
And all these, through her eyes, have stopt her ears.

Another poem, remarkable for its sense, vigour and felicity, is written *Against Jealousy* :

Wretched and foolish jealousy,
How cam'st thou thus to enter me ?
    I ne'er was of thy kind ;
    Nor have I yet the narrow mind
        To vent that poor desire,
That others should not warm them at my fire ;
    I wish the sun should shine
On all men's fruit and flowers, as well as mine.

But under the disguise of love,
Thou say'st, thou only cam'st to prove
    What my affections were.
    Think'st thou that love is helped by fear ?
        Go, get thee quickly forth,
Love's sickness, and his noted want of worth.
    Seek doubting men to please,
I ne'er will owe my health to a disease.

Anthology

Jonson, writing of jealousy, speaks for the renaissance. Jealousy short of madness or malady, is for him, as for all the comic poets, essentially ridiculous. The puritan ethic of jealousy, based in varying degrees on the sense of property and envy of the sexually happy, is unknown to him except as a " humour " to be chastised. There is a companion piece to the poem against jealousy written in defence of inconstancy in women. It should be read with attention by those who think that the times in which we live are in any real sense modern or exceptional :

> Hang up those dull and envious fools
>   That talk abroad of woman's change.
> We were not bred to sit on stools,
>   Our proper virtue is to range ;
>   Take that away, you take our lives,
>   We are no women then, but wives.
>
> Such as in valour would excel,
>   Do change, though man, and often fight,
> Which we in love must do as well,
>   If ever we will love aright ;
>   The frequent varying of the deed,
>   Is that which doth perfection breed.
>
> Nor is't inconstancy to change
>   For what is better, or to make,
> By searching, what before was strange,
>   Familiar, for the uses sake ;
>   The good from bad is not descried,
>   But as 'tis often vext and tried.
>
> And this profession of a store
>   In love doth not alone help forth
> Our pleasure ; but preserves us more
>   From being forsaken, than doth worth ;
>   For were the worthiest woman curst
>   To love one man, he'd leave her first.

The normal quality of Jonson's formal poetry, with its merits and defects, is most usefully illustrated by examples which express a mood or opinion of interest to the biographer. Of such verse enough has been given incidentally in following his career. Appropriate to this anthology, however, are the verses which he wrote in a " fit of rhyme against rhyme ". They are a good specimen of a style, ingenious, precise, angular, with no easy graces to carry it or winged words to lift it over difficult places, which reminds us, among modern poets, now of Robert Browning, or again of Thomas Hardy :

> Rhyme, the rack of finest wits,
> That expresseth but by fits
> > True conceit,
> Spoiling senses of their treasure,
> Cozening judgment with a measure,
> > But false weight ;
>
> Wresting words from their true calling ;
> Propping verse for fear of falling
> > To the ground ;
> Jointing syllables, drowning letters,
> Fastening vowels, as with fetters
> > They were bound !
>
> . . . . . .
>
> Vulgar languages that want
> Words, and sweetness, and be scant
> > Of true measure,
> Tyrant rhyme hath so abused,
> That they long since have refused
> > Other cesure.
>
> He that first invented thee,
> May his joints tormented be,
> > Cramped for ever ;
> Still may syllables jar with time,
> Still may reason war with rhyme,
> > Resting never !
>
> May his sense when it would meet
> The cold tumour in his feet,
> > Grow unsounder ;
> And his title be long fool,
> That in rearing such a school
> > Was the founder! "

Anthology

We will conclude with a single strophe from the first Pindaric Ode in the English language, written to the immortal memory of that noble pair Sir Lucius Cary and Sir Henry Morison. Sir Lucius Cary, better known as Lord Falkland, was the most faithful and discerning of the sons of Ben. He left many tokens of his admiration for " Our metropolitan in poetry " and in an " epistle to his noble father ", even defends him from the charge of insolence :

> I thought you proud, for I did surely know
> Had I Ben Jonson been, I had been so :
> Now I recant.

Falkland was sincerely grieved by Jonson's poverty and the neglect in which he lived during his last years. He found it a scandal—

> That want should a quotidian trouble be
> To such a Zeno in philosophy.

Sir Henry Morison, the close friend of Falkland in his early youth, died at twenty and Jonson mourned him in an ode modelled upon Pindar with a remarkable exactitude of form and feeling. The strophe, counter-strophe and epode—all are there. But not only is the skeleton true to form. Jonson had a natural affinity with his model and reproduces, without violence to his own style or habit of mind, Pindar's most notable qualities as aptly scheduled by Gifford—the artful plan, the regular returns of metre, the interesting pathos, the lofty morality and the sacred tone. Jonson never wrote better than when he followed a classic model and delivered himself of the echoes that slept perpetually in his ear :

> It is not growing like a tree
> In bulk, doth make man better be ;
> Or standing long an oak, three hundred year,
> To fall a log at last, dry, bald, and sear :

Ben Jonson

A lily of a day,
Is fairer far, in May,
Although it fall and die that night;
It was the plant and flower of light.
In small proportions we just beauties see ;
And in short measures life may perfect be.

Do we detect here the regret of a poet, declined into the vale of years, feeling perhaps that in a shorter measure his own life might have been more perfect and left a sweeter memory ? Such a personal application is the more justified when we remember, once again, that Jonson is never more personal than when he speaks with the voice of antiquity.

CHAPTER XVII

Green Fields

FROM January 14th, 1634, when the King and Queen witnessed *A Tale of a Tub*, to August 6th, 1637, when Jonson died, the personal glimpses are few. The King, in September, 1634, commanded the City aldermen to restore his pension as City chronologer. On New Year's Day and on the King's birthday, 1635, the poet expressed his gratitude to King Charles for the last time. On November 20th of the same year he lost his only surviving son, for whom he had secured the reversion of his post as Master of the Revels not yet inherited from Sir John Astley.

Two intimate references are historical. Howell records that on April 4th, 1636, Ben gave a solemn supper with " good company, excellent cheer, choice wines and jovial welcome ". The priest of the Devil Tavern truculently remembered ancient glories. He " began to vapour extremely of himself and, by vilifying others, to magnify his own muse ". This almost spoiled the " relish " of the evening ; but all might be forgiven " now that time hath snowed upon his pericranium ". The second glimpse is not so happy. Among the sons of Ben was one George Morley who afterwards became Bishop of Winchester. Years later he told Izaak Walton that he had often visited Ben Jonson in his " long retirement and sickness " in his lodging near Westminster. Morley states that " so much as came in " of his pension was given

311

to a woman " that governed him ; that neither he nor she took much care for next week but would be sure not to want wine, of which he took too much before he went to bed, if not oftener and sooner ".

What was the mood of these last years, apart from such fitful feasting and truculent reminiscence as Howell records ?

That Jonson, released from his theory of comedy, could delight in pastoral simplicities, in woods and flowers, in shepherds, young love and the coming of spring, was evident in his masks and occasional passages of his plays. We have even glanced at a theory that in the author of *Volpone* we are to look for a romantic poet who wilfully destroyed himself by inventing and practising the rigid theory of humours. Those who accept this view, in reading the early plays and fragments, will inevitably be drawn to it again in contrasting *The Magnetic Lady*, where the author lies stiff and stark in the strait-waistcoat of his method, with *The Sad Shepherd*, in which he escapes from his method into the green fields. They would discover an essential Jonson in *The Case is Altered*, before he had fitted his features to the comic mask, and in an unfinished fragment written when the mask was finally removed. *Volpone* and the great works of his prime would thus be aberrations and least expressive of the man himself. Such a theory would never have been invented but for the farewell mood in which we find him at the close. Is it, however, necessary ? Falstaff wandered into the green fields at his latter end, but no one has ever suggested that he was an arcadian astray in Eastcheap.

Jonson, towards the end of his life, was an enforced spectator of the active world. He had come to rest like his host of *The New Inn* :

Green Fields

Where I imagine all the world's a play ;
The state and men's affairs all passages
Of life to spring new scenes ; come in, go out,
And shift and vanish ; and if I have got
A seat to sit at ease here, in mine inn,
To see the comedy ; and laugh and chuck
At the variety and throng of humours
And dispositions that come justling in
And out still, as they one drive hence another,
Why will you envy me my happiness ?

Fixed to his tenement in Westminster, Jonson was reviewing his life and bringing an old man's philosophy to bear upon his recollections. Sometimes we hit upon a phrase which shows us, embedded in the generalities of a wiseacre, a memory of wrongs once suffered but to be borne in retrospect with a laugh :

I am kept out a mask, sometime *thrust out*,
Made wait a day, two, three, for a great word,
Which when it comes forth is all frown and forehead.
What laughter should this breed rather than anger !
Out of the tumult of so many errors,
To feel with contemplation mine own quiet !

It was nearly thirty years since Jonson had been ejected with his friend Roe from *A Vision of Twelve Goddesses* at Hampton Court. The poet has discovered how such incidents should be met, but the deep impression they had made upon him in occurrence may be judged from the fact that, in a speech of general application concerning true valour delivered thirty years later, they are still remembered.

Lovel on true valour advances the wisdom of the stoic. There is no valour in a private cause. True valour must distinguish between good and evil ; it must fear to do unworthy things, preserve its dignity under affront, be never angry or rash. True valour is untroubled with injuries inflicted by a fool. Jonson

313

at last has leisure to be wise—in precept. He utters as an observer what his reason commends as right and proper.

Lovel on true valour is proof that the best sermons are often preached by the biggest sinners. The ink was scarcely dry upon this philosophic page before Jonson took pen and paper and indited the *Ode to Himself*, as angry a piece as he ever wrote. Lovel on true love is a more difficult case. Those who admire the robust sensuality of Jonson's earlier studies in the gentle passion are saddened by the platonic discourses of *The New Inn*. They would ascribe them less to a change in the poet himself than to a cunning wish to be in the fashion. The Court of Charles, in its gallantries, had definitely changed for better or for worse. The King's Reader was expunging the more masculine forms of asseveration by oath from the texts of plays submitted for his approval, and his courtiers were learning to profess a disembodied ardour in their amatory diversions in striking contrast with the Jacobean habit of approach. Admittedly the court of love at *The New Inn* reflects this change of manners, but it is equally clear that the author was not unwilling to celebrate the new fashion of loving for its own sake. Jonson, at sixty, was disposed to look quietly for the more abiding elements of a passion which he had so often satirised as an appetite or a frailty. He has come piously to distinguish the essentials of love from the accidents. Men are naturally drawn to what is outwardly fair :

> But put the case, in travel I may meet
> Some gorgeous structure, a brave frontispiece ;
> Shall I stay captive in the outer court,
> Surprised with that, and not advance to know
> Who dwells there and inhabiteth the house ?
> There is my friendship to be made, within,
> With what can love me again : not with the walls,

Doors, windows, architraves, the frieze and cornice.
My end is lost in loving of a face,
An eye, lip, nose, hand, foot or other part,
Whose all is but a statue, if the mind
Move not, which only can make the return.
The end of love is to have two made one
In will and in affection, that the minds
Be first inoculated, not the bodies.

This is an old man's wisdom, phrased in Jonsonian metaphor. Protest was inevitable. " Give me the body, if it be a good one," exclaims my lord Beaufort, and the lovers of good life, who have hitherto found in Jonson their comfort and support, endorse the sentiment and deplore in their poet a tardy conversion to the platonic faith. Yet it should be noted that Lovel's courtship ends in kissing which was not less welcome to the lady for being so finely urged. Nor should it be forgotten that Lovel's rhapsodies are spoken under a running fire of hearty and disrespectful comment from Beaufort whereby Jonson corrects his hero and shows that, for all these higher flights, he is not yet disembodied.

Neither the platonism of *The New Inn*, nor the elegiac scenes of *The Sad Shepherd*, are to be regarded as the expression of romantic yearnings long suppressed, still less of an increasing impotence. The satirist has laid aside his weapons. These late works are a quiet disarming of the spirit. The poet at the last would use his art, no longer as a panoply, no more as a means of discovery or attack, but as offering him a shelter from affliction, an escape from the bed and boards to which his muse was fixed. They are works of meditation and retreat. During the last seven years of his life, but for strong flashes of rebellion, Jonson was turning his face to the wall. Already in 1632 he was living so retired that Mr. Pory, on hearing of the production of *The Magnetic Lady* expressed surprise at the news. He had believed Jonson to be already dead. The melancholy fall of a chance phrase in the induction of *The Magnetic Lady* will perhaps have lingered in the reader's ear : *finding himself near the close, or shutting up of his circle.* It was a long farewell. Jonson was more than seven years a-dying.

**

Such was the mood in which death, so long in coming, at last surprised him composing a naughty speech for the witch in a fairy tale. In *The Sad Shepherd* Jonson dreams of a spell which will restore to the world its first and tuneful planeting. He listens for new concords,

> to rock old sages,
> Twice infants, in the cradle of speculation,
> And throw a silence upon all the creatures.

We feel this silence as we read—a silence of the spirit, broken only by Arcadian voices plaintive or merry, devout or mocking, but never arresting or harsh. Lightly he follows the maiden of his pastoral :

> Here she was wont to go ! and here ! and here !
> Just where those daisies, pinks and violets grow.
> The world may find the spring by following her ;
> For other print her airy steps ne'er left.
> Her treading would not bend one blade of grass,
> Or shake the downy blowbell from his stalk,
> But like the soft west wind she shot along,
> And where she went, the flowers took thickest root,
> As she had sowed them with her odorous foot.

The Sad Shepherd is almost free of the blemishes due to Jonson's habit of elaboration. To remind us, however, that this was still the author of the hideous passage on Sejanus' death we find Aeglamour drawing a picture of Earinë drowned and her corpse thrown

up by the waters. His ecstasy prompts him to fancy
how he will make the beholders mad,

> To see how I will hug it in mine arms !
> And hang upon her looks, dwell on her eyes,
> Feed round about her lips, and eat her kisses,
> Suck off her drownèd flesh.

But such lapses are quite contrary to the free flow of
fancy and spirit which distinguishes this last play
from its predecessors. Jonson came nearest here to
" gentle " Shakespeare, though his music and turn of
thought are entirely his own :

> A spring, now she is dead ! of what ? of thorns ?
> Briars, and brambles ? thistles ? burs, and docks ?
> Cold hemlock ? yew ? the mandrake, or the box ?
> These may grow still ; but what can Spring beside ?
> Did not the whole earth sicken when she died ?
> As if there since did fall one drop of dew,
> But what was wept for her ! or any stalk
> Did bear a flower, or any branch a bloom,
> After her wreath was made !

And again he mourns :

> Earinë,
> Who had her very being and her name
> With the first knots or buddings of the Spring,
> Born with the primrose and the violet,
> Or earliest roses blown ; when Cupid smiled
> And Venus led the Graces out to dance,
> And all the flowers and sweets in Nature's lap
> Leaped out, and made their solemn conjuration
> To last but while she lived ! Do not I know
> How the vale withered the same day ? how Dove,
> Dean, Eye and Erwash, Idel, Snite, and Soare
> Each broke his urn, and twenty waters more,
> That swelled proud Trent, shrunk themselves dry ? that since,
> No sun or moon, or other cheerful star,
> Looked out of heaven, but all the cope was dark,
> As it were hung so for her exequies ?
> And not a voice or sound to ring her knell,
> But of that dismal pair, the scritching owl,
> And buzzing hornet ? Hark ! hark ! hark ! the foul
> Bird ! how she flutters with her wicker wings !
> Peace ! you shall hear her scritch.

Ben Jonson

There is a prologue to *The Sad Shepherd*. It has a dying fall. The inevitable challenge is delivered, for Jonson to the last must defy his audience; but the author is broad, mild, almost impersonal:

> But here's an heresy of late let fall
> That mirth by no means fits a pastoral;
> Such say so who can make none, he presumes,
> Else there's no scene more properly assumes
> The sock. For whence can sport in kind arise
> But from the rural routs and families?
> Safe on this ground then, we not fear to-day
> To tempt your laughter by our rustic play.

The challenge is on a general issue. Personally the author is resigned and friendly: " He that hath feasted you these forty years ", thus he begins and prays his public " to hear him this once more." His Muse is to pull her wool from English flocks, but the fleece will be made in the pattern of Greece or Sicily.

Jonson for the plot of *The Sad Shepherd* went to Sherwood. Robin Hood is lord of the forest. Between him and Maid Marian the witch Maudlin provokes dissension, but we know at once that all difficulties will be happily resolved. Aeglamour, the sad shepherd, must ultimately find and release from the cleft oak, wherein Maudlin has imprisoned her, his lost Earinë. Meanwhile, the poet sweetens the lorn mouth of his swain with pleasing numbers and, as Shakespeare filled his island, reached after tempest, with sweet noises, so Jonson surprisingly breaks forth in a stage direction, never, alas, to be fulfilled: *music of all sorts is heard.*

The Sad Shepherd is Jonson's elegy. With it he passed from the age which he had helped to fill. But it is also an elegy of the age itself. Aeglamour laments his vanished maiden of the spring and

318

Green Fields

Robin Hood rebukes a world whose pastimes are threatened with eclipse :

> Now that the shearing of your sheep is done,
> And the washed flocks are lighted of their wool,
> The smoother ewes are ready to receive
> The mounting rams again, and both do feed,
> As either promised to increase your breed
> At eaning time, and bring you lusty twins.
> Why should or you or we so much forget
> The season in ourselves as not to make
> Use of our youth and spirits to awake
> The nimble horn-pipe and the timburine,
> And mix our songs and dances in the wood,
> And each of us cut down a triumph-bough ?

Such are the rites which June allows to youth and plenty. But one protests :

> They *were*, gay Robin ; but the sourer sort
> Of shepherds now disclaim in all such sport ;
> And say our flocks the while are poorly fed
> When with such vanities the swains are led.

And Robin answers :

> I do not know what their sharp sight may see
> Of late, but I should think it still might be
> As't was, a happy age, when on the plains
> The woodman met the damsels, and the swains
> The neat-herds, ploughmen and the pipers loud,
> And each did dance, some to the kit or crowd,
> Some to the bag-pipe ; some the tabret moved,
> And all did either love or were beloved.

Jonson completed but two acts of *The Sad Shepherd*. Alken, wise in country lore, has seen the witch, Maudlin, sitting within a gloomy dimble in the shape of a hare. For the last time Jonson remembers his witchcraft, thinks perhaps of the dead king with whom he had talked as one adept to another. We read of the sad mandrake,

Whose groans are deathful ; the dead-numbing night-shade,
The stupefying hemlock, adders tongue,
And martagan : the shrieks of luckless owls
We hear and croaking night crows in the air,
Green-bellied snakes, blue fire-drakes in the sky
And giddy flitter-mice with leather wings ;
The scaly beetles with their habergeons,
That make a humming murmur as they fly.

Good sport is promised in Sherwood. For Alken
will lead the huntsmen to where the witch is waiting,
fearful and melancholy, in the wicked seat of all her
mischiefs :

> I will find her for you
> And show her sitting in her fourm ; I'll lay
> My hand upon her, make her throw her skut
> Along her back, when she does start before us.
> But you must give her law ; and you shall see her
> Make twenty leaps and doubles ; cross the paths
> And then squat down beside us.

Whereat Will Scarlet exclaims :

> We'll make this hunting of the witch as famous
> As any other blast of venery.

There was to be no meet in Sherwood nor blast
of venery. Jonson set down the argument of the
third act in full but completed only the second. The
rest is silence. We know nothing of the manner of
his death or burial. His busy pen was arrested in
the middle of a phrase, and we find him next in
Westminster, lying under a plain stone.

* *

For over a year before the poet's death Brian
Duppa, Bishop of Winchester, had been collecting
what Jonson had himself described on a previous
occasion as a " packet of commendations ". These
were duly published early in 1638 under the title,

suggested by Falkland, of *Jonsonus Virbius*. Howell, sending his contribution, wrote to the Editor : " It is a well-becoming and a very worthy work you are about, not to suffer Mr. Ben Jonson to go so silently to his grave or to rot so suddenly." Jonson was borne to the Abbey, set down, and then somehow forgotten. Sir John Young of Great Milton, passing shortly afterwards, found no epitaph or inscription on the slab which covered his grave and gave eighteenpence to a mason to carve the words which we read to-day : O rare Ben Jonson. Perhaps he had seen them inscribed over the door of the Apollo Room in the Devil Tavern. They had in any case been current for over twenty years, ever since the production of *Bartholomew Fair* in 1614.

The incident of the carving and the reference of Howell to the neglect into which the memory of Jonson had fallen within a year of his death point to a public indifference which is not difficult to understand. He had been intermittently an invalid for over ten years. His masterpieces were nearly a generation old when he passed away. His " sons " had grown up, and some of them had grown judicious, as had become painfully evident during the final battle of the Odes. *Jonsonus Virbius* is ceremonious rather than enthusiastic or searching. The sons of Ben gathered round. An institution had passed away. " Mirror of poets, mirror of our age "— Waller set the tune. Such sentiments are frequent, but not revealing. Over thirty poets, not half a dozen of them above thirty-five, contributed as friends of the muses. They say or sing what is expected, celebrating their master as a wonder of the time, defending him from the common charges to which he had answered all his life—his borrowings, his excess of learning, his failure to please the public.

Y

Ben Jonson

It is clear from these tributes that Jonson's work was not, even in his own generation of scholars and minds alert and clean to new impressions, always too easy of approach. Jonson is praised for his solidity, permanence, high-thinking and noble ethic. That he was difficult is not denied. Even Francis Beaumont admitted it :

> But thou hast squared thy rules by what is good
> And art three ages yet from understood ;
> And (I daresay) in it there lies much wit
> Lost, till the readers can grow up to it.

All insist on his art, judgment, industry and learning. To him poets would always turn for a model. He is the giver of laws, the founder of good practice. Such was the attitude to Jonson in his time, and as long as his influence lasted. It culminated in Dryden, for whom Jonson was the formal master and fundamental source of English comedy.

The two fullest tributes were from Falkland, who headed the list and found a name for the collection, and from Owen Feltham. Falkland contributed an eclogue between Meliboeus and Hylas. He is biographical rather than critical. He celebrates the accepted virtues of his master, laying special emphasis on the moral improvement to be derived from " the ethic lectures of his comedies," in which the age,

> Blusheth to meet her follies on the stage ;
> Where each man finds some light he never sought,
> And leaves behind some vanity he brought.

But he passes quickly from the poet to the contemporary figure. The wise had flocked to do him reverence. Those who had censured him had desired the

Green Fields

glory of having so great a foe. Three sovereigns
had in three generations united to do him honour,
last of all being the mighty Charles, who—

> Found still some time to hear and to admire
> The happy sounds of his harmonious lyre,
> And oft hath left his bright exalted throne
> And to his muse's feet combined his own,
> As did his Queen, whose person so disclosed
> A brighter nymph than any part imposed,
> When she did join, by an harmonious choice,
> Her graceful motions to his powerful voice.

Falkland here betrays the hand of his master. Admiration and grief are remotely expressed in careful numbers
in which each fancy is clearly defined and adequately
exploited.

Feltham's tribute has been noted in another connection. His lines *To the Memory of Immortal Ben*
are an atonement for his parody of Jonson's *Ode to
Himself*, though even in commemoration Feltham
could not forbear to glance at his master's habit of
self-praise and he ended with a complaint that Jonson,
having said so much for himself, had left little for
his friends. But the tribute was generous and apt.
Slow are substantial bodies. Admit that the muse
of Jonson was laboursome. His fame would outlive
that of kings and princes :

> And to write things that time can never stain
> Will require sweat and rubbing of the brain ;
> Such were the things he left.

Not included in the *Jonsonus Virbius* was a tribute
which cannot be omitted. Clarendon, writing of
friends in his autobiography, puts Jonson first among
those who, while he stood at gaze, irresolute what
corner of life to take, were to be reckoned among his
chief acquaintance :

323   Y*

Ben Jonson

Ben Jonson's name can never be forgotten, having by his very good learning, severity of his nature and manners very much reformed the stage and indeed the English poetry itself; his natural advantages were judgment to order and govern fancy, rather than excess of fancy; his productions being slow and upon deliberation, yet then abounding with great wit and will live accordingly; and, surely as he did exceedingly exalt the English language in eloquence, propriety and masculine expression, so he was the best judge and fittest to prescribe rules to Poetry and Poets of any man who had lived with or before him or since.

* *

To sum up is out of fashion. It is a textbook habit which standardises the approach of hasty scholars to great movements and figures. The longer we remain with any period or person the more impertinent it seems to generalise. Enough of Jonson's work has been described and quoted in these pages to present him directly. Such general impressions concerning the bent of his genius and method of work as suggested themselves have been conveyed in dealing with particular passages or plays. He may be left without place or label—sufficiently large and living to escape definition or summary. He closed a chapter in English life, and the poets mourned in him the eclipse of the English theatre :

> After the rare arch-poet Jonson died,
> The sock grew loathsome, and the buskin's pride,
> Together with the stage's glory, stood
> Each like a poor and pitied widowhood.

Herrick, looking at the theatre, with the writers of a later generation, felt that something was wrong. Even Dryden was aware of it. The theatre, however, was not to blame. The stage is never a cause but a consequence. Something had passed out of English life and letters and Herrick, writing of plays and players, was speaking to a wider theme :

> All wit
> In utter darkness did, and still will, sit,
> Sleeping the luckless age out, till that she
> Her resurrection has again with thee.

The poet writes in hyperbole, but conveys a truth more fatal than he suspected. With Jonson's death the English Renaissance had ceased to be an inspiration and became an episode.

INDEX

327

Index

Index

Index